Access 2007 for Starters

THE MISSING MANUAL

D1536835

Access 2007 for Starters

THE MISSING MANUAL

Matthew MacDonald

Beijing • Cambridge • Farnham • Köln • Paris • Sebastopol • Taipei • Tokyo

Access 2007 for Starters: THE MISSING MANUAL

by Matthew MacDonald

Copyright © 2007 O'Reilly Media, Inc. All rights reserved.
Printed in the United States of America.

Published by O'Reilly Media, Inc., 1005 Gravenstein Highway North, Sebastopol, CA 95472.

O'Reilly books may be purchased for educational, business, or sales promotional use. Online editions are also available for most titles (*safari.oreilly.com*). For more information, contact our corporate/institutional sales department: (800) 998-9938 or *corporate@oreilly.com*.

Printing History:

January 2007:   First Edition.

RepKover™ This book uses RepKover™, a durable and flexible lay-flat binding.
ISBN-10: 0-596-52833-7
ISBN-13: 978-0-596-52833-1
[M]

TABLE OF CONTENTS

PART TWO: MANIPULATING DATA WITH QUERIES

PART THREE: PRINTING REPORTS AND USING FORMS

PART FOUR: SHARING ACCESS WITH THE REST OF THE WORLD

THE MISSING CREDITS

About the Author

 Matthew MacDonald is an author and programmer extraordinaire. He's the author of *Excel 2007: The Missing Manual, Creating Web Sites: The Missing Manual,* and over a dozen books about programming with the Microsoft .NET Framework. In a dimly remembered past life, he studied English literature and theoretical physics.

About the Creative Team

Peter Meyers (editor) works as an editor at O'Reilly Media on the Missing Manual series. He lives with his wife and cats in New York City. Email: *peter.meyers@gmail.com.*

Sanders Kleinfeld (editor) is a production editor for the Head First series at O'Reilly Media. In addition to copyediting lengthy technical books, he enjoys British crosswords and *Buffy the Vampire Slayer* reruns. Email: *sanders@oreilly.com*

Juel Bortolussi (technical reviewer) has worked as an Access database developer for inventory and asset management systems in the design, beverage, and publishing industries. She thinks this book would make a great classroom textbook, providing students with database skills. Email: *juel@oreilly.com*

Michael Schmalz (technical reviewer) works in banking and performs business and technology consulting in a variety of industries. He has done technical editing for O'Reilly on Microsoft Office books. Michael has a degree in finance from Penn State. He lives with his wife and daughter in Pennsylvania.

Sohaila Abdulali (copy editor) is a freelance writer and editor. She has published a novel, several children's books, and numerous short stories and articles. She recently finished an ethnography of an aboriginal Indian woman. She lives in New York City with her husband Tom and their small but larger-than-life daughter, Samara. She can be reached through her Web site at *www.sohailaink.com*.

Jill Steinberg (copy editor) is a freelance writer and editor based in Seattle, and has produced content for O'Reilly, Intel, Microsoft, and the University of Washington. Jill was educated at Brandeis University, Williams College, and Stanford University. Email: *saysjill@mac.com*.

Acknowledgements

Writing a book about a program as sprawling and complex as Access is a labor of love (love of pain, that is). I'm deeply indebted to a whole host of people, including those who helped me track down all the neat and nifty things you can do with the latest version of Office (including bloggers extraordinaire Jensen Harris and Erik Rucker), those who kept the book clear, concise, and technically accurate (Peter Meyers, Sarah Milstein, Brian Sawyer, Juel Bortolussi, and Michael Schmalz), and those who put up with me while I wrote it (more on that in a moment). I also owe thanks to many people who worked to get this book formatted, indexed, and printed—you can meet many of them on the Missing Credits page.

Completing this book required a few sleepless nights (and many sleep-deprived days). I extend my love and thanks to my daughter Maya, who put up with it without crying most of the time; my dear wife Faria, who mostly did the same; and our moms and dads (Nora, Razia, Paul, and Hamid), who contributed hours of babysitting, tasty meals, and general help around the house that kept this book on track. So thanks everyone—without you half of the book would still be trapped inside my brain!

The Missing Manual Series

Missing Manuals are witty, superbly written guides to computer products that don't come with printed manuals (which is just about all of them). Each book features a handcrafted index and RepKover, a detached-spine binding that lets the book lie perfectly flat without the assistance of weights or cinder blocks.

Recent and upcoming titles include:

Access 2003 for Starters: The Missing Manual by Kate Chase and Scott Palmer

Access 2007 for Starters: The Missing Manual by Matthew MacDonald

Access 2007: The Missing Manual by Matthew MacDonald

Digital Photography: The Missing Manual by Chris Grover and Barbara Brundage

Excel 2003 for Starters: The Missing Manual by Matthew MacDonald

Excel 2003: The Missing Manual by Matthew MacDonald

Excel 2007 for Starters: The Missing Manual by Matthew MacDonald

Excel 2007: The Missing Manual by Matthew MacDonald

Google: The Missing Manual, Second Edition by Sarah Milstein, J.D. Biersdorfer, and Matthew MacDonald

iMovie 6 & iDVD: The Missing Manual by David Pogue

iPhoto 6: The Missing Manual by David Pogue

iPod: The Missing Manual, Fifth Edition by J.D. Biersdorfer

PCs: The Missing Manual by Andy Rathbone

Photoshop Elements 5: The Missing Manual by Barbara Brundage

PowerPoint 2007 for Starters: The Missing Manual by E. A. Vander Veer

PowerPoint 2007: The Missing Manual by E. A. Vander Veer

Quicken for Starters: The Missing Manual by Bonnie Biafore

The Internet: The Missing Manual by David Pogue and J.D. Biersdorfer

Windows XP for Starters: The Missing Manual by David Pogue

Windows XP Home Edition: The Missing Manual, Second Edition by David Pogue

Windows XP Pro: The Missing Manual, Second Edition by David Pogue, Craig Zacker, and Linda Zacker

Windows Vista: The Missing Manual by David Pogue

Windows Vista for Starters: The Missing Manual by David Pogue

Word 2007 for Starters: The Missing Manual by Chris Grover

Word 2007: The Missing Manual by Chris Grover

INTRODUCTION

- ▶ What You Can Do with Access
- ▶ The New Face of Access 2007
- ▶ About This Book

IN THE PAST, PEOPLE HAVE TRIED A VARIETY OF TECHNIQUES to organize information. They've used Rolodexes, punch cards, cardboard boxes, vertical files, Post-it notes, 10,000-page indexes, and (when all else failed) large piles on top of flat surfaces. But after much suffering, people discovered that computers were far better at dealing with information, especially when that information's large, complex, or changes frequently.

That's where Microsoft Access comes into the picture. Access is a tool for managing *databases*—carefully structured catalogs of information (or *data*). Databases can store just about any type of information, including numbers, pages of text, and pictures. Databases also range wildly in size—they can handle everything from your list of family phone numbers to a ginormous product catalog for Aunt Ethel's Discount Button Boutique.

In this book, you'll learn how to design complete databases, maintain them, search for valuable nuggets of information, and build attractive forms for quick and easy data entry.

Best of all, this book was written from scratch for Access 2007, the latest and greatest incarnation of Microsoft's bestselling database software. Access 2007's quite a bit different from previous versions, with a slick new interface that has computer geeks buzzing. And for once, it's not just a gimmick. As you'll see in this book, once you master Access's new style, you'll be able to build great databases in record time.

What You Can Do with Access

The modern world is filled with information. A Web search for a ho-hum topic like "canned carrots" nets more than a million Web pages. As a result, it's no surprise that people from all walks of life need great tools to store and manage information.

It's impossible to describe even a fraction of the different databases that Access fans create every day. But just to get you thinking like a database maven, here are some common types of information that you can store handily in an Access database:

▶ Catalogs of books, CDs, rare wine vintages, risqué movies, or anything else you want to collect and keep track of

▶ Mailing lists that let you keep in touch with friends, family, and co-workers

- Business information, like customer lists, product catalogs, order records, and invoices
- Lists of guests and gifts for weddings and other celebrations
- Lists of expenses, investments, and other financial planning details

Think of Access as a personal assistant that can help you organize, update, and find any type of information. This help isn't just a convenience—it also lets you do things you could never accomplish on your own.

Imagine you've just finished compiling a database for your collection of 10,000 rare comic books. On a whim, you decide to take a look at all the books written in 1987. Or just those that feature Aquaman. Or those that contain the words "special edition" in the title. Performing these searches with a paper catalog would take days. On an average computer, Access can perform all three searches in under a second.

Access is also the king of small businesses, because of its legendary powers of customization. After all, you can use virtually any database product to create a list of customer orders. But only Access makes it easy to build a full *user interface* for that database (as shown in Figure I-1).

The Two Sides of Access

As you'll see, there are actually two separate tasks you'll perform with Access:

- **Designing your database.** This task involves creating *tables* to hold data, *queries* that can ferret out important pieces of information, *forms* that make it easy to enter information, and *reports* that produce attractive printouts.
- **Dealing with data.** This task involves adding new information to the database, updating what's there, or just searching for the details you need. In order to do this work, you use the tables, queries, forms, and reports that you've already built.

Most of this book's dedicated to task #1—creating and perfecting your database. This job's the heart of Access, and it's the part that initially seems the most daunting. It's also what separates the Access masters from the neophytes.

Once you've finished task #1, you're reading to move on to task #2—actually *using* the database in your day-to-day life. Although task #1 is more challenging, you'll (eventually) spend more time on task #2. For example, you might spend a couple of

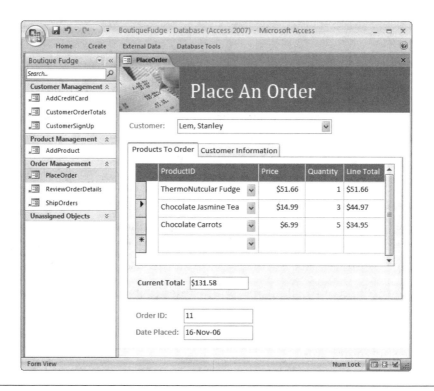

Figure I-1. This sales database includes handy forms that sales people can use to place new orders (shown here), customer service representatives can use to sign up new customers, and warehouse staff can use to review outgoing shipments. Best of all, the people who are using the forms in the database don't need to know anything about Access. As long as a database pro (like your future self, once you've finished this book) has designed these forms, anyone can use them to enter, edit, and review data.

hours creating a database to keep track of your favorite recipes, but you'll wind up entering new information and looking up recipes for *years* (say, every time you need to cook up dinner).

Access vs. Excel

Access isn't the only Office product that can deal with lists and tables of information. Microsoft Excel also includes features for creating and managing lists. So what's the difference?

The Benefits of a Good Database

Many people use an address book to keep track of close friends, distant relatives, or annoying co-workers. For the most part, the low-tech address book works great. But consider what happens if you decide to store the same information in an Access database. Even though your contact list isn't storing Google-sized volumes of information, it still offers a few features that you wouldn't have without Access:

* **Backup.** If you've ever tried to decipher a phone number through a coffee stain, you know that sometimes it helps to have things in electronic form. Once you place all your contact information into a database, you'll be able to preserve it in case of disaster, and print up as many copies as you need (each with some or all of the information showing). You can even share your list with a friend who needs the same numbers.

* **Space.** Although most people can fit all the contacts they need into a small address book, a database ensures you'll never fill up that "M" section. Not

to mention that there are only so many times you can cross out and rewrite the address for your itinerant Uncle Sy before you run out of room.

* **Searching.** An address book organizes contacts in one way—by name. But what happens once you've entered everyone in alphabetical order by last name, and you need to look up a contact you vaguely remember as Joe? Access can effortlessly handle this search. It can also find a matching entry by phone number, which is great if your phone gives you a log of missed calls and you want to figure out who's been pestering you.

* **Integration with other applications.** Access introduces you to a realm of timesaving possibilities, like mail merge. You can feed a list of contacts into a form letter you create in Word, and automatically generate dozens of individually addressed letters. You'll see how to do this in Chapter 10.

All these examples demonstrate solid reasons to go electronic with almost any type of information.

Although Excel's perfectly good for small, simple amounts of information, it just can't handle the same *quantity* and *complexity* of information as Access. Excel also falters if you need to maintain multiple lists with related information (for example, if you want to track a list with your business customers, and a list of the orders they've made). Excel forces you to completely separate these lists, which makes it harder to analyze your data and introduces the possibility of inconsistent information. Access lets you set up strict *links* between tables, which prevents these problems.

Access also provides all sorts of features that don't have any parallel in the spreadsheet world, such as the ability to create customized search routines, design fine-tuned forms for data entry, and print a variety of snazzy reports.

> **NOTE**
>
> Looking to polish up your Excel skills? Check out *Excel 2007: The Missing Manual.*

The New Face of Access 2007

Ever since Microsoft Office conquered the world (way back in the 1990s), programs like Word, Excel, and Access haven't changed a lot. Although a genuinely useful new feature appears once in a while, Microsoft spends more time wedging in odd gimmicks like a talking paper clip.

Access 2007 breaks this pattern and introduces some of the most dramatic changes Office fans have seen since Office 95. The most obvious change is the thoroughly revamped *user interface* (the windows, toolbars, menus, and keyboard shortcuts you use to interact with Access). After spending far too long trying to simplify the haphazard, toolbar-choked interfaces in most Office applications, Microsoft finally worked up the courage to redesign it all from scratch.

The Ribbon

The Access 2007 ribbon is a super-toolbar that replaces the various toolbars and menus in previous versions.

> **NOTE**
>
> Access doesn't show the ribbon until you create a database. If you can't stand the suspense any longer, and you want to be able to look at the ribbon on your monitor as you read the next couple of pages, follow the instructions on page 28 to create a blank database.

The ribbon's divided into task-specific *tabs*—Home, Create, External Data, and so on. Initially, Access starts out with four tabs (although other tabs appear when you perform specific tasks). When you launch Access, you start at the Home tab. Click Create (as shown in Figure I-2), and you get access to a slew of powerful commands that let you add new database components.

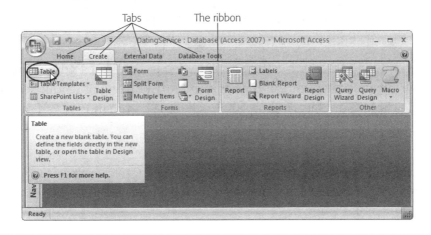

Figure I-2. *The ribbon's full of craftsman-like detail. When you hover over a button, you don't see a paltry two- or three-word description in a yellow box. Instead, you see a friendly pop-up box with a complete mini-description. Here, the mouse is hovering over the Table command.*

___ TIP ___

Want to reclaim the screen real estate that the ribbon occupies? Just double-click the current tab, and the ribbon collapses, leaving only the row of tab titles visible. Double-click the tab again to pop the buttons back into sight. Page 55 has more about this feature.

Here's a quick snapshot of the four basic ribbon tabs:

▶ **Home** gathers together a variety of common commands, including the familiar copy-and-paste tools and formatting commands for tweaking fonts and colors. You'll also find handy features like sorting, searching, and filtering, all of which you'll tackle in Chapter 3.

▶ **Create** has commands for inserting all the different database objects you'll learn about in this book (see page 24 for the lowdown). These include the tables that store data, the queries that search it, the forms that help you edit it, and the reports that help you print it.

- **External Data** has commands for importing data into Access and exporting it to other programs. You'll use these commands in Chapter 10.

- **Database Tools** features the pro tools that help experts perform deep-tissue data analysis and add Visual Basic code (a scripting language). Most civilians can safely avoid this tab, although you will tap into its abilities occasionally in Chapter 5, when you learn about linking tables.

It's worth spending some time getting accustomed to the tab-based ribbon. Try clicking one tab after the other, rifling back and forth through the four sections to see what they hold. You'll learn more about all these commands as you make your way through this book.

TIP

If you have a scroll mouse, you can breeze through the tabs even faster by moving the mouse pointer over the ribbon, and then moving the scroll wheel up or down.

One nice ribbon tab feature is that they never change—in other words, you don't see commands mysteriously moving around or winking out of existence. Microsoft designed the ribbon to be predictable, so commands always remain in the same place. However, commands *will* change their arrangement a bit if you resize the Access window, so that they better use the available space (Figure I-3).

Using the Ribbon with the Keyboard

If you're a diehard keyboard lover, you'll be happy to hear that you can trigger ribbon commands with the keyboard. The trick's using *keyboard accelerators*, a series of keystrokes that starts with the Alt key (the same keys you *used* to use to get to a menu). When using a keyboard accelerator, you *don't* hold down all the keys at the same time. (As you'll soon see, some of them have enough letters to tie your fingers up better than the rowdiest game of Twister.) Instead, you hit the keys one after the other.

The trick to keyboard accelerators is to understand that once you hit the Alt key, you do two things, in this order:

1. **Pick the correct ribbon tab.**

2. **In that tab, choose a command.**

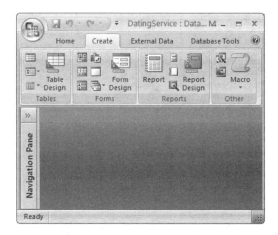

Figure I-3. This super-skinny Access window doesn't have much room for ribbon buttons. All the same commands that you saw in Figure I-2 are still in the ribbon, but now you see only small icons with no text. When you're in doubt about a button, hover over it to see its name.

Before you can trigger a specific command, you *must* select the right tab (even if you're already there). Every accelerator requires at least two key presses after you hit the Alt key. You'll need even more if you need to dig through a submenu.

By now, this whole process probably seems hopelessly impractical. Are you really expected to memorize dozens of different accelerator key combinations?

Fortunately, Access is ready to help you out with a new feature called *KeyTips*. Here's how it works: Once you press the Alt key, letters magically appear over every tab in the ribbon. Once you hit a key to pick a tab, letters appear over every button in that tab. You can then press the corresponding key to trigger the command. Figure I-4 shows how it works.

> **NOTE**
>
> In some cases, a command may have two letters, and you need to press both keys, one after the other. You can back out of KeyTips mode at any time without triggering a command by pressing the Alt key again.

Some other shortcut keys don't use the ribbon. These key combinations start with the Ctrl key. For instance, Ctrl+C copies highlighted text, and Ctrl+S saves your

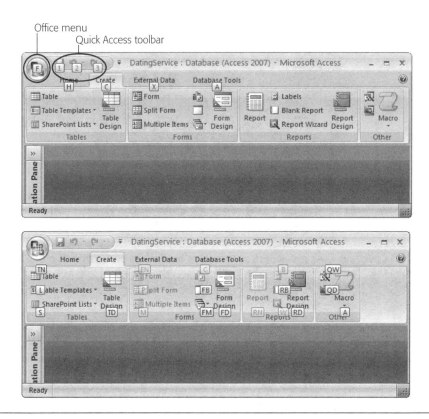

Office menu

Quick Access toolbar

Figure I-4. Top: When you press Alt, Access pins KeyTips next to every tab, over the Office menu, and over the buttons in the Quick Access toolbar (more about the Office menu and the Quick Access toolbar in a moment).

Bottom: If you follow up with C (for the Create tab), you'll see letters next to every command in that tab. Now you can click another button to run a command. Don't bother trying to match letters with tab or button names; the ribbon's got so many features packed into it that in many cases, the letters don't mean anything at all.

current work. Usually, you find out about a shortcut key by hovering over a command with the mouse. Hover over the Paste button in the ribbon's Home tab, and you see a tooltip that tells you its timesaving shortcut key is Ctrl+V. And if you've worked with a previous version of Access, you'll find that Access 2007 keeps most of the same shortcut keys.

Access 2003 Menu Shortcuts

If you've worked with a previous version of Access, you may have trained yourself to use menu shortcuts—key combinations that open a menu and pick out the command you want. When you press Alt+E in Access 2003, the Edit menu pops open (in the main menu). You can then press the S key to choose the Paste Special command.

At first glance, it doesn't look like these keyboard shortcuts amount to much in Access 2007. After all, Access 2007 doesn't even have a main menu! Fortunately, Microsoft went to a little extra trouble to make life easier for longtime Access aficionados. You can still use your menu shortcuts, but they work in a slightly different way.

If you hit Alt+E in Access 2007, a tooltip appears over the top of the ribbon (Figure I-5) that lets you know you've started to enter an Access 2003 menu shortcut. If you go on to press S, then you wind up at the familiar Paste Special dialog box, because Access knows what you're trying to do. It's almost as though Access has an invisible menu at work behind the scenes.

Of course, this feature can't help you out all the time. It doesn't work if you're trying to use one of the few commands that don't exist any longer. And if you need to see the menu to remember what key to press next, you're out of luck. Access just gives you the tooltip.

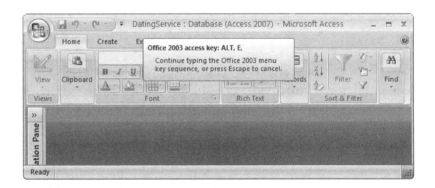

Figure I-5. By pressing Alt+E, you've triggered the "imaginary" Edit menu. You can't actually see it (because it doesn't exist in Access 2007). However, the tooltip lets you know that Access is paying attention. You can now complete your action by pressing the next key for the menu command.

Why Reinvent the Wheel?

Some Access veterans are understandably skeptical about the new Access interface. After all, we've had to suffer through some painful experiments. Past versions of Access have introduced kooky ideas like personalized menus that always seem to hide just the command you need, pop-up side panels that appear when you least expect them, and floating toolbars that end up strewn across the screen.

In reality, all the Office applications have been struggling to keep up with more than a decade's worth of new features. The menus in most Office programs haven't changed since Word 2.0 hit the scene in the early 1990s. In those days, a basic menu and a single toolbar were just the ticket, because the number of commands was relatively small.

Today, the Office programs are drowning in features—and they're crammed into so many different nooks and crannies that even pros don't know where to look.

That's where the new ribbon fits in. Not only can you easily understand and navigate it, it provides one-stop shopping for everything you need to do. Microsoft's user interface designers have a new mantra: *It's all in the ribbon.* In other words, if you need to find a feature, then look for it in one of the tabs at the top of the Access window. As you get accustomed to this new system, you'll find it not only helps you quickly use your favorite features, it also helps you discover new features just by browsing.

The Office Menu

One small part of the traditional Access menu's left in Access 2007—sort of. The traditional File menu that lets you open, save, and print files has been transformed into the *Office menu.* You get there using the Office button, which is the big, round logo in the window's top-left corner (Figure I-6).

You generally use the Office menu for three things:

▶ Opening, creating, and saving your database. You'll do plenty of this in Chapter 1.

▶ Printing your work (Chapter 3) and sending it off to other people by email.

▶ Configuring how Access behaves. Choose Access Options at the bottom of the menu to get to the Access Options dialog box, an all-in-one hub for configuring Access settings.

Figure I-6. The Office menu's bigger and easier to read than a traditional menu. When you click it, it displays a list of menu commands (on the left) and a list of the databases you used recently (on the right).

There's one menu quirk that takes a bit of getting used to. Some Office menu commands hide submenus that have more commands. Take the Print command. You can choose Print from the Office menu to fire off a quick printout of your work. But if you click the right-pointing arrow at the edge of the Print command (or if you hover over it for a moment), then you see a submenu with more options, as shown in Figure I-7.

The Quick Access Toolbar

Keen eyes will have noticed the tiny bit of screen real estate that sits on the Office button's right side, just above the ribbon (Figure I-8). This bit of screen holds a series of tiny icons, like the toolbars in older versions of Access. This area's the Quick Access toolbar (or QAT to Access nerds).

Figure I-7. Print's both a clickable menu command and a submenu. To see the submenu, you need to hover over Print (without clicking), or click the arrow at the right edge (shown here). The ribbon also has a few buttons that work this way.

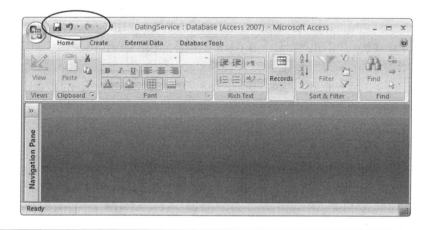

Figure I-8. The Quick Access toolbar puts the Save, Undo, and Redo commands right at your fingertips. Access singles out these commands because people use them more frequently than any other commands.

About This Book

Despite the many improvements in software over the years, one feature hasn't improved a bit: Microsoft's documentation. In fact, with Office 2007, you get no printed user guide at all. To learn about the thousands of features included in this software collection, Microsoft expects you to read the online help.

Occasionally, these help screens are actually helpful, like when you're looking for a quick description explaining a mysterious new function. On the other hand, if you're trying to learn how to, say, create an attractive chart, you'll find nothing better than terse and occasionally cryptic instructions.

This book is the manual that *should* have accompanied Access 2007. In these pages, you'll find step-by-step instructions and tips for using almost every Access feature, including those you haven't (yet) heard of.

> **NOTE**
>
> This book is based on *Access 2007: The Missing Manual* (O'Reilly). That book is a truly complete reference for Access 2007, covering every feature, including geeky stuff like XML, VBA, SQL Server, and other things you'll probably never encounter—or even want to. But if you get really deep into Access and want to learn more, *Access 2007: The Missing Manual* can be your trusted guide.

About the Outline

This book's divided into four parts:

▶ **Part One: Storing Information in Tables.** In this part, you'll build your first database and learn how to add and edit tables that store information. Then you'll pick up the real-world skills you need to stop mistakes before they happen, browse around your database, and link tables together.

▶ **Part Two: Manipulating Data with Queries.** In this part, you'll build *queries*: specialized commands that can hunt down the data you're interested in, apply changes, and summarize vast amounts of information.

▶ **Part Three: Printing Reports and Using Forms.** This part shows you how to use reports to take the raw data in your tables and format it into neat printouts, complete with fancy formatting and subtotals.You'll also learn how to build forms—customized windows that make data entry easy, even for Access newbies.

▶ **Part Four: Sharing Access with the Rest of the World.** In this part, you'll learn how to pull your data out of (or put your data into) other types of files, like text documents and Excel spreadsheets.

About → These → Arrows

Throughout this book, you'll find sentences like this one: "Choose Create → Tables → Table." This method's a shorthand way of telling you how to find a feature in the Access ribbon. It translates to the following instructions: "On the ribbon, click the **Create** tab. On the tab, look for the **Tables** section. In the Tables box, click the **Table** button." (Look back to Figure I-2 to see the button you're looking for.)

As you saw back in Figure I-3, the ribbon adapts itself to different screen sizes. Depending on your Access window's size, the button you need to click may not include any text. Instead, it shows up as a small icon. In this situation, you can hover over the mystery button to see its name before deciding whether or not to click it.

If you resize the Access window so that it's *really* small, you might run out of space for a section altogether. In that case, you get a single button that has the section's name. Click this button, and the missing commands appear in a drop-down panel (Figure I-9).

Contextual tabs

Although nice, predictable tabs are a great idea, some features obviously make sense only in specific circumstances. Say you start designing a table. You may have a few more features than when you're entering data. Access handles this situation by adding one or more *contextual tabs* to the ribbon, based on your current task. These tabs have additional commands that are limited to a specific scenario (Figure I-10).

When dealing with contextual tabs, the instructions in this book always include the title of the tab section (it's Table Tools in Figure I-10). Here's an example: "Choose Table Tools | Datasheet → Fields & Columns → New Fields." Notice that this instruction's first part includes the contextual tab title (Table Tools) and the tab name (Datasheet), separated by the | character.

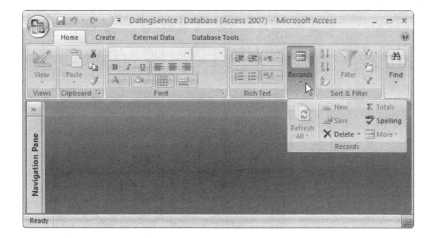

Figure I-9. In this example, Access doesn't have the room to display the Home tab's Views, Records, or Find sections, so they're all replaced with buttons. If you click any of these buttons, then a panel appears with the content you're looking for.

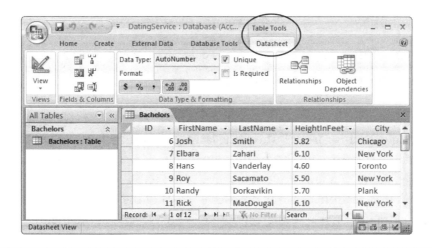

Figure I-10. When you're designing a form, a new contextual tab appears, named Datasheet, under the heading Table Tools. Contextual tabs always appear on the ribbon's right side.

Drop-down buttons

From time to time you'll encounter buttons in the ribbon that have short menus attached to them. Depending on the button, this menu appears as soon as you click the button, or it appears only if you click the button's drop-down arrow, as shown in Figure I-11.

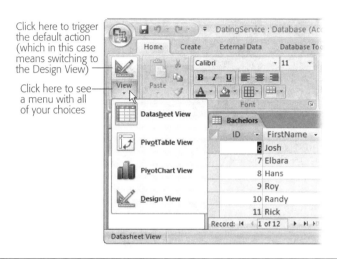

Click here to trigger the default action (which in this case means switching to the Design View)

Click here to see a menu with all of your choices

Figure I-11. Access lets you switch between several different views of your database. Click the bottom part of the View button to see the menu of choices shown here, or click the top part to switch to the next view in the list, with no questions asked.

When dealing with this sort of button, the last step of the instructions in this book tells you what to choose from the drop-down menu. For example, say you're directed to "Home → Views → View → Design View." That tells you to select the Home tab, look for the Views section, click the drop-down part of the View button (to reveal the menu with extra options), and then choose Design View from the menu.

> **NOTE**
>
> Be on the lookout for drop-down arrows in the ribbon—they're tricky at first. You need to click the *arrow* part of the button to see the full list of options. If you click the other part of the button, then you don't see the list. Instead, Access fires off the standard command (the one Access thinks is the most common choice), or the command you used most recently.

About Shortcut Keys

Every time you take your hand off the keyboard to move the mouse, you lose a few microseconds of time. That's why many experienced computer fans use keystroke combinations instead of toolbars and menus wherever possible. Ctrl+S, for one, is a keyboard shortcut that saves your current work in Access (and most other programs).

When you see a shortcut like Ctrl+S in this book, it's telling you to hold down the Ctrl key, and, while it's down, press the letter S, and then release both keys. Similarly, the finger-tangling shortcut Ctrl+Alt+S means hold down Ctrl, then press and hold Alt, and then press S (so that all three keys are held down at once).

About Clicking

This book gives you three kinds of instructions that require you to use your computer's mouse or trackpad. To *click* means to point the arrow cursor at something on the screen and then—without moving the cursor at all—press and release the left-side clicker button on the mouse (or laptop trackpad). To *double-click*, of course, means to click twice in rapid succession, again without moving the cursor at all. And to *drag* means to move the cursor while holding down the button.

Examples

As you read this book, you'll see a number of examples that demonstrate Access features and techniques for building good databases. Many of these examples are available as Access database files in a separate download. Just surf to *www.missingmanuals.com*, click the link for this book, and then click the "Missing CD" link to visit a page where you can download a zip file that includes the examples, organized by chapter.

About MissingManuals.com

At *www.missingmanuals.com*, you'll find news, articles, and updates to the books in the Missing Manual and For Starters series.

But the Web site also offers corrections and updates to this book (to see them, click the book's title, and then click Errata). In fact, you're invited and encouraged to submit such corrections and updates yourself. In an effort to keep the book as up to date and accurate as possible, each time we print more copies of this book, we'll make any confirmed corrections you've suggested. We'll also note such changes on the Web site, so that you can mark important corrections into your own copy of the book, if you like.

In the meantime, we'd love to hear your own suggestions for new books in the Missing Manual and For Starters lines. There's a place for that on the Web site, too, as well as a place to sign up for free email notification of new titles in the series.

Safari® Enabled

 When you see a Safari® Enabled icon on the cover of your favorite technology book, that means the book is available online through the O'Reilly Network Safari Bookshelf.

Safari offers a solution that's better than e-books. It's a virtual library that lets you easily search thousands of top tech books, cut and paste code samples, download chapters, and find quick answers when you need the most accurate, current information. Try it for free at *http://safari.oreilly.com*.

PART ONE: STORING INFORMATION IN TABLES

CREATING YOUR FIRST DATABASE

- ▶ Understanding Access Databases
- ▶ Getting Started
- ▶ Saving and Opening Access Databases
- ▶ The Navigation Pane

ALTHOUGH MICROSOFT WON'T ADMIT IT, Access can be intimidating—intimidating enough to trigger a cold sweat in the most confident office worker. Even though Microsoft has spent millions making Access easier to use, most people still see it as the most complicated Office program on the block. They're probably right.

Access seems more daunting than any other Office program because of the way that databases work. Quite simply, databases *need strict rules*. Other programs aren't as obsessive. For example, you can fire up Word, and start typing a letter straight away. Or you can start Excel, and launch right into a financial report. But Access isn't nearly as freewheeling. Before you can enter a stitch of information into an Access database, you need to create that database's *structure*. And even after you've defined that structure, you'll probably want to spend more time creating other useful tools, like handy search routines and friendly forms that you can use to simplify data lookup and data entry. All of this setup takes effort, and a good understanding of how databases work.

In this chapter, you'll conquer any Access resistance you have and learn to create a simple but functional database. Along the way, you'll get acquainted with the slick new Access user interface, and you'll learn exactly what you can store in a database. You'll then be ready to tackle the fine art of database design, covered in more detail throughout this book.

Understanding Access Databases

As you already know, a database is a collection of information. In Access, every database is stored in a single file. That file contains *database objects,* which are simply the components of a database.

Database objects are the main players in an Access database. Altogether, you have six different types of database objects:

▶ **Tables** store information. Tables are the heart of any database, and you can create as many tables as you need to store different types of information. A fitness database could track your daily running log, your inventory of exercise equipment, and the number of high-protein whey milkshakes you down each day, as three separate tables.

- ▶ **Queries** let you quickly perform an action on a table. Usually, this action involves retrieving a choice bit of information (like the 10 top-selling food items at Ed's Roadside Dinner, or all the purchases you made in a single day). However, you can also use queries to apply changes.

- ▶ **Forms** are attractive windows that you create, arrange, and colorize. Forms provide an easy way to view or change the information in a table.

- ▶ **Reports** help you print some or all of the information in a table. You can choose where the information appears on the printed page, how it's grouped and sorted, and how it's formatted.

- ▶ **Macros** are mini-programs that automate custom tasks. Macros are a simple way to get custom results without becoming a programmer.

- ▶ **Modules** are files that contain Visual Basic code. You can use this code to do just about anything—from updating 10,000 records to firing off an email. For more on Visual Basic, see *Access 2007: The Missing Manual*.

Access gurus refer to all these database ingredients as objects because you manage them all in essentially the same way. If you want to use a particular object, then you add it to your database, give it a name, and then fine-tune it. Later on, you can view your objects, rename them, or delete ones you don't want anymore.

___ TIP _____

Designing a database is the process of adding and configuring database objects. For those keeping score, an Access database can hold up to 32,768 separate objects.

_____

In this chapter, you'll consider only the most fundamental type of database object: *tables*. But first, you need to learn a bit more about databases and the Access environment.

Getting Started

It's time to begin your journey and launch Access. You'll start at a spiffy Getting Started page (Figure 1-1).

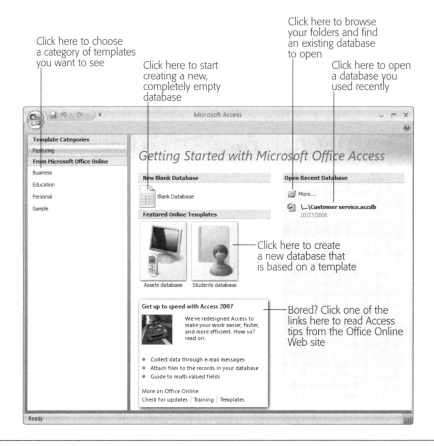

Figure 1-1. The Getting Started page is a bit of a cross between a Windows program and a Web page. Use the links on the left to browse through different categories of templates (ready-to-go databases that you can download and fill with your own information). Or check out the links on the bottom, which show you the latest Access news and tips.

The Getting Started page looks a little dizzying at first glance, but it really serves just three purposes:

▶ **It shows you recent content from Microsoft's Office Online Web site.** For example, you can read helpful articles about Access, find timesaving tips, or download updates. All links open in a separate browser window.

▶ **It lets you open a database you used recently.** Look for the Open Recent Database section on the right, which gives you a list.

Using Someone Else's Database

Can I use an Access database I didn't design?

Although every database follows the same two-step process (first somebody creates it, and then people fill it with information), the same person doesn't need to perform both jobs. In fact, in the business world, different people often work separately on these two tasks.

For example, a summer student whiz kid at a beer store may build a database for tracking orders (task #1). The sales department can then use the database to enter new orders (task #2), while other employees look up orders and fill them (also task #2). Warehouse staff can make sure stock levels are OK (again, task #2), and the resident accountant can keep an eye on total sales (task #2).

If task #1 (creating the database) is done well, task #2 (using the database) can be extremely easy. In fact, if the database is well designed, people who have little understanding of Access can still use it to enter, update, and look up information. Amazingly, they don't even need to know they're running Access at all!

▶ **It lets you create a new database.** You can start off with an empty database (use the Blank Database button), or you can try to find a ready-made *template* that fits the bill.

You may think that it would be nice to customize the Getting Started page. Access does let you do so, but it's not all that easy—and it's recommended only for organizations that want to standardize the Getting Started page to better suit their employees. A business could add links to a company Web site or a commonly used database template. If you're interested in this feature, you'll need another tool: the freely downloadable Access Developer's Toolkit, which you can search for at *http://msdn.microsoft.com*. (This tool wasn't yet released at the time of this writing.)

The Getting Started page is only the front door to the features in Access—there's lot more in store once you get rolling. You won't be able to try out other parts of the Access until you create a new database, and the next section shows you how.

Templates: One Size Fits Some

Templates are prebuilt databases. Templates aim to save you the work of creating your database, and let you jump straight to the fine-tuning and data-entry stage.

As you might expect, there's a price to be paid for this convenience. Even if you find a template that stores the type of information you want to track, you might find that the predefined structure isn't quite right. For example, if you choose to use the Home Inventory template to track all the stuff in your basement, you might find that it's missing some information

you want to use (like the projected resale value of your stuff on eBay) and includes other details you don't care about (like the date you acquired each item). To make this template work, you'll need to change the design of your table, which involves the same Access know-how as creating one.

In this book, you'll learn how to build your own databases from the ground up. Once you're an Access master, you can spend many fun hours playing with the prebuilt templates and adapting them to suit your needs.

Creating a New Database

In this chapter, you'll slap together a fairly straightforward database. The example's designed to store a list of prized bobblehead dolls. (For those not in the know, a bobblehead doll is a toy figure with an outsize head on a spring, hence the signature "bobbling" motion. Bobblehead dolls usually resemble a famous celebrity, politician, athlete, or fictional character.)

> **TIP**
>
> You can get the Bobblehead database, and all the databases in this book, on the Web. Check out page 19 in the Introduction for more details.

Here's how to create a blank new database:

1. **On the Getting Started page, click the Blank Database button.**

   A side panel appears on the right (see Figure 1-2).

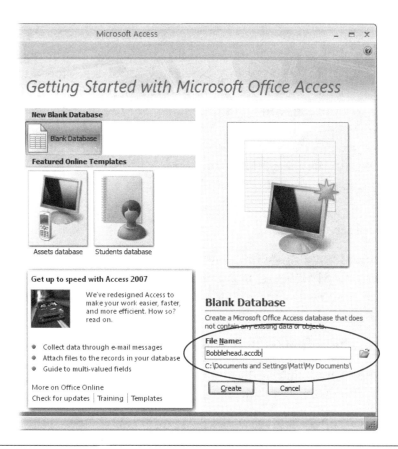

Figure 1-2. The database Bobblehead.accdb will be placed in the folder C:\Documents and Settings\Matt\My Documents. You can edit the file name by clicking in the File Name box, and you can browse to a different folder by clicking the folder icon.

2. **Type in a file name.**

Access stores all the information for a database in a single file with the extension *.accdb* (which stands for Access database). Don't stick with the name Access picks automatically (like Database1.accdb). Instead, pick something more suitable. In this example, Bobblehead.accdb does the trick.

As with any other file, Access files can contain a combination of letters, spaces, numbers, parentheses, hyphens (-), and the underscore (_). It's generally safest to stay away from other special characters, some of which aren't allowed.

> Depending on your computer settings, Windows may hide file exten-
> sions. Instead of seeing the Access database file MyScandalous-
> Wedding.accdb in file-browsing tools like Windows Explorer, you may
> just see the name MyScandalousWedding (without the .accdb part on
> the end). In this case, you can still tell the file type by looking at the
> icon. If you see a small Access icon next to the file name (which looks
> like a key), that's your signal that you're looking at an Access database.
> If you see something else (like a tiny paint palette), you need to make a
> logical guess about what type of file it is.

3. **Choose a folder.**

   Like all Office programs, Access assumes you want to store every file you create
   in your personal My Documents folder. If this isn't the case, click the folder icon
   to show the File New Database dialog box, browse to the folder you want (Figure
   1-3), and then click OK.

4. **Click the Create button (at the bottom-right of the Access window).**

   Access creates your database file and then pops up a datasheet where you can get
   to work creating your first table.

Once you create or open a database, the Access window changes quite a bit. An
impressive-looking toolbar (the *ribbon*) appears at the top of your screen, and a navigation pane shows up on the left. You're now in the control center where you'll perform all your database tasks (as shown in Figure 1-4).

The Introduction covers the basics of how the ribbon works. (Jump to page 6 for the
full details.) But first, it's time to consider how you can make use of your brand-
new, empty database by adding a table.

Understanding Tables

Tables are information containers. Every database needs at least one table—without
it, you can't store any data. In a simple database, like the Bobblehead database, a single table (which we'll call Dolls) is enough. But if you find yourself wanting to store
several lists of related information, then you need more than one table. In the

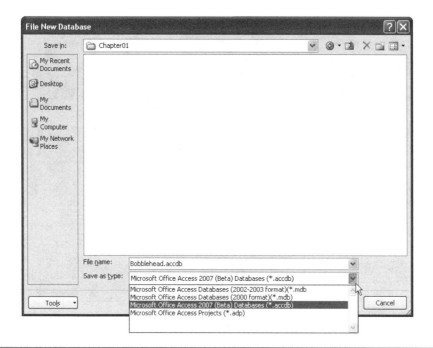

Figure 1-3. The File New Database dialog box lets you choose where you'll store a new Access database file. It also gives you the option to create your database in the format used by previous versions of Access (.mdb). To do so, you need to choose either the 2000 or 2002-2003 format options from the "Save as type" list, as shown here. If you're running Windows Vista, you'll notice that the File New Database dialog box has a whole different look, but all the same features.

database BigBudgetWedding.accdb, you might want to keep track of the guests that you invited to your wedding, the gifts that you requested, and the loot that you actually received. In Chapter 5, you'll see plenty of examples of databases that use multiple tables.

Figure 1-5 shows a sample table.

Before you start designing this table, you need to know some very basic rules:

▶ **A table's nothing more than a group of *records*.** A record's a collection of information about a single thing. In the Dolls table, for example, each record represents a single bobblehead doll. In a Family table, each record would represent a single relative. In a Products table, each record would represent an item that's for sale. You get the idea.

The ribbon ⟶

The navigation pane ⟶

The document window

Figure 1-4. The navigation pane on the left lets you see different items (or objects) in your database. You can use the navigation pane to jump from a list of products to a list of customers and back again. The ribbon along the top groups together every Access command. This ribbon's the mission control that lets you perform various tasks with your database.

▶ **Each record's subdivided into *fields*.** Each field stores a distinct piece of information. For example, in the Dolls table, one field stores the person on whom the doll's based, another field stores the price, another field stores the date you bought it, and so on.

▶ **Tables have a rigid structure.** In other words, you can't bend the rules. If you create four fields, *every* record must have four fields (although it's acceptable to leave some fields blank if they don't apply).

Creating a Simple Table

When you first create a database, it's almost empty. But in order to get you started, Access creates your first database object—a table named Table1. The problem is, this table begins life completely blank, with no defined fields (and no data).

If you followed the steps to create a new database (page 28), you're already at the *Datasheet view* (Figure 1-5), which is where you enter data into a table. All you need to do is customize this table so that it meets your needs.

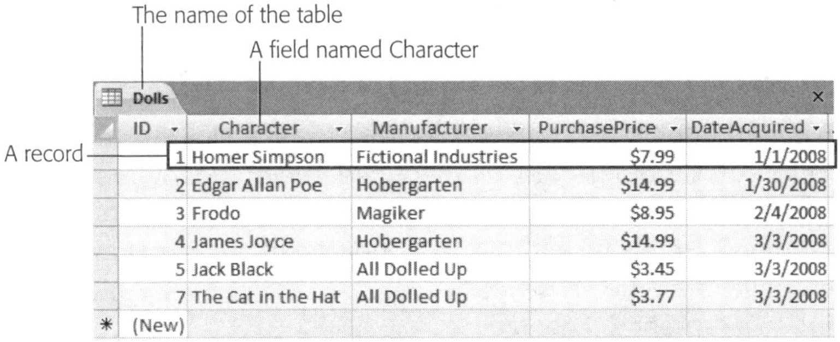

The name of the table

A field named Character

ID	Character	Manufacturer	PurchasePrice	DateAcquired
1	Homer Simpson	Fictional Industries	$7.99	1/1/2008
2	Edgar Allan Poe	Hobergarten	$14.99	1/30/2008
3	Frodo	Magiker	$8.95	2/4/2008
4	James Joyce	Hobergarten	$14.99	3/3/2008
5	Jack Black	All Dolled Up	$3.45	3/3/2008
7	The Cat in the Hat	All Dolled Up	$3.77	3/3/2008
*	(New)			

A record

Figure 1-5. In a table, each record occupies a separate row. Each field is represented by a separate column. In this table, it's clear that you've added six bobblehead dolls. You're storing information for each doll in five fields (ID, Character, Manufacturer, PurchasePrice, and DateAcquired).

WORD TO THE WISE

Sharing Databases with Older Versions of Access

Older versions of Access don't use the .accdb format. If you try to open Bobblehead.accdb in Access 2003, you'll get nothing more than a blank stare and an error message.

Earlier versions of Access use the *.mdb* file format (which stands for Microsoft database). Although Access 2007 is happy using both .accdb and .mdb files, previous versions of Access recognize only .mdb. (And just to make life more interesting, the .mdb format actually has *three* versions: the really, really old original format, a retooled version that appeared with Access 2000, and the improved-yet-again version that Microsoft introduced with Access 2002 and reused for Access 2003.)

Here's what you need to know to choose the right format for your new databases. The standard .accdb format's the best choice if you don't need to worry about compatibility, because it has the best performance and a few extra features. But if you need to share databases with other versions of Access, skip the new kid on the block, and rely instead on the tested-and-true .mdb format.

To create an old-style .mdb database file in Access 2007, use the "Save as type" option shown in Figure 1-3. You can choose the Access 2002-2003 file format, or the even older Access 2000 format. (If you're set on going back any further, say the Access 95 format, your best bet's a time machine.)

Database Planning for Beginners

Many database gurus suggest that before you fire up Access, you should decide exactly what information you want to store by brainstorming. Here's how it works. First, determine the type of list you want by finishing this sentence "I need a list of ...." (One example: "I need a list of all the bobblehead dolls in my basement.")

Next, jot down all your must-have pieces of information on a piece of paper. Some details are obvious. For example, for the bobblehead doll collection, you'll probably want to keep track of the doll's name, price, and date you bought it.

Other details, like the year it was produced, the company that created it, and a short description of its appearance or condition may require more thought.

Once you've completed this process and identified all the important bits of data you need, you're ready to create the corresponding table in Access. The bobblehead doll example demonstrates an important theme of database design: First you plan the database, and then you create it using Access. In Chapter 5, you'll learn a lot more about planning more complex databases.

There are two ways to customize a table:

▶ **Design view** lets you precisely define all aspects of a table before you start using it. Almost all database pros prefer Design view, and you'll start using it in Chapter 2.

▶ **Datasheet view** is where you enter data into a table. Datasheet view also lets you build a table on the fly as you insert new information. You'll use this approach in this chapter.

The following steps show you how to turn a blank new table (like Table1) into the Dolls table using the Datasheet view:

1. **To define your table, you need to add your first record.**

   In this case, that means mentally picking a bobblehead doll to add to the list. For this example, you'll use a nifty Homer Simpson replica.

   ___ NOTE _____

   It doesn't matter which doll you enter first. Access tables are *unsorted*, which means they have no underlying order. However, you can sort them any way you want when you need to retrieve information later on.

2. **In the datasheet's Add New Field column, type the first piece of information for the record (see Figure 1-6).**

   Based on the simple analysis you performed earlier (page 34), you know that you need to enter four fields of information for every doll. For the Homer Simpson doll, this information is: "Homer Simpson" (the name), "Fictional Industries" (the manufacturer), $7.99 (the price), and today's date (the purchase date). Although you could start with any field, it makes sense to begin with the name, which is clearly an identifying detail.

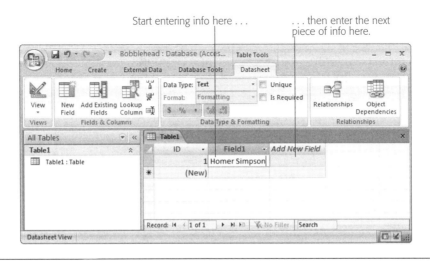

Figure 1-6. To fill in your first record, start by entering something in the first field of information (like the doll name "Homer Simpson"). Then, hit Tab to jump to the second column, and then enter the second piece of information. Ignore the ID column for now—Access adds that to every table to identify your rows.

3. **Press Tab to move to the next field, and return to step 2.**

   Repeat steps 2 and 3 until you've added every field you need, being careful to put each separate piece of information into a different column.

   If you want to get a little fancier, include the currency symbol ($) when you enter the price, and make sure you put the data in a recognized date format (like *January 1, 2008* or *01-01-2008*). These clues tell Access what type of information you're putting in the column. (In Chapter 2, you'll learn how to take complete control of the type of data in each column and avoid possible misunderstandings.) Figure 1-7 shows the finalized record.

Putting Big Values in Narrow Columns

A column can hold entire paragraphs of information, so you may find yourself running out of space once you start typing. This phenomenon isn't a problem (after all, you can just scroll through your field itself while you're editing it), but it *is* annoying. Most people prefer to see the entire contents of a column at once.

Fortunately, you don't need to suffer in silence with cramped columns. To expand a column, just position your mouse at the right edge of the column header. (To expand a column named

Field1, move your mouse to the right edge of the Field1 box.) Then, drag the column to the right to resize it as big as you want.

If you're just a bit impatient, there's a shortcut. Double-click the right edge of the column to resize it to fit the largest piece of information that's in the column (provided this doesn't stretch the column beyond the edge of the Access window). That way, you automatically get all the room you need.

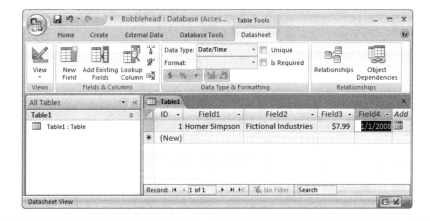

Figure 1-7. The only problem with the example so far is that as you enter a new record, Access creates spectacularly useless field names. You'll see its choices at the top of each column (they'll have names like Field1, Field2, Field3, and so on). The problem with using these meaningless names is that they might lead you to enter a piece of information in the wrong place. You could all too easily put the purchase price in the date column. To prevent these slip-ups, you need to set better field names.

If you hit Tab without entering any information, you'll move to the next row and start inserting a new record. If you make a mistake, you can backtrack using the arrow keys.

4. **It's time to fix your column names. Double-click the first column title (like Field1).**

   The field name switches into Edit mode.

5. **Type in a new name, and then press Enter. Return to step 4.**

   Repeat this process until you've cleaned up all the field names. The proper field names for this example are Character, Manufacturer, PurchasePrice, and Date-Acquired. Figure 1-8 shows how it works.

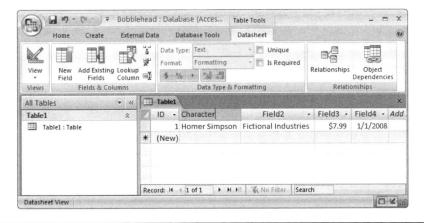

Figure 1-8. To choose better field names, double-click the column title. Next, type in the real field name, and then press Enter. Page 93 has more about field naming, but for now just stick to short, text-only titles that don't include any spaces, as shown here.

Don't be too timid about tweaking your table. You can always rename fields later, or even add entirely new fields. (It's also possible to *delete* existing fields, but that has the drawback of also clearing out all the data that's stored in that field.)

6. **Choose Office button → Save (or use the Ctrl+S shortcut) to save your table.**

Access asks you to supply a table name (see Figure 1-9).

Figure 1-9. A good table name's a short text title that doesn't have any spaces (like Dolls here).

7. **Type a suitable table name, and then click OK.**

Congratulations! The table's now a part of your database.

___ **NOTE** _____

Technically, you don't need to save your table right away. Access prompts you to save it when you close the datasheet (by clicking the X at the document window's top-right corner), or when you close Access.

As you can see, creating a simple table in Access is almost as easy as laying out information in Excel or Word. If you're itching to try again, you can create *another* table in your database by choosing Create → Table from the ribbon. But before you get to that stage, it makes sense to take a closer look at how you edit your table.

Editing a Table

You now have a fully functioning (albeit simple) database, complete with one table, which in turn contains one record. Your next step's filling your table with useful information. This often-tedious process is *data entry*.

To fill the Dolls table, you use the same datasheet you used to define the table. You can perform three basic tasks:

▶ **Editing a record.** Move to the appropriate spot in the datasheet (using the arrow keys or the mouse), and then type in a replacement. You may also want to use Edit mode, which is described in the next section.

- **Inserting a new record.** Move down to the bottom of the table, to the row that has an asterisk (*) on the left. This row doesn't actually exist until you start typing in some information. At that point, Access creates the row and moves the asterisk down to the next row underneath. You can repeat this process endlessly to add as many rows as you want (Access can handle millions).

- **Deleting a record.** You have several ways to remove a record, but the easiest is to right-click the margin immediately to the left of the record, and then choose Delete Record. Access asks you to confirm that you really want to remove the selected record, because you can't reverse the change later on.

WORD TO THE WISE

When in Doubt, Don't Delete

Most seasoned database designers rarely delete records from their databases. Every ounce of information is important.

For example, imagine you have a database that lists the products that a mail-order origami company has for sale. You might think it makes sense to delete products once they've been discontinued and can't be ordered anymore. But it turns out that it makes sense to keep these old product records around. For example, you might want to find out what product categories were the best sellers over the previous year. Or maybe a manufacturer issues a recall of asbestos-laced paper, and you need to track down everyone who ordered it. To perform either of these tasks, you need to keep your product records.

This hang-onto-everything rule applies to any kind of database. For example, imagine you're tracking student enrollment at a top-flight culinary academy. When a class is finished, you can't just delete the class record. You might need it to find out if a student has the right prerequisites for another course, what teachers she's had in the past, and so on.

The same is true for employees who retire, promotions that end, items that you used to own but you've sold, and so on. You need them all (and you probably need to keep them indefinitely).

In many cases, you'll add extra fields to your table to help you separate old data from the new. For example, you can create a Discontinued field in the Products table that identifies products that aren't available anymore. You can then ignore those products when you build an order-placement form.

Edit mode

You'll probably spend a lot of time working with the datasheet. So settle in. To make your life easier, it helps to understand a few details.

As you already know, you can use the arrow keys to move from field to field or row to row. However, you might have a bit of trouble editing a value. When you start typing, Access erases any existing content. To change this behavior, you need to switch into *Edit mode* by pressing the F2 key; in Edit mode, your typing doesn't delete the stuff that's already in that field. Instead, you get to change or add to it. To switch out of Edit mode, you press F2 again. Figure 1-10 shows a closeup look at the difference.

TIP

You can also switch in and out of Edit mode by double-clicking a cell.

Figure 1-10. Top: Normal mode. If you start typing now, you'll immediately erase the existing text ("Hobergarten"). The fact that all the text in the field's selected is a big clue that you're about to wipe it out.

Bottom: Edit mode. The cursor shows where you're currently positioned in the current field. If you start typing now, you'll insert text in between "Hober" and "garten".

Edit mode also affects how the arrow keys work. In Edit mode, the arrow keys move through the current field. For example, to move to the next cell, you need to move all the way to the end of the current text, and then press the right arrow (→) key again. But in Normal mode, the arrow keys always move you from cell to cell.

Shortcut keys

Power users know the fastest way to get work done is to use tricky keyboard combinations like Ctrl+Alt+Shift+*. Although you can't always easily remember these combinations, a couple of tables can help you out. Table 1-1 lists some useful keys that can help you whiz around the datasheet.

Table 1-1. Keys for Moving Around the Datasheet

Key	Result
Tab (or Enter)	Moves the cursor one field to the right, or down when you reach the edge of the table. This key also turns off Edit mode if it's currently switched on.
Shift+Tab	Moves the cursor one field to the left, or up when you reach the edge of the table. This key also turns off Edit mode.
→	Moves the cursor one field to the right (in Normal mode), or down when you reach the edge of the table. In Edit mode, this key moves the cursor through the text in the current field.
←	Moves the cursor one field to the left (in Normal mode), or up when you reach the edge of the table. In Edit mode, this key moves the cursor through the text in the current field.
↑	Moves the cursor up one row (unless you're already at the top of the table). This key also turns off Edit mode.
↓	Moves the cursor down one row (or it moves you to the "new row" position if you're at the bottom of the table). This key also turns off Edit mode.
Home	Moves the cursor to the first field in the current row. This key brings you to beginning of the current field if you're in Edit mode.
End	Moves the cursor to the last field in the current row. This key brings you to end of the current field if you're in Edit mode.
Page Down	Moves the cursor down one screenful (assuming you have a large table of information that doesn't all fit in the Access window at once). This key also turns off Edit mode.
Page Up	Moves the cursor up one screenful. This key also turns off Edit mode.
Ctrl+Home	Moves the cursor to the first field in the first row. This key doesn't do anything if you're in Edit mode.
Ctrl+End	Moves the cursor to the last field in the last row. This key doesn't do anything if you're in Edit mode.

Table 1-2 lists some convenient keys for editing records.

Table 1-2. Keys for Editing Records

Key	Result
Esc	Cancels any changes you've made in the current field. This key works only if you use it in Edit mode. Once you move to the next cell, change is applied. (For additional cancellation control, try the Undo feature, described next.)
Ctrl+Z	Reverses the last edit. Unfortunately, the Undo feature in Access isn't nearly as powerful as it is in other Office programs. For example, Access allows you to reverse only one change, and if you close the datasheet, you can't even do that. You can use Undo right after you insert a new record to remove it, but you can't use the Undo feature to reverse a delete operation.
Ctrl+"	Copies a value from the field that's immediately above the current field. This trick's handy when you need to enter a batch of records with similar information. Figure 1-11 shows this often-overlooked trick in action.
Ctrl+;	Inserts today's date into the current field. The date format's based on computer settings, but expect to see something like 24-12-2007. You'll learn more about how Access works with dates on page 78.
Ctrl+Alt+Space	Inserts the default value for the field. You'll learn how to designate a default value on page 134.

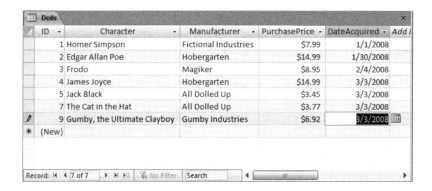

Figure 1-11. An Access user has been on an eBay buying binge and needs to add several dolls at once. With a quick Ctrl+" keystroke, the acquire date from the previous record's pasted into the current field.

Cut, copy, and paste

Access, like virtually every Windows program, lets you cut and paste bits of information from one spot to another. This trick's easy using just three shortcut keys: Ctrl+C to copy, Ctrl+X to cut (similar to copy, but the original content's deleted), and Ctrl+V to paste. When you're in Edit mode, you can use these keys to copy whatever you've selected. If you're not in Edit mode, the copying or cutting operation grabs all the content in the field.

GEM IN THE ROUGH

Copying an Entire Record in One Step

Usually, you'll use copy and paste with little bits and pieces of data. However, Access has a little-known ability that lets you copy an *entire record*. To pull it off, follow these steps:

1. Click the margin to the left of the record you want to copy.

2. This selects the record. (If you want to copy more than one adjacent record, hold down Shift, and then drag your mouse up or down until they're all selected.)

3. Right-click the selection, and then choose Copy.

This copies the content to the clipboard.

4. Scroll to the bottom of the table until you see the new-row marker (the asterisk).

5. Right-click the margin just to the left of the new-row marker, and then choose Paste.

Presto—an exact duplicate. (Truth be told, one piece of data doesn't match exactly. Access updates the ID column for your pasted record, giving it a new number. That's because every record needs to have a unique ID. You'll learn why on page 91.)

Saving and Opening Access Databases

Unlike other programs, Access doesn't require that you save your work. It automatically saves any changes you make.

When you create a new database (page 28), Access saves your database file. When you add a table or another object to the database, Access saves the database again. And when you enter new data or edit existing data, Access saves the database almost instantaneously.

Shrinking a Database

When you add information to a database, Access doesn't always pack the data as compactly as possible. Instead, Access is more concerned with getting information in and out of the database as quickly as it can.

After you've been working with a database for a while, you might notice that its size bloats up like a week-old fish in the sun. If you want to trim your database back to size, you can use a feature called *compacting*. To do so, just choose Office button → Manage → Compact and Repair Database. The amount of space you reclaim varies widely, but it's not uncommon to have a 10 MB database shrink down to a quarter of its size.

The only problem with the database compacting feature is that you need to remember to use it. If you want to keep your databases as small as possible at all times, you can switch on a setting that tells Access to compact the current database every time you close it. Here's how:

1. Open the database that you want to automatically compact.

2. Choose Office button → Access Options. Access opens the Access Options window where you can make a number of configuration changes.

3. In the list on the left, choose Current Database.

4. In the page on the right, turn on the "Compact on Close" checkbox.

5. Click OK to save your changes.

You can set the "Compact on Close" setting on as few or as many databases as you want. Just remember, it's not switched on when you first create a new database.

This automatic save process takes place behind the scenes, and you probably won't notice anything. But don't be alarmed when you exit Access and it doesn't prompt you to save changes, as *all changes are saved the moment you make them*.

Making Backups

The automatic save feature can pose a problem if you make a change mistakenly. If you're fast enough, you can use the Undo feature to reverse your last change (Figure 1-12). However, the Undo feature reverses only your most recent edit, so it's no help if you edit a series of records and then discover the problem. It also doesn't help if you close your table and then reopen it.

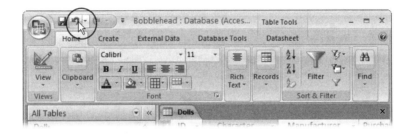

Figure 1-12. The Undo command appears in the Quick Access toolbar at the top left of the Access window (circled), so it's always available.

For these reasons, it's a good idea to make frequent database backups. To make a backup, you simply need to copy your database file to another folder, or make a copy with another name (like Bobblehead_Backup1.accdb). You can perform these tasks with Windows Explorer, but Access gives you an even easier option. Just choose Office button → Manage → Back Up Database, and Access creates a copy of your database for you, in the location you choose (Figure 1-13).

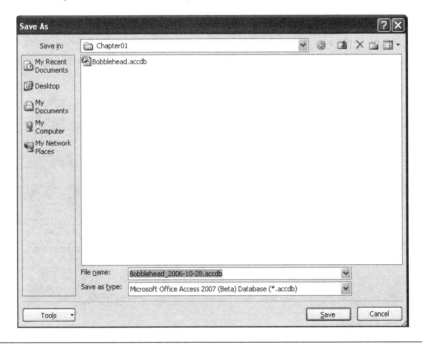

Figure 1-13. When you choose Office button → Manage → Back Up Database, Access fills in a suggested file name that incorporates the current date. That way, if you have several backup files, you can pick out the one you want.

It's still up to you to *remember* to back up your database. Access doesn't include an automatic backup feature, but you can use another tool to periodically copy your database file. One example is the Windows Task Scheduler that's included with most versions of Windows. (You can read a quick no-nonsense Task Scheduler tutorial at *www.pctechguide.com/tutorials/ScheduleTasks.htm.*)

Saving a Database with a Different Name or Format

If you want to save your database with a different name, in a different place, or using an older Access file format, you can use the trusty Save As command. Choose Office button → Save As, and then use one of the options in Figure 1-14. Note that, once Access creates the new database file, that file's the one it keeps using. In other words, when you create a table or edit some data, Access updates the *new* file. (If you want to go back to the old file, you either need to open it in Access, or use Save As again.)

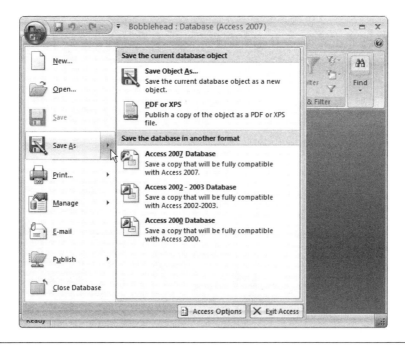

Figure 1-14. Make sure you click the right-pointing arrow next to the Save As menu command to see this submenu of choices. (Just clicking Save As performs the default option, which saves a copy of the currently selected database object, not your entire database.) Then, choose one of the options under the "Save the database in another format" heading.

Opening a Database

Once you've created a database, it's easy to open it later. You can use any of these approaches:

▶ Double-click a database file. (You can browse to it using My Computer, Windows Explorer, or just plop in on your desktop.) Remember, Access databases have the file extension .accdb or .mdb.

▶ Launch Access, and then look for your database in the Open Recent Database section on the right of the Getting Started page. (The same list's available through the Office menu, as shown in Figure 1-15.)

▶ Launch Access, choose Office button → Open, and then browse for your Access database file.

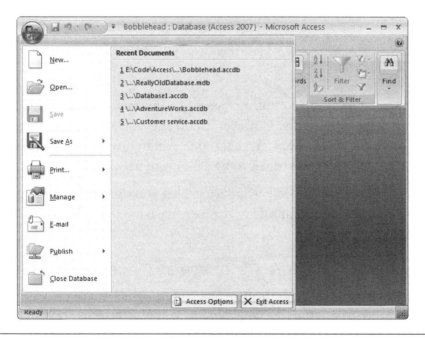

Figure 1-15. The Office menu's Recent Documents list has the same list of files as the Open Recent Database section on the Getting Started page. But if you already have a database open, the Recent Documents list's more convenient, because you don't need to head back to the Getting Started page.

When you open a database, you'll notice something a little bizarre. Access pops up a message bar with a scary-sounding security warning (Figure 1-16).

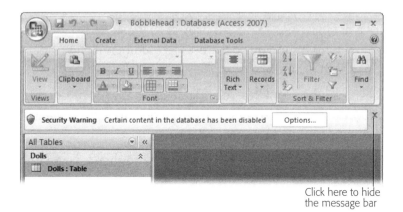

Click here to hide
the message bar

Figure 1-16. This security warning tells you that Access doesn't trust your database—in other words, it's opened your file in a special safe mode that prevents your database from performing any risky operations.

The security warning's a bit confusing, because right now your database doesn't even *attempt* do anything risky. However, when you start using action queries (Chapter 7), it's a different story. At that point, you may want to reconfigure Access so it recognizes your files and learns to be a bit more trusting.

In the meantime, you're probably wondering what you should do about the message bar. Just click the X at the right side of the message bar to banish it. (It'll reappear the next time you open the database.)

Opening More Than One Database at Once

Every time you use the Office button → Open command, Access closes the current database, and then opens the one you chose. If you want to see more than one database at a time, you need to fire up more than one copy of Access at the same time. (Computer geeks refer to this action as starting more than one *instance* of a program.)

It's almost embarrassingly easy. If you double-click another database file while Access is already open, then a second Access window appears in the taskbar for that database. You can also launch a second (or third, or fourth…) instance of Access

What's with the .laccdb File?

I see an extra file with the extension .laccdb. What gives?

So far, you've familiarized yourself with the .accdb file type. But if you're in the habit of browsing around with Windows Explorer, you may notice another file that you didn't create, with the cryptic extension .laccdb. Along with Bobble-head.accdb, you may spot the mysterious Bobblehead.laccdb.

Access creates a .laccdb file when you open a database file and removes it when you close the database, so you'll see it only while you (or someone else) is browsing the database.

Access uses the .laccddb to track who's currently using the database. The *l* stands for *lock*, and it's used to make sure that if more than one person's using the database at once, people can't make changes to the same record at the same time (which could cause all manner of headaches).

Access 2007: The Missing Manual covers more on how Access works with multiple users. All you need to know is that it's safe to ignore the .laccddb file. You don't need to include it in your backups.

---

from the Start menu, and then use Office button → Open to load up a different database in each one.

Opening a Database Created in an Older Version of Access

You can use the Office button → Open command to open an Access database that somebody created with a previous version of Access. (See the box "Sharing Databases with Older Versions of Access" on page 33 for more about different Access file formats.)

Access handles old database files differently, depending on just how old they are. Here's how it works:

▶ If you open an Access 2002-2003 file, you don't get any notification or warning. Access keeps the current format, and you're free to make any changes you want.

▶ If you open an Access 2000 file, you're also in for smooth sailing. However, if you change the design of the database, the new parts you add may not be accessible in Access 2000.

▶ If you open an older Access file (like one created for Access 97, 95, or 2.0), Access asks whether you want to convert the database or just open it (see Figure 1-17).

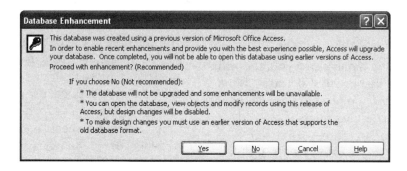

Figure 1-17. Access gives you a choice when you open a database file that was created in Access 97, 95, or 2.0. If you choose to convert the database (click Yes), Access copies the existing database into a new database file, in Access 2002-2003 format. You can then edit this copy normally. If you choose to open the database (click No), Access opens the original file without making a copy. You can still edit existing data and add new data, but you can't change the database's design.

POWER USERS' CLINIC

Changing the Folder Access Uses for Databases

Access always assumes you want to store databases in the My Documents folder. And though you can choose a different location every time you save or open a database, if there's another folder you need to visit frequently, then it makes sense to make that your standard database storage location. You can configure Access to use this folder with just a few steps:

1. Choose Office button → Access Options. The Access Options window appears.

2. In the list on the left, choose Popular.

3. In the page on the right, look for the "Creating databases" heading. Underneath, you'll find a "Default database folder" text box. Type in the folder you want to use (like C:\MyDatabases), or click Browse to navigate to it.

When you're finished, click OK to save your changes.

___ TIP ___

You can always tell the current database's format by looking at the text in brackets in the Access window's title bar. If you open an Access 2002-2003 file, the title bar might read "Bobblehead: Database (Access 2002-2003 file format)".

When you open an old-school Access database, you'll notice something else has changed. When you open a table, it won't appear in a tabbed window (like the ones shown in Figure 1-20). Instead, the table opens in an ordinary window that can float wherever it wants *inside* the main Access window. This seems fine at first, until you open several tables at once. Then, you're stuck with some real clutter, as shown in Figure 1-18.

Figure 1-18. In an old-style Access database, different windows can overlap each other. It's not long before the table you want is buried at the bottom of a stack of windows.

This somewhat unfriendly behavior is designed to be more like previous versions of Access. But don't worry—you can get back to the slick tabs even if you don't convert your database to the new format. All you need to do is set a single configuration option for your database:

1. **Choose Office button → Access Options. The Access Options window appears.**

2. **In the list on the left, choose Current Database.**

3. **Under the Application Options heading, look for the Document Windows Options setting, where you can choose Overlapping Windows (the Access 2003 standard) or Tabbed Windows (the wave of the future).**

4. **Click OK.**

5. **Close and open your database so the new setting takes effect.**

For a retro touch, you can use the same setting to make a brand new Access database use overlapping windows instead of tabs.

Creating Another Database

Creating a new database is the easiest task yet. You simply need to choose Office button → New. Access takes you back to the Getting Started page, where you can create a blank database by clicking the familiar Blank Database button, as described earlier (page 28).

The Navigation Pane

It's time to step back and take a look at what you've accomplished so far. You've created the Bobblehead database, and added a single database object: a table named Dolls. You've filled the Dolls table with several records. You don't have the fancy windows, reports, and search routines that make a database work really smoothly, but you do have the most important ingredient—organized data.

One issue you haven't tackled yet is how you manage the objects in your database. For example, if you have more than one table, you need a way to move back and forth between the two. That tool's the navigation pane, shown in Figure 1-19.

Browsing Tables with the Navigation Pane

The navigation pane shows the objects (page 24) that are part of your database, and it lets you manipulate them. However, you don't necessarily see all your database objects at all times. The navigation pane has several different viewing modes, so you can home in on exactly what interests you.

When you first create a database, the navigation pane shows only the tables in your database. That's good enough for now—after all, your database doesn't contain anything but the tables you've created.

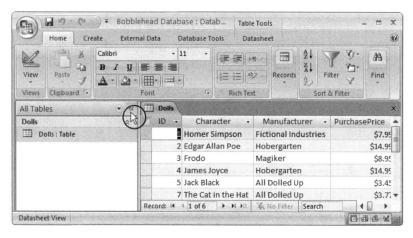

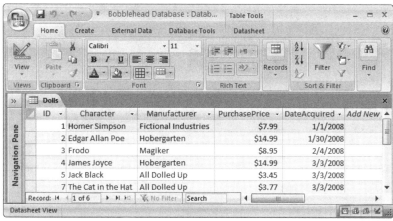

Figure 1-19. Unhappy with the space consumed by the navigation pane? Click the Open/Close button in the top-right corner (top), and the navigation bar slides out of the way to give more room for the datasheet (bottom). Click the button again to expand it back into view.

To really try out the navigation pane, you need a database with more than one table. To give it a whirl, choose Create → Table from the ribbon to add a new blank table. Follow all the steps on page 34 to define the table and insert a record or two.

— TIP

Not sure what table to create? Try creating a Collectors table that tracks all the friends you know who share the same bobbleheaded obsession. Now try to come up with a few useful fields for this table (while remembering that there's no need to go crazy with the details yet), and then compare your version to the example in Figure 1-20.

Once you've added the new table, you see both the new table and the old in the navigation pane at the same time. If you want to open a table, then, in the navigation pane, just double-click it. If you have more than one datasheet open at once, then Access organizes them into tabs (see Figure 1-20).

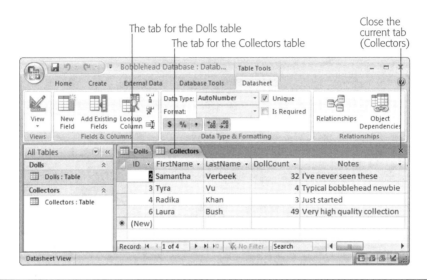

Figure 1-20. Using the navigation pane, you can open as many tables at once as you want. Access gives each datasheet a separate tabbed window. To move from one window to another, you just click the corresponding tab. If you're feeling a bit crowded, just click the X at the far right of the tab strip to close the current datasheet.

If you open enough tables, eventually all the tabs you need won't fit. In this situation, Access adds tiny scroll buttons to the left and right of the tab strip. You can use these buttons to move through all the tabs, but it takes longer.

Managing Database Objects

So far, you know how to open a table using the navigation pane. However, opening tables isn't all you can do with the navigation pane. You can actually perform three more simple tasks with any database object that shows up in the navigation pane:

▶ **Rename it**. Right-click the object, and then choose Rename. Then, type in the new name, and then press Enter. Go this route if you decide your Dolls table would be better off named DollsInMyWorldRenownedCollection.

Collapsing the Ribbon

Most people are happy to have the ribbon sit at the top of the Access window, with all its buttons on hand. However, serious data crunchers demand maximum space for their data. They'd rather look at another record of information than a pumped-up toolbar. If this preference describes you, then you'll be happy to find out you can *collapse* the ribbon, which shrinks it down to a single row of tab titles, as shown in Figure 1-21. To do so, just double-click any tab title.

Even when the ribbon's collapsed, you can still use all its features. Just click a tab. If you click Home, the Home tab pops up over your worksheet. As soon as you click the button you want in the Home tab (or click somewhere else in

the Access window), the ribbon collapses itself again. The same trick works if you trigger a command in the ribbon using the keyboard, as described on page 8.

If you use the ribbon only occasionally, or if you prefer to use keyboard shortcuts, it makes sense to collapse the ribbon. Even when collapsed, the ribbon commands are available; it just takes an extra click to open the tab. On the other hand, if you make frequent trips to the ribbon, or if you're learning about Access and you like to browse the ribbon to see the available features, don't bother collapsing it. The extra space that you'll lose is well worth it.

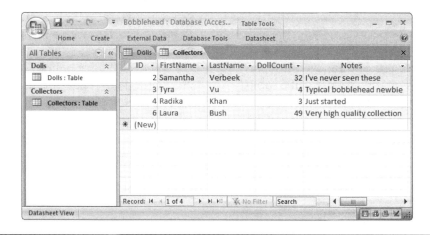

Figure 1-21. Do you want to use every square inch of screen space for your data? You can collapse the ribbon (as shown here) by double-clicking any tab. Click a tab to pop it open temporarily, or double-click a tab to bring the ribbon back for good. And if you want to perform the same trick without raising your fingers from the keyboard, then you can use the shortcut key Ctrl+F1.

- **Create a copy.** Right-click the object, and then choose Copy. Right-click anywhere in the navigation pane, and then choose Paste. Access prompts you to supply the new copy's name. The copy-an-object feature's useful if you want to take an existing table and try redesigning it, but you're not ready to remove the original copy just yet.

- **Delete it.** Right-click the object, and then choose Delete. Access asks you to confirm this operation, because you can't reverse it.

Access gives you a few more options for transferring database objects and tucking them out of sight. You'll consider these features later in the book.

TIMESAVING TIP

Creating a Shortcut to a Table

You probably already know that you can place a Windows shortcut on your desktop that points to your database file. To do so, just right-click your desktop, choose New → Shortcut, and then follow the instructions to pick your database file and choose a shortcut name. Now, any time you want to jump back into your database, you can double-click your shortcut.

You probably don't know that you can create a shortcut that opens a database *and* navigates directly to a specific table. In fact, this maneuver's even easier than creating a plain-vanilla shortcut. Just follow these steps:

1. Resize the Access window so it doesn't take up the full screen, and then minimize any other programs. This way, you can see the desktop behind Access, which is essential for this trick.

2. Find the table you want to use in the navigation pane. Drag this table out of Access and over the desktop.

3. Release the mouse button. Access creates a shortcut with a name like "Shortcut to Dolls in Bobblehead.accdb". Double-click this shortcut to load the Bobblehead database and open a datasheet right away for the Dolls table.

BUILDING SMARTER TABLES

- ▶ Understanding Data Types
- ▶ Design View
- ▶ Access Data Types
- ▶ The Primary Key
- ▶ Six Principles of Database Design

IN THE PREVIOUS CHAPTER, you learned how to dish out databases and pop tables into them without breaking a sweat. However, there's bad news. The tables you've been creating so far aren't up to snuff.

Most significantly, you haven't explicitly told Access what *type* of information you intend to store in each field of your table. A database treats text, numbers, dates, and other types of information differently. If you store numeric information in a field that expects text, then you can't do calculations later on (like find the average value of your bobblehead dolls), and you can't catch mistakes (like a bobblehead with a price value of "fourscore and twenty").

To prevent problems like these, you need to define the *data type* of each field in your table. This is the central task you'll tackle in this chapter. Once you've mastered data types, you're ready to consider some of the finer points of database design.

Understanding Data Types

All data's not created equal. Consider the Dolls table you created in Chapter 1 (page 32). Its fields actually contain several different types of information:

▶ **Text**. The Character and Manufacturer fields.

▶ **Numbers**. The ID and PurchasePrice fields.

▶ **Dates**. The DateAcquired field.

You may naturally assume that the PurchasePrice field always includes numeric content, and the DateAcquired field always includes something that can be interpreted as a date. But if you haven't set the data types correctly, Access doesn't share your assumptions, and doesn't follow the same rules.

When you create a new field in Datasheet view, Access makes an educated guess about the data type by examining the information you've just typed in. If you type 44, then Access assumes you're creating a number field. If you type *Jan 6, 2007*, then Access recognizes a date. However, it's easy to confuse Access, which leads to the problems shown in Figure 2-1.

In order to prevent invalid entries, you need to tell Access what each field *should* contain. Once you set the rules, Access enforces them rigorously. You put these requirements in place using another window—the Design view of your table.

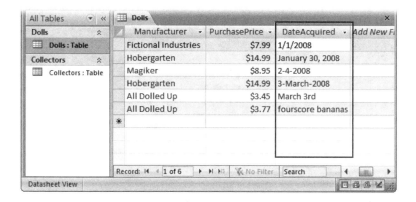

Figure 2-1. Here, Access doesn't recognize the date format used for the DateAcquired field when it was created. As a result, Access treats that field as ordinary text. You can enter dates in several different formats (which makes the DateAcquired information harder to read and impossible to sort). You also let in completely nonsensical entries, like "fourscore bananas."

Design View

When you create a new database, Access starts you off with a single table and shows that table in Datasheet view. (As you learned last chapter, Datasheet view is the grid-like view where you can create a table *and* enter data.) To switch to Design view, right-click the tab name (like "Dolls: Table"), and then choose Design View. (Or you can use the Home → View command, the Table Tools | Datasheet → View command, or the View buttons at the bottom of the Access window. Figure 2-2 shows all your options. All of these commands do the same thing, so pick whichever approach seems most convenient.)

— **NOTE** ———————————————————————————————————

If you've opened an old Access 2003 database, you won't see any tabs. Instead, you'll get a bunch of overlapping windows. You can remedy this problem and get your tabs back by following the instructions on page 51. Or, if you want to keep the overlapping windows, just use the view buttons or the ribbon to change views (instead of the right-click-the-tab-title approach described above).

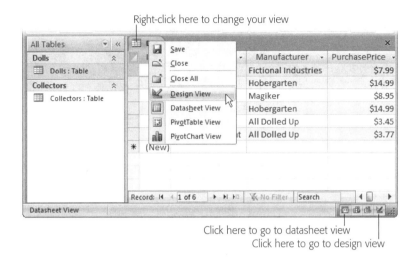

Right-click here to change your view

Click here to go to datasheet view
Click here to go to design view

Figure 2-2. Right-click the tab name to see this menu. You can switch to Design view (choose Design View) and back again (choose Datasheet View). Alternatively, you can use the tiny view buttons in the window's bottom-right corner to jump back and forth. (Don't worry about the other two view buttons. Those are used to analyze data in a pivot table, an advanced form of data presentation covered in *Access 2007: The Missing Manual*.)

If you switch to Design view on a brand-new table that you haven't saved yet, Access asks you for a table name. Access then saves the table before switching you to Design view.

— TIP

For a handy shortcut, you can create a new table and automatically start in Design view. To do this, choose Create → Tables → Table Design. However, when you take this route, your table doesn't include the very important ID column, so you need to add one, as described on page 91.

While Datasheet view shows the content in your table, Design view shows only its *structure* (see Figure 2-3).

You can use Design view to add, rearrange, and remove fields, but you can't use it to add new records. In the Dolls table, you can use Design view to add a Quantity field to keep track of doll duplicates. However, you can't add your newly purchased Bono

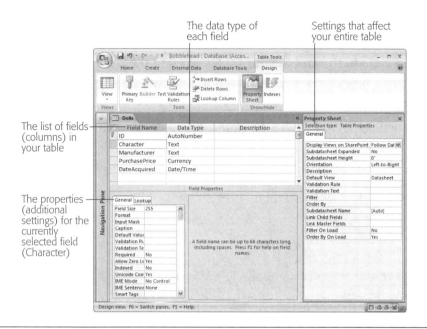

The data type of each field

Settings that affect your entire table

The list of fields (columns) in your table

The properties (additional settings) for the currently selected field (Character)

Figure 2-3. Design view lists the fields in your table, putting each in a separate row. Fields here are listed from top to bottom, but they appear in datasheet view ordered from left to right. Next to each field is its data type and an optional description. Underneath the field list, the Field Properties section shows more information about the currently selected field. Here, the navigation pane has been collapsed (page 53) to provide extra space.

bobblehead without switching back to the Datasheet view. Design view isn't intended for data entry.

At first, Design view seems quite intimidating. To simplify what you're looking at, you should start by closing the Property Sheet box on the window's right side. (The Property Sheet lets you set a few highly technical table settings, none of which you need to consider right now.) To banish it, choose Table Tools | Design → Property Sheet. If you want to bring it back later, then just repeat the same command.

Organizing and Describing Your Fields

Design view allows you to rearrange the order of your fields, add new ones, rename the existing ones, and more. You can also do all these things in Datasheet view, but Access gurus usually find it's easier to work in Design view, because you won't be distracted by the data in the table.

Here are a few simple ways you can change the structure of your table in Design view:

▶ **Add a new field to the end of your table.** Scroll to the last row of the field list, and then type in a new field name. This action's equivalent to adding a new field in Datasheet view.

▶ **Add a new field between existing fields.** Move to the field that's just *under* the place where you want to add the new field. Right-click the field, and then choose Insert Rows. Then, type a field name in the new, blank row.

▶ **Move a field.** Drag the gray square immediately to the left of the field you want to move, to the new position.

> **NOTE**
>
> Remember, the fields' order isn't all that important, because you can change the order in which you view the fields in Datasheet view. However, most people find it's easier to design a table if you organize the fields from the very start.

▶ **Delete a field.** Right-click the gray square immediately to the left of the field you want to remove, and then choose Delete Rows. Keep in mind that when you remove a field, you also wipe out any data that was stored in that field. This action isn't reversible, so Access prompts you to confirm it's really what you want to do.

▶ **Add a description for a field.** Type in a sentence or two in the Description column next to the appropriate field (see Figure 2-4).

How Updates Work in Design View

Access doesn't immediately apply the changes you make in Design view. Instead, it waits until you close the table or switch back to Datasheet view. At that point, Access asks whether you want to save the table. (The answer, of course, is Yes.)

Sometimes, you may apply a change that causes a bit of a problem. You could try to change the data type of a field so that it stores numbers instead of text. (The box on page 68, "Changing the Data Type Can Lose Information," discusses this problem in more detail.) In this situation, you won't discover the problem until you close the table or switch back to the Datasheet view, which might be a little later than you expect.

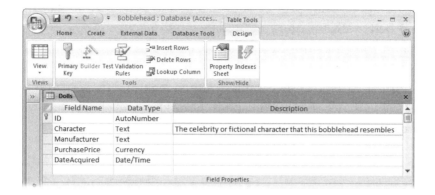

Figure 2-4. Descriptions can help you remember what's what if you need to modify a table later on. Descriptions are a great idea if more than one person maintains the same database, in which case you need to make sure your fields are as clear as possible. Descriptions also appear in the status bar when you're entering information in a table (see Figure 2-5).

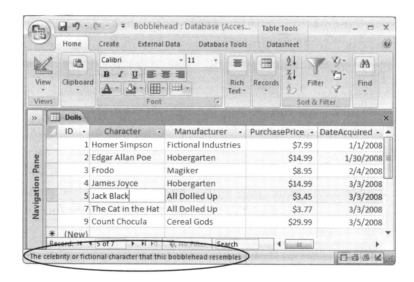

Figure 2-5. The status bar text tells you what goes in this column, based on the field description. Sadly, this feature isn't as useful as it seems, because most people never think to look down in the status bar.

If you've made a potentially problematic change and you just can't take the suspense, you're better off applying your update *immediately,* so you can see if there's a problem before you go any further. To do so, click the Quick Access toolbar's Save button (it's the diskette icon in the Access window's top-left corner), or just use the keyboard shortcut Ctrl+S. Access applies your change, and then saves the table. If it runs into a problem, Access tells you about it (and lets you choose how you want to fix it) before you do anything else with the table.

Access Data Types

Design view's a much more powerful place for defining a table than Datasheet view. As you'll see throughout this chapter, Design view allows you to tweak all sorts of details that are hidden in Datasheet view (or just awkward to change).

One of these is the *data type* of your field—a setting that tells Access what type of information you're planning to store. To change the data type, make a selection in the Data Type column next to the appropriate field (Figure 2-6). Here's where you separate the text from numbers (and other data types). The trick's choosing the best data type from the long list Access provides—you'll get more help in the following section.

Depending on the data type you choose, there are other *field properties* that you can adjust to nail down your data type even more precisely. If you use a text data type, then you use field properties to set the maximum length. If you choose a decimal value, then you use field properties to set the number of decimal places. You set field properties in the Field Properties part of the Design view, which appears just under the field list. You'll learn more about field properties throughout this chapter (and you'll consider them again in Chapter 4).

The most important decision you'll make for any field is choosing its data type. The data type tells Access what sort of information you plan to store in that field. Access uses this information to reject values that don't make sense (see Figure 2-7), to perform proper sorting, and to provide other features like calculations, summaries, and filtering.

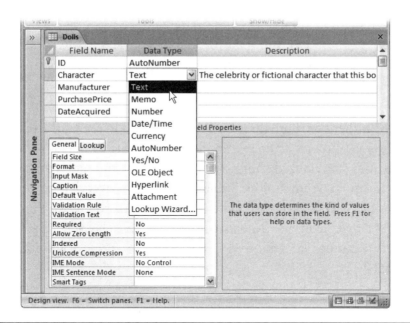

Figure 2-6. To choose a data type, click the Data Type column next to the appropriate field. A drop-down list box appears, with 11 choices.

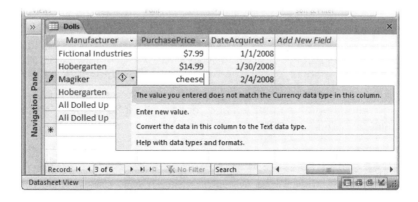

Figure 2-7. This currency field absolutely does not allow text. Access lets you fix the problem by entering a new value (the right choice) or changing the field data type to text so that it allows anything (the absolutely wrong choice).

NOTE

A field can have only one data type. You can't create a field that can store two or three different data types, because Access wouldn't have enough information to manage the field properly. (Instead, in this situation, you probably need two separate fields.)

As you learned earlier, there are three basic types of data in the world: text, numbers, and dates. However, Access actually provides a whopping *11* data types, which include many more specialized choices. Before you pick the right data type, it's a good idea to review all your choices. Table 2-1 shows an overview of the first 10 menu options in the Data Type list. (The Lookup wizard choice isn't included, because it isn't a real data type. Instead, this menu option launches the Lookup wizard, which lets you set a list of allowed values. You'll learn more about this on page 159 in Chapter 4.)

Table 2-1. Access Data Types

Data Type	Description	Examples
Text	Numbers, letters, punctuation, and symbols, up to a maximum of 255 characters (an average-sized paragraph).	Names, addresses, phone numbers, and product descriptions. This data type's the most common.
Memo	Large amounts of unformatted text, up to 65,536 characters (an average-sized chapter in a novel).	Articles, memos, letters, arrest warrants, and other short documents.
Number	A variety of different kinds of numbers, including negative numbers and those that have decimal places.	Any type of number except dollar values. Stores measurements, counts, and percentages.
Currency	Similar to Number, but optimized for numbers that represent values of money.	Prices, payments, and expenses.
Date/Time	A calendar date or time of day (or both). Don't use this field for time *intervals* (the number of minutes in a song, the length of your workout session)—instead, use the Number data type.	Birthdates, order dates, ship dates, appointments, and UFO sighting times.
Yes/No	Holds one of two values: Yes or No. (You can also think of this as True or False.)	Fields with exactly two options, like male/female or approved/unapproved.

Table 2-1. Access Data Types (continued)

Data Type	Description	Examples
Hyperlink	A URL to a Web site, an email address, or a file path.	www.FantasyPets.com, noreplies@antisocial.co.uk, f:\Documents\Report.doc.
Attachment	One or more separate files. The content from these files is copied into the database.	Pictures, Word documents, Excel spreadsheets, sound files, and so on.
AutoNumber	Stores a number that Access generates when you insert a new record. Every record automatically gets a unique number that identifies it.	Used to uniquely identify each record, especially for a primary key (page 90). Usually, the field's named ID.
OLE Object	Holds embedded binary data, according to the Windows OLE (object linking and embedding) standard. Rarely used, because it leads to database bloat and other problems. The Attachment field's almost always a better choice.	Some types of pictures and documents from other programs. Mostly used in old-school Access databases. Nowadays, database designers use the Attachment data type instead of the OLE Object data type.

The following sections describe each data type except for OLE Object, which is a holdover from the dark ages of Access databases. Each section also describes any important field properties that are unique to that data type.

Text

Text is the all-purpose data type. It accepts any combination of letters, numbers, and other characters. So you can use a text field for a word or two (like "Mary Poppins"), a sentence ("The candidate is an English nanny given to flights of song."), or anything else ("@#$d sf_&!").

___ NOTE _____

Because text fields are so lax, you can obviously enter numbers, dates, and just about anything else in them. However, you should use text only when you're storing some information that can't be dealt with using another data type, because Access always treats the contents of a text field as plain, ordinary text. In other words, if you store the number 43.99 in a text field, Access doesn't realize you're dealing with numbers, and it doesn't let you use it in a calculation.

_____

Changing the Data Type Can Lose Information

The best time to choose the data types for your fields is when you first create the table. That way, your table's completely empty, and you won't run into any problems.

If you add a few records, and *then* decide to change the data type in one of your fields, life becomes a little more complicated. You can still use Design view to change the data type, but Access needs to go through an extra step and *convert* the existing data to the new data type.

In many cases, the conversion process goes smoothly. If you have a text field that contains only numbers, you won't have a problem changing the data type from Text to Number. But in other cases, the transition isn't quite so seamless. Here are some examples of the problems you might run into:

* You change the data type from Text to Date, but Access can't interpret some of your values as dates.

* You change the data type from Text to Number, but some of your records have text values in that field (even though they shouldn't).

* You change the data type from Text to Number. However, your field contains fractional numbers (like 4.234), and you forget to change the Field Size property (page 75). As a result, Access assumes you want to use only whole numbers, and chops off all your decimal places.

The best way to manage these problems is to make a backup (page 44) before you make any drastic changes, and be on the lookout for changes that go wrong. In the first two cases in the list above, Access warns you that it needs to remove some values because they don't fit the data type rules (see Figure 2-8). The third problem's a little more insidious—Access gives you a warning, but it doesn't actually tell you whether or not a problem occurred. If you suspect trouble, switch to Design view, and then check out your data before going any further.

Sometimes it seems that the Text data type's just too freewheeling. Fortunately, you can apply some stricter rules that deny certain characters or force text values to match a preset pattern. For example, Access usually treats phone numbers like text, because they represent a series of characters like 123-4444 (not the single number 1,234,444). However, you don't want to let people put letters in a phone number, because they

Figure 2-8. Don't say you weren't warned. Here, Access lets you know (in its own slightly obscure way) that it can't make the change you want—modifying the data type of field from Text to Date—without throwing out the values in four records. The best course of action is to click No to cancel the change and then take a closer look at your table in Datasheet view to track down the problematic values.

obviously don't belong. To put this restriction into action, you can use input masks (page 140) and validation (page 147), two features discussed in Chapter 4.

Text length

Every text field has a *maximum length*. This trait comes as a great surprise to many people who aren't used to databases. After all, with today's gargantuan hard drives, why worry about space? Can't your database just expand to fit whatever data you want to stuff inside?

The maximum length matters because it determines how *densely* Access can pack your records together. For performance reasons, Access needs to make sure that an entire record's stored in one spot, so it always reserves the maximum amount of space a record might need. If your table has four fields that are 50 characters apiece, Access can reserve 200 characters worth of space on your hard drive for each record. On the other hand, if your fields have a maximum 100 characters each, Access holds on to twice as much space for each record, even if you aren't actually using that space. The extra space isn't a major issue (you probably have plenty of room on your computer), but the more spread out a database, the slower your searches.

The standard maximum length is 50, a good starting point. The box "Maximum Length Guidelines" (page 72) has some more recommendations.

To set the maximum length, enter a number in the Field Size box, in the Field Properties section (Figure 2-9). The largest maximum you're allowed is 255 characters. If you need to store a large paragraph or an entire article's worth of information, then you need the Memo data type instead (page 70).

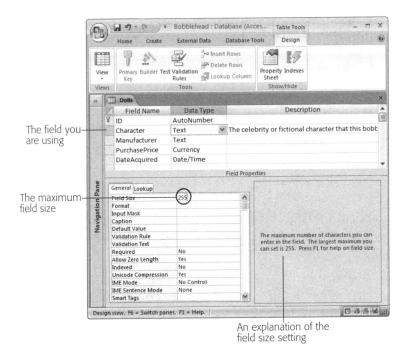

The field you are using

The maximum field size

An explanation of the field size setting

Figure 2-9. To set a maximum length, choose your field, and then click the Field Size box in the Field Properties list (shown here). (All the field properties you need in this chapter are on the General tab.) When you click a field property box, that field property's description appears on the right.

TIP

It's worthwhile being a little generous with maximum lengths to avoid the need to modify the database later on.

Memo

Microsoft designed the Memo data type to store large quantities of text. If you want to place a chapter from a book, an entire newspaper article, or just several paragraphs into a field, you need the Memo data type. The name's a little odd—although a memo field could certainly store the information from an inter-office memorandum, it's just as useful any time you have large blocks of text.

When creating a memo field, you don't need to supply a maximum length, because Access stores the data in a memo field differently from other data types. Essentially, it stuffs memo data into a separate section, so it can keep the rest of the record as compact and efficient as possible, but accommodate large amounts of text.

A memo field tops out at 65,536 characters. To put it in perspective, that's about the same size as this chapter. If you need more space, then add more than one memo field.

If you need to edit a large amount of text while you're working on the datasheet, then you can use the Zoom box (Figure 2-10). Just move to the field you want to edit, and then press Shift+F2.

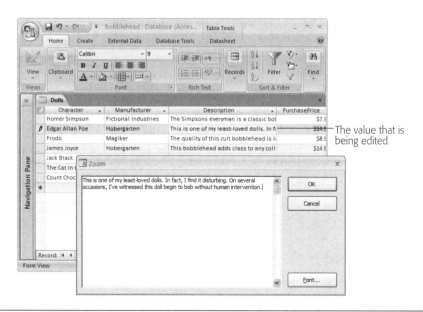

Figure 2-10. If you have lengthy text in a field, it's hard to see it all at once without a lot of scrolling. By opening a Zoom box (Shift+F2), you can see more content and edit it more easily. You'll need to click OK (to accept your edits) or Cancel (to abandon them) to get back to the datasheet.

Maximum Length Guidelines

Here are some recommended maximum lengths:

* **First names and last names.** 25 characters handles a first name, while 50 characters each plays it safe for a long, hyphenated last name.

* **Middle initial.** One character. (Sometimes common sense is right.)

* **Email address.** Go with 50 characters. Email addresses closer to 100 characters have turned up in the wild (Google "world's longest email address" for more), but they're unlikely to reach your database.

* **Cities, states, countries, and other places.** Although a Maori name for a hill in New Zealand tops out at over 80 characters (see *http://en.wikipedia.org/wiki/Longest_word_in_English*), 50 is enough for most practical purposes.

* **Street address.** A street address consists of a number, followed by a space, then the street name, another space, and the street abbreviation (like Rd or St). Fifty characters handles it, as long as you put postal codes, cities, and other postal details in other fields.

* **Phone numbers, postal codes, credit card numbers, and other fixed-length text.** Count the number characters and ignore the placeholders, and set the maximum to match. If you want to store the phone number (123) 456-7890, make the field 10 characters long. You can then *store* the phone number as 1234567890, but use an input mask (page 140) to add the parentheses, spaces, and dash when you *display* it. This approach is better because it avoids the headaches that result from entering similar phone numbers in different ways.

* **Description or comments.** 255 characters fits three or four average sentences of information. If you need more, consider the memo data type instead (page 70).

Formatted text

Like a text field, the memo field stores *unformatted* text. However, you can also store *rich text* in a memo field—text that has different fonts, colors, text alignment, and so on. To do so, set the Text Format setting to Rich Text (rather than Plain Text).

To format part of your text, you simply need to select it and then choose a formatting option from the ribbon's Home → Font Home → Rich Text sections. However, most of the time you won't take this approach, because it's difficult to edit large amounts of text in the datasheet's narrow columns. Instead, use Shift+F2 to open a Zoom box, and then use the minibar (Figure 2-11).

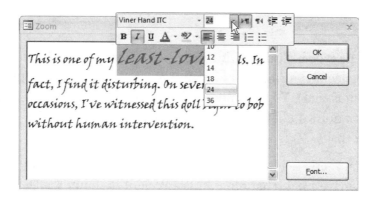

Figure 2-11. To show the minibar (sadly, of the non-alcoholic variety), select some text, and then hover over it with the mouse. The minibar—a compact toolbar with formatting options—gradually fades into view. The minibar's sometimes a little finicky, and you may need to reselect the text more than once to get it to appear.

TIP

There's another, even easier way to get formatted text into a memo field. Create the text in a word processing program (like Word), format it there, and then copy and paste it into the field. All the formatting comes with it.

As neat as this feature may seem at first glance, it's rarely worth the trouble. Database purists believe that tables should store raw information and let other programs (or fancy forms) decide how to format it. The problem is that once you've created your formatted text, it can be quite a chore to maintain it. Just imagine having to change the font in 30,000 different records.

If you really do want to store formatted content, then consider linking your database to a separate document, like a Word file. In Access, you can do this in two ways:

▶ **Create a field that points to the file.** For example, c:\myfile\BonoBobblehead-Description.docx). For this trick, use the Text or Hyperlink data type (page 83).

▶ **Embed the file inside your database.** This way, it's impossible to lose the file (or end up pointing to the wrong location). However, you'll need to pull the file out every time you want to update it. To do this, you need to use the Attachment data type (page 84).

Number

The Number data type includes a wide variety of differently sized numbers. You can choose to allow decimal numbers, and you can use negative values (just precede the value with a minus sign). You should use the Number data type for every type of numeric information you have—except currency amounts, in which case the Currency data type (page 77) is a better match.

When you use numeric fields, you don't include information about the units you're using. You may have a field that represents a Weight in pounds, a Height in Meters, or an Age in Years. However, these fields contain only a number. It's up to you to know what that number signifies. If you think other people may be confused, consider explaining the units in the description (page 62), or incorporate it into the field name (like HeightInMeters).

___ NOTE _____

Your field should never, ever contain values like "44 pounds." Access treats this value as a text value, so if you make this mistake, you can't use all the important number crunching and validation tools you'll learn about later in this book.

_____

Number size

As with a text field, when you create a number field, you need to set the Field Size property to make sure Access reserves the right amount of space. However, with numbers your options are a little more complicated than they are for ordinary text.

Essentially, numbers are divided into several subgroups, depending on whether or not they support fractional values (numbers to the right of a decimal point) and how many *bytes* of space Access uses to store them.

__ NOTE _____

A byte's a group of eight bits, which is the smallest unit of storage in the computer world. For example, a megabyte's approximately one million bytes.

Table 2-2 lists the different Field Size options you can choose for the Number data type, and explains when each one makes most sense. Initially, Access chooses Long Integer for all fields, which gives a fair bit of space but doesn't allow fractional values.

Table 2-2. Field Size Options for the Number Data Type.

Field Size	Contains	When to Use It
Byte	An integer (whole number) from 0 to 255. Requires just one byte of space.	This size is risky, because it fits only very small numbers. Usually, it's safer to use Integer for small numbers and give yourself a little more breathing room.
Integer	An integer (whole number) from –32,768 to 32,767. Requires two bytes of space.	Useful if you need small numbers with no decimal part.
Long Integer	An integer (whole number) from –2,147,483,648 to 2,147,483,647. Requires four bytes of space.	The Access standard. A good choice with plenty of room. Use this to store just about anything without hitting the maximum, as long as you don't need decimals.
Single	Positive or negative numbers with up to 38 zeroes and 7 decimal places of accuracy. Requires four bytes of space.	The best choice if you need to store fractional numbers or numbers that are too large to fit in a Long Integer.
Double	Positive or negative numbers with up to 308 zeroes and 15 decimal places of accuracy. Requires eight bytes of space.	Useful if you need ridiculously big numbers.
Decimal	Positive or negative numbers with up to 28 zeroes and 28 decimal places of accuracy. Requires eight bytes of space.	Useful for fractional numbers that have lots of digits to the right of the decimal point.

> Table 2-2 doesn't include Replication ID, because you use that option only with the AutoNumber data type (page 87).

Number formatting

The Field Size determines how Access stores your number in the table. However, you can still choose how it's *presented* in the datasheet. For example, 50, 50.00, 5E1, $50.00, and 5000% are all the same number behind the scenes, but people interpret them in dramatically different ways.

To choose a format, you set the Format field property. Your basic built-in choices include:

▶ **General Number.** Displays unadorned numbers, like 43.4534. Any extra zeroes at the end of a number are chopped off (so 4.10 becomes 4.1).

▶ **Currency and Euro.** Both options display numbers with two decimal places, thousands separators (the comma in $1,000.00), and a currency symbol. These choices are used only with the Currency data type (page 77).

▶ **Fixed.** Displays numbers with the same number of decimal places, filling in zeroes if necessary (like 432.11 and 39.00). A long column of numbers lines up on the decimal point, which makes your tables easier to read.

▶ **Standard.** Similar to Fixed, except it also uses thousands separators to help you quickly interpret large numbers like 1,000,000.00.

▶ **Percent.** Displays fractional numbers as percentages. For example, if you enter 0.5, that translates to 50%.

▶ **Scientific.** Displays numbers using scientific notation, which is ideal when you need to handle numbers that range widely in size (like 0.0003 and 300). Scientific notation displays the first non-zero digit of a number, followed by a fixed number of digits, and then indicates what power of ten that number needs to be multiplied by to generate the specified number. For example, 0.0003 becomes 3.00×10^{-4}, which displays as 3.00E-4. The number 300, on the other hand, becomes 3.00×10^{2}, or 3E2.

▶ **A custom format string.** This is a cryptic code that tells Access exactly how to format a number. You need to type the format string you need into the Format box. For example, if you type in the weird-looking code *#,##0,* (including the comma at the end) Access hides the last three digits of every number, so 1 million appears as 1,000 and 15,000 as 15.

Currency

Currency's a slight variation on the Number data type that's tailored for financial calculations. Unlike the Number data type, here you can't choose a Field Size for the Currency data type—Access has a one-size-fits-all policy that requires eight bytes of storage space.

You can adjust the number of decimal places Access shows for currency values on the datasheet by setting the Decimal Places field property. Usually, it's set to 2.

The formatting that Access uses to display currency values is determined by the Regional and Language Options settings on your computer (page 82). However, these settings might produce results you don't want—for example, say you run an artisanal cereal business in Denmark that sells all its products overseas in U.S.

dollars (not kroner). You can control exactly how currency values are formatted by setting the Format field property, which gives you the following options:

▶ **Currency.** This option is the standard choice. It uses the formatting based on your computer's regional settings.

▶ **Euro.** This option always uses the Euro currency symbol (€).

▶ **A custom format string.** This option lets you get any currency symbol you want (as described below). You need to type the format string you need into the Format box.

There's a simple recipe for cooking up format strings with a custom currency symbol. Start by adding the character for the currency symbol (type in whatever you want) and then add #,###.## which is Access code for "give me a number with thousands separators and two decimal places."

For example, the Danish cereal company could use a format string like this to show the U.S. currency symbol:

```
$#,###.##
```

Whereas a U.S. company that needs to display a Danish currency field (which formats prices like *kr 342.99*) would use this:

```
kr #,###.##
```

___ NOTE _____

> Enterprising users can fiddle around with the number format to add extra text, change the number of decimal places (just add or remove the number signs), and remove the thousands separators (just take out the comma).

_____

Date/Time

Access uses the Date/Time data type to store a single instant in time, complete with the year, month, day, and time down to the second. Behind the scenes, Access stores dates as numbers, which lets you use them in calculations.

Although Access always uses the same amount of space to store date information in a field, you can hide some components of it. You can choose to display just a date (and ignore any time information) or just the time (and ignore any date information). To do this, you simply need to set the Format field property. Table 2-3 shows your options.

Table 2-3. Date/Time Formats

Format	Example
General Date	2/23/2008 11:30:15 PM
Long Date	February 23, 2008 11:30:15 PM
Medium Date	23-Feb-08
Short Date	2/23/2008
Long Time	11:30:15 PM
Medium Time	11:30 PM
Short Time	23:30

__ NOTE __

Both the General Date and Long Date show the time information only if it's not zero.

The format affects only how the date information's displayed—it doesn't change how you type it in. Access is intelligent enough to interpret dates correctly when you type any of the following:

▶ 2008-23-2 (the international year-month-day standard always works)

▶ 2/23/2008 (the most common approach, but you might need to flip the month and day on non-U.S. computers)

▶ 23-Feb-08

▶ Feb 23 (Access assumes the current year)

▶ 23 Feb (ditto)

To add date and time information, just follow the date with the time, as in 23-Feb-08 5:06 PM. Make sure to include the AM/PM designation at the end, or use a 24-hour clock.

If it's too much trouble to type in a date, then consider using the calendar smart tag instead. The smart tag is an icon that appears next to the field whenever you move to it, as shown in Figure 2-12.

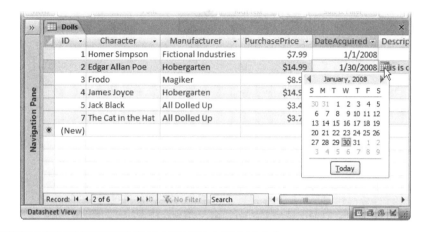

Figure 2-12. Access automatically pops up the calendar smart tag for all date fields. Click the calendar icon to pop up a mini calendar where you can browse to the date you want. However, you can't use the calendar to enter time information.

Yes/No

A Yes/No field is a small miracle of efficiency. It's the leanest of Access data types, because it allows only two possible values: Yes or No.

When using a Yes/No field, imagine that your field poses a yes or no question by adding an imaginary question mark at the end of your field name. You could use a field named InStock to keep track of whether or not a product's in stock. In this case, the yes or no question is "in stock?" Other examples include Shipped (in a list of orders), Male (to separate the boys from the girls), and Republican (assuming you're willing to distinguish between only two political orientations).

Dating Your Computer

Windows has regional settings for your computer, which affect the way Microsoft programs display things like dates and currencies. In Access, the regional settings determine how the different date formats appear. In other words, on a factory-direct U.S. computer, the Short Date format shows up as 2/23/2008. But on a British computer, it may appear as 23/2/2008. Either way, the information that's stored in the database is the same. However, the way it appears in your datasheet changes.

You can change the regional settings, and they don't have to correspond to where you live—you can set them for your company headquarters on another continent, for instance. But keep in mind that these settings are global, so if you alter them, you affect all your programs.

To make a switch, head to Control Panel. (In Windows XP, click the Start menu and choose Settings → Control Panel. In Windows Vista, click Start and look for the Control Panel option on the right side.) Once you've opened the Control Panel, double-click Regional and Language Options, which brings up a dialog box. The first tab has all the settings you want. The most important setting's in the first box, which has a drop-down list you can use to pick the region you want to use, like English (United States) or Swedish (Finland).

You can fine-tune the settings in your region, too. This makes sense only if you have particular preferences about how dates should be formatted that don't match the standard options. Click the Customize button next to the region box to bring up a new dialog box, and then click the Date tab (shown in Figure 2-13).

Although every Yes/No field is essentially the same, you can choose to format it slightly differently, replacing the words "Yes" and "No" with On/Off or True/False. You'll find these three options in the Format menu. However, it doesn't make much difference because on the datasheet, Yes/No fields are displayed with a checkbox, as shown in Figure 2-14.

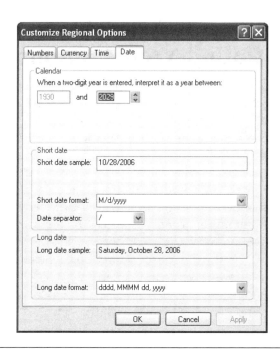

Figure 2-13. The Customize Regional Options dialog box lets you customize how dates appear on your computer. Use the drop-down lists to specify the date separator; order of month, day, and year components in a date; and how Access should interpret two-digit years. You can mix and match these settings freely, although you could wind up with a computer that's completely counterintuitive to other people.

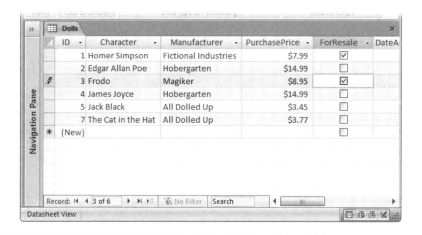

Figure 2-14. In this example, ForResale is a Yes/No field. A checked checkbox represents Yes (or True or On). An unchecked checkbox represents No (or False or Off).

Hyperlink

The Hyperlink data type comes in handy if you want to create a clickable link to a Web page, file, or email address. You can mix and match any combination of the three in the same table.

Access handles hyperlinks a little differently in the Datasheet view. When you type text into a hyperlink field, it's colored blue and underlined. And when you click the link, Access pops it open in your browser (Figure 2-15).

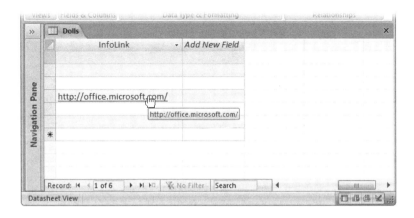

Figure 2-15. *Click this hyperlink, and you'll head straight to the welcoming arms of Office Online.*

One hyperlink field feature isn't immediately obvious. Hyperlink fields actually store more than one piece of information. Every hyperlink includes these three components:

▶ The text you see in the cell

▶ The destination you go to when you click the cell (the URL or file path)

▶ The text you see when you hover over the link with your mouse (the tooltip)

When you type a link into the datasheet, all three of these are set to the same value—what you just typed in. That is, when you type *http://www.FantasyPharmacologists.com*, the text you see, the URL link, and the tooltip are all set to hold the same content, which is the URL *http://www.FantasyPharmacologists.com*.

Most of the time, this approach is good, because it lets you quickly size up a link. However, you aren't limited to this strategy. If you want to set these three components to have different values, move to the value, and then hit Ctrl+K to pop up the Edit Hyperlink window (see Figure 2-16). Or right-click it, and then choose Hyperlink → Edit Hyperlink.

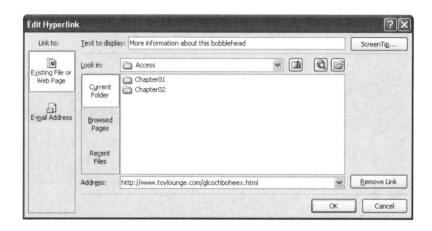

Figure 2-16. Using the Edit Hyperlink window, you can change the text that appears in the cell (at the top of the window) and the page that Access opens when you click it (at the bottom). You can also create links that use email addresses (in which case Access opens the email program that's configured on your computer) or links to file paths (use the folder browsing area to pick the file you want).

Attachment

The Attachment data type's new in Access 2007. It lets you add files to your database record in much the same way that you tack on attachments to your email messages. Access stores the files you add to an attachment field as part of your table, embedded inside your database file.

The Attachment data type's a good choice if you need to insert a picture for a record, a short sound file, or even a document from another Office application, like Word or Excel. You could create a People table with a picture of each person in your contact list, or a product catalog with pictures of the wares you're selling. In these cases, attachments have an obvious benefit—because they're stored inside your database file, you'll never lose track of them.

However, attachments aren't as graceful with large files, or files you need to modify frequently. If you place a frequently modified document into an Access database, it isn't available on your hard drive for quick editing, printing, and searching. Instead, you'll need to fire up Access, and then find the corresponding record before you can open your document. If you want to make changes, then you'll also need to keep Access open so it can take the revised file and insert it back into the database.

WARNING

Think twice before you go wild with attachments. As you've already learned, an Access database is limited to two gigabytes of space. If you start storing large files in your tables, you just may run out of room. Instead, store large documents in separate files, and then record the file name in a text or hyperlink field.

When you use the Attachment data type, make sure you set the Caption field property, which determines the text that appears in the column header for that field. (Often, you'll use the field name as the caption.) If you don't set a caption, the column header shows a paper clip but no text.

You'll recognize an attachment field in the datasheet because it has a paper clip icon next to it (Figure 2-17).

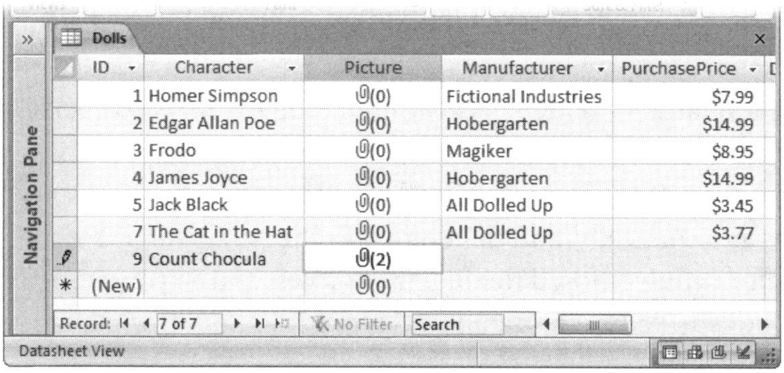

Figure 2-17. Attachments are flagged with a paper clip icon and a number in brackets, which tells you how many files are attached. In this example, all the values in the Picture attachment field are empty except Count Chocula, which has two.

To attach a file or review the list of attached files, double-click the paper clip icon. You'll see the Attachments dialog box (see Figure 2-18).

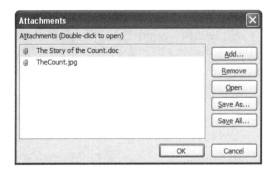

Figure 2-18. The Attachments dialog box shows you all the files that are linked to your field.

Here's what you can do in the Attachments window:

▶ **Add a new attachment.** Click the Add button. Then browse to a new file, and then click OK. You'll see it appear at the bottom of the list.

▶ **Delete an attachment.** Select the attachment in the list, and then click Remove.

▶ **Save a copy of an attachment.** Select the attachment, click Save, and then browse to a location on your computer. Or, click Save All to save copies of all the attachments in this field. If you change these copies, you don't change the attachment in the database.

▶ **Edit or view an attachment.** Select the attachment, and then click Open. Access copies the attachment to a temporary folder on your computer, where Internet content is cached. If you save the file, then Access notices the change, updates the attachment automatically, and then removes the file. If you close the Attachments window before you've closed the file, then Access warns you that your updates might not be reflected in the database. Figure 2-19 shows what happens.

Unfortunately, the Attachment data type doesn't give you a lot of control. Here are some of its limitations:

▶ You can't restrict the number of attachments allowed in an attachment field. All attachment fields allow a practically unlimited number of attachments (although you can't attach two files with the same name).

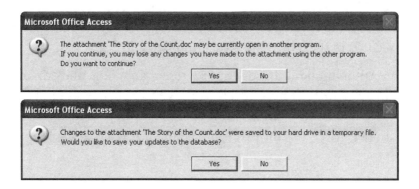

Figure 2-19. Top: In this example, the file "The Story of the Count.doc" is still open. If you continue, then any changes you make (or any changes you've made so far and haven't saved) aren't reflected in the database.

Bottom: If Access notices you've saved your file since you first opened it, then Access also asks if you want to update the database with the last saved version. (To avoid such headaches, attach only files that you don't plan to edit.)

▶ You also can't restrict the types of files used for an attachment.

▶ You can't restrict the size of the files used for an attachment.

AutoNumber

An AutoNumber is a special sort of data type. Unlike all the other data types you've seen, you can't fill in the value for an AutoNumber field. Instead, Access does it automatically whenever you insert a new record. Access makes sure that the Auto-Number value is unique—in other words, it never gives two records the same AutoNumber value.

___ **NOTE** _____

Every table can have no more than one AutoNumber field.

_____

Ordinarily, the AutoNumber field looks like a *sequence* of numbers—Access tends to give the first record an AutoNumber value of 1, the second an AutoNumber of 2, and so on. However, the truth isn't so straightforward. Sometimes, Access skips a number. This skipping could happen when several people are using a database at once, or if you start adding a new record, and then cancel your action by pressing the Esc key. You may also delete an existing record, in which case Access never reuses that AutoNumber value. As a result, if you insert a new record and you see it's assigned an AutoNumber value of 401, then you can't safely assume that there are already 400 records in the table. The actual number's probably less.

Truthfully, an AutoNumber value doesn't represent anything, and you probably won't spend much time looking at it. The AutoNumber field's sole purpose is to make sure you have a unique way to point to each record in your table. Usually, your AutoNumber field's also the primary key for your table, as explained on page 90.

Using AutoNumbers without revealing the size of your table

AutoNumber values have one minor problem: they give a clue about the number of records in a table. You may not want a customer to know that your brand-new food and crafts company, Better Butter Sculptures, hasn't cracked 12 customers. So you'll be a little embarrassed to tell him he's customer ID number 6.

The best way to solve this problem is to start counting at a higher number. You can fool Access into generating AutoNumber values starting at a specific minimum. For example, instead of creating customer IDs 1, 2, and 3, you could create the ID values 11001, 11002, 11003. This approach also has the advantage of keeping your IDs a consistent number of digits, and it allows you to distinguish between IDs in different tables by starting them at different minimums. Unfortunately, in order to pull this trick off, you need to fake Access out with a specially designed query that requires some power-user skills beyond the scope of this book. (Budding power users should check out *Access 2007: The Missing Manual* for details.)

Fortunately, you can tell Access to generate AutoNumber values in a different way. You have two choices:

▶ **Random AutoNumber value.** To use random numbers, change the New Values field property from Increment to Random. Now you'll get long numbers for each record, like 212125691, 1671255778, and −1388883525. You might use random AutoNumber to create values that other people can't guess. (For example, if you have an Orders table that uses random values for the OrderID field, you can use those values as confirmation numbers.) However, random AutoNumbers are rarely used in the Access world.

▶ **Replication IDs.** Replication IDs are long, obscure codes like 38A94E7B-2F95-4E7D-8AF1-DB5B35F9700C that are statistically guaranteed to be unique. To use them, change the Field Size property from Long Integer to Replication ID. Replication IDs are really used only in one scenario—if you have separate copies of a database and you need to merge the data together in the future. The next section explains that scenario.

Both of these options trade the easy-to-understand simplicity of the ordinary AutoNumber with something a little more awkward, so evaluate them carefully before using these approaches in your tables.

Using Replication IDs

Imagine you're working at a company with several regional sales offices, each with its own database for tracking customers. If you use an ordinary AutoNumber field, then you'll end up with several customers with the same ID, but at different offices. If you ever want to compare data, you'll quickly become confused. And you can't combine all the data into one database for further analysis later on.

Access gives you another choice—a *replication ID*. A replication ID's a strange creation—it's an extremely large number (16 bytes in all) that's represented as a string of numbers and letters that looks like this:

```
38A94E7B-2F95-4E7D-8AF1-DB5B35F9700C
```

This ID's obviously more cumbersome than an ordinary integer. After all, it's much easier to thank someone for submitting Order 4657 than Order 38A94E7B-2F95-4E7D-8AF1-DB5B35F9700C. In other words, if you use the AutoNumber value for tracking or bookkeeping, then the replication ID's a bad idea.

However, the replication ID solves the problem described earlier, where multiple copies of the same database are being used in different places. That's because replication IDs are guaranteed to be *statistically unique*. In other words, there are so many possible replication IDs that it's absurdly unlikely that you'll ever generate the same replication ID twice. So even if you have dozens of separate copies of your database, and they're all managing hundreds of customers, you can rest assured that each customer has a unique customer ID. Even better, you can periodically fuse the separate tables together into one master database. (This process is called *replication*, and it's the origin of the term replication ID. You'll learn more about transferring data from one database to another in Chapter 10.)

Figure 2-20 shows a table that uses replication IDs.

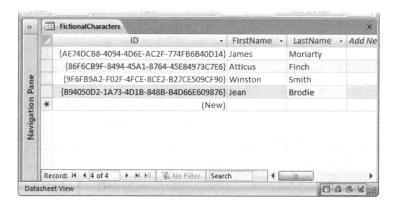

Figure 2-20. This figure shows four records in the FictionalCharacters table, each with a statistically unique AutoNumber value.

The Primary Key

Design view also allows you to set a table's *primary key*, which is a field (or a combination of fields) that's unique for each record. Every table must have a primary key. To understand why the primary key's important, you need to consider a little bit more about how databases work. The box "How Access Prevents Duplicate Records" on page 91 has the full story.

Choosing a primary key is trickier than it seems. Imagine you have a list of friends (and their contact information) in a table named People. You may logically assume that you can create a primary key using a combination of first and last name. Unfortunately, that just won't do—after all, some address books have two Sean Smiths.

Your best solution's to *invent* a new piece of information. You can label every individual in your contact list with a unique ID number. Best of all, you can get Access to automatically create this number for you (and make sure that no two people get the same number), so you don't even need to think about it. That way, if you have two Sean Smiths, each one has a different ID. And even if Ferris Wheel Simpson decides to change his first name, the ID remains the same.

How Access Prevents Duplicate Records

In order to function correctly, a database program like Access needs to be able to tell the difference between each and every record in your table. In other words, you can't insert two records with *exactly* the same information. Databases are notoriously fussy, and they don't tolerate this sort of sloppiness.

The challenge of preventing duplicates isn't as easy as it seems. Access is designed to be blisteringly fast, and it can't afford to double-check your new record against every other record in the table to see if there's a duplicate. So instead, it relies on a *primary key*. As long as every record in a table

has a unique, never-duplicated primary key, you can't have two identical records. (At worst, they'll be two almost identical records that have the same information in all their other fields, but have different primary keys. And this is perfectly acceptable to Access.)

In an Employees table, the Social Security number could serve as the primary key. This method works well, because when you insert a new record, Access can check for duplicates by breezing through the list of Social Security numbers, which is much faster than scanning through the entire table.

This approach is exactly the one Access uses when you create a table using the Datasheet view. Consider the Dolls table you built in Chapter 1. You'll notice that it includes a field named ID, which Access fills automatically. You can't set the ID value in a new record, or change it in an existing record. Instead, Access takes complete control, making sure each bobblehead has a different ID number. This behavior's almost always what you want, so don't try to change it or delete the ID field.

However, there's one exception. If you *create* a table in Design view by choosing Create → Tables → Table Design, then Access assumes you know what you're doing, and it doesn't create an ID field for you. You need to add an ID field (or something like it).

Creating Your Own Primary Key Field

If your database doesn't have an ID field (perhaps because you created it using the Create → Tables → Table Design command), it's up to you to create one and set the primary key.

Here's how to do it:

1. **Create a new field by typing a name in the Field Name column.**

   For automatically generated values, the name ID is the best choice. Some people prefer to be a little more descriptive (for example, BobbleheadID, CustomerID, and so on), but it's unnecessary.

2. **In the Data Type column, choose AutoNumber.**

   By choosing the AutoNumber data type, you make sure that Access generate a unique ID value for every new record you insert. If you don't want this process to happen, you can choose something else (like the Text or Number data type). You'll be responsible for entering your own unique value for each record, which is more work that it seems.

3. **Right-click the field, and then choose Primary Key.**

   This choice designates the field as the primary key for the table. Access doesn't allow duplicate values in this field.

NOTE _____

If you want to make a primary key that includes more than one field, then you need to take a slightly different approach. First, click the margin next to the field name, and then drag the mouse to select more than one field. Then, hold down Shift, and then right-click your selection. Now you can choose Primary Key.

Six Principles of Database Design

With great power comes great responsibility. As a database designer, it's up to you to craft a set of properly structured tables. If you get it right, you'll save yourself a lot of work in the future. Well-designed databases are easy to enhance, simpler to work with, and lead to far fewer mind-bending problems when you need to extract information.

Sadly, there's no recipe for a perfect database. Instead, a number of recommendations can guide you on the way. In this section, you'll learn about a few of the most important.

Why It's Important to Be Unique

You won't completely understand why it's so important for each record to have a unique ID number until you work with the more advanced examples in later chapters. However, one of the reasons is that other programs that use your database need to identify a record *unambiguously*.

To understand why there's a problem, imagine that you've built a program for editing the Dolls table. This program starts by retrieving a list of all your table's bobbleheads. It displays this list to the person using the program, and lets her make changes. Here's the catch—if a change is made, the program needs to be able to apply the change to the corresponding record in the database. And in order to apply the change, it needs some unique piece of information that it can use to locate the record. If you've followed the best design practices described above, the unique "locator" is the bobblehead's ID.

TIP

Building a good database is an art that takes practice. For best results, read these guidelines, and then try building your own test databases.

---

1. Choose Good Field Names

Access doesn't impose many rules on what field names you can use. It lets you use 64 characters of your choice. However, field names are important. You'll be referring to the same names again and again as you build forms, create reports, and even write code. So it's important to choose a good name from the outset.

Here are some tips:

▶ **Keep it short and simple.** The field name should be as short as possible. Long names are tiring to type, more prone to error, and can be harder to cram into forms and reports.

▶ **CapitalizeLikeThis.** It's not a set-in-stone rule, but most Access fans capitalize the first letter of every word (known as CamelCase), and then cram them all together to make a field name. Examples include UnitsInStock and DateOf-Expiration.

- **Avoid spaces.** Spaces are allowed in Access field names, but they can cause problems. In SQL (the database language you'll use to search for data), spaces aren't kosher. That means you'll be forced to use square brackets when referring to field name that includes spaces (like [Number Of Guests]), which gets annoying fast. If you really must have spaces, then consider using underscores instead.

- **Be consistent.** You have the choice between the field names Product_Price and ProductPrice. Either approach is perfectly reasonable. However, it's not a good idea to mingle the two approaches in the same database—doing so's a recipe for certain confusion. Similarly, if you have more than one table with the same sort of information (for example, a FirstName field in an Employees table and a Customers table), use the same field name.

- **Don't repeat the table name.** If you have a Country field in a Customers table, it's fairly obvious that you're talking about the Country where the customer lives. The field name CustomerCountry would be overkill.

- **Don't use the field name Name.** Besides being a tongue-twister, Name is an Access keyword. Instead, use ProductName, CategoryName, ClassName, and so on. (This is one case where it's OK to violate the previous rule and incorporate the table name in the field name.)

You should also give careful thought to naming your tables. Once again, consistency is king. For example, database nerds spend hours arguing about whether or not to pluralize table names (like Customers instead of Customer). Either way's fine, but try to keep all your tables in line.

2. Break Down Your Information

Be careful that you don't include too much information in a single field. You want to have each field store a single piece of information. Rather than have a single Name field in a table of contacts, it makes more sense to have a FirstName and a LastName field.

There are many reasons for breaking down information into separate fields. First of all, it stops some types of errors. With a Name field, the name could be entered in several different ways (like "Last, First" or "First Last"). Splitting the name avoids these issues, which can create headaches when you try to use the data in some sort of automated task (like a mail merge). But more importantly, you can more easily work with data that's broken down into small pieces. Once the Name field's split into FirstName and LastName, you can perform sorts or searches on just one of these two pieces of information, which you couldn't otherwise do. Similarly, you should split address information into columns like Street, City, State, and Country—that way, you can far more easily find out who lives in Nantucket.

Figure 2-21 (top) shows an example of proper separation. Figure 2-21 (bottom) shows a dangerous mistake—an attempt to store more than one piece of information in a single field.

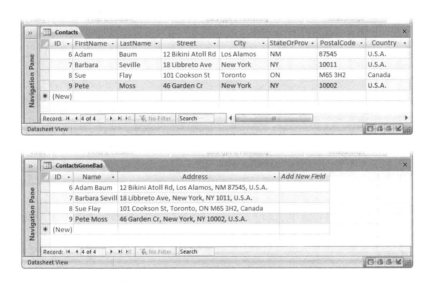

Figure 2-21. This example shows the right way to subdivide information in the Contacts table (top), and the wrong way (bottom).

3. Include All the Details in One Place

Often, you'll use the same table in many different tasks. You may use the Dolls table to check for duplicates (and avoid purchasing the same bobblehead twice), to identify the oldest parts of your collection, and to determine the total amount of money you've spent in a given year (for tax purposes). Each of these tasks needs a slightly different combination of information. When you're calculating the total money spent, you aren't interested in the Character field that identifies the doll. When checking for a duplicate, you don't need the DateAcquired or PurchasePrice information.

Even though you don't always need all these fields, it's fairly obvious that it makes sense to put them all in the same table. However, when you create more detailed tables, you may not be as certain. It's not difficult to imagine a version of the Dolls table that has 30 or 40 fields of information. You may use some of these fields only occasionally. However, you should still include them all in the same table. All you'll see in this book, you can easily filter out the information you don't need from the datasheet, as well as in your forms and printed reports.

4. Avoid Duplicating Information

As you start to fill a table with fields, it's sometimes tempting to include information that doesn't really belong. This inclusion causes no end of headaches, and it's a surprisingly easy trap to fall into. Figure 2-22 shows this problem in action with a table that tries to do too much.

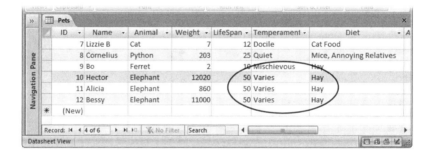

Figure 2-22. This table lists the available pets at an exotic animal breeder's. It also lists some helpful information about the life expectancy, temperament, and meal requirements of each type of animal. Initially, this design seems fairly reasonable. However, a problem appears when you have several of the same type of animals (in this case, three elephants). Now the elephant-specific details are repeated three separate times.

Duplicate data like that shown in Figure 2-22 is inefficient. You can easily imagine a table with hundreds of similar records, needlessly wasting space repeating the same values over and over again. However, this concern's minor compared to the effort of updating that information, and the possibility of inconsistency. What happens if you want to update the life expectancy information for every elephant based on new studies? Based on the current design of the table, you need to change each record that has the same information. Even worse, it's all too easy to change some records but leave others untouched. The overall result's inconsistent data—information in more than one spot that doesn't agree—which makes it impossible to figure out the correct information.

This problem occurs because the information in the Pets table doesn't all belong. To understand why, you need to delve a little deeper into database analysis.

As a rule, every table in a database stores a single *thing*. In the Pets table, that thing is pets. Every field in a table is a piece of information about that thing.

In the Pets table, fields like Name, Animal, and Weight all make sense. They describe the pet in question. But the LifeSpan, Temperament, and Diet fields aren't quite right. They don't describe the individual pet. Instead, they're just standards for that species. In other words, these fields aren't based on the *pet* (as they should be)— they're based on the *animal type*. The only way to solve this problem is to create two tables: Pets and AnimalTypes (Figure 2-23).

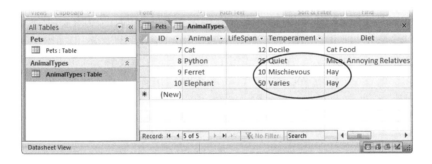

Figure 2-23. Now the animal-specific information is maintained in one place, with no duplicates. It takes a little more work to get all the pet information you need—for example, to find out the life expectancy for Beatrice, you need to check out the Elephant record in the AnimalTypes table—but the overall design's more logical.

It takes experience to spot fields that don't belong. And in some cases, breaking a table down into more and more sub-tables isn't worth the trouble. You could theoretically separate the address information (contained in fields like Street, City, Country, and PostalCode) from a Customers table, and then place it into a separate Addresses table. However, it's relatively uncommon for two customers to share the same address, so this extra work isn't likely to pay off. You'll consider how to define formal relationships between tables like Pets and AnimalTypes in Chapter 5.

5. Avoid Redundant Information

Another type of data that just doesn't belong is redundant information—information that's already available elsewhere in the database, or even in the same table, sometimes in a slightly different form. As with duplicated data, this redundancy can cause inconsistencies.

Calculated data's the most common type of redundant information. An Average-OrderCost field in a Customers table is an example. The problem here is that you can determine the price of an average order by searching through all the records in the Orders table for that customer, and averaging them. By adding an AverageOrderCost field, you introduce the possibility that this field may be incorrect (it may not match the actual order records). You also complicate life, because every time a customer places an order, you need to recalculate the average, and then update the customer record.

Here are some more examples of redundant information:

▶ **An Age and a DateOfBirth field (in a People table).** Usually, you'll want to include just a DateOfBirth field. If you have both, then the Age field contains redundant information. But if you have only the Age field, you're in trouble—unless you're ready to keep track of birthdays and update each record carefully, your information will soon be incorrect.

▶ **A DiscountPrice field (in a Products table).** You should be able to calculate the discount price as needed based on a percentage. In a typical business, markups and markdowns change frequently. If you calculate 10 percent discounts and store the revised prices in your database, then you'll have a lot of work to do when the discount drops to nine percent.

6. Include an ID Field

As you learned earlier (page 90), Access automatically creates an ID field when you create a table in Datasheet view and sets it to be the primary key for the table. But even now that you've graduated to Design view, you should still add an ID field to all your tables. Make sure it uses the AutoNumber data type so Access fills in the numbers automatically, and set it to be the primary key.

In some cases, your table may include a unique field that you can use as a primary key. *Resist the temptation.* You'll always buy yourself more flexibility by adding an ID field. You never need to change an ID field. Other information, even names and social insurance numbers, may change. And if you're using table relationships, Access copies the primary key into other tables. If a primary key changes, you'll need to track down the value in several different places.

—— **NOTE** ——————————————————————————————————

It's a good idea to get into the habit of using ID fields in all your tables. In Chapter 5, you'll see the benefits when you start creating table relationships.

MASTERING THE DATASHEET: SORTING, SEARCHING, FILTERING, AND MORE

▶ Datasheet Customization

▶ Datasheet Navigation

▶ Printing the Datasheet

IN CHAPTER 1, YOU TOOK YOUR FIRST LOOK AT THE DATASHEET—a straightforward way to browse and edit the contents of a table. As you've learned since then, the datasheet isn't the best place to build a table. (Design view's a better choice for database control freaks.) However, the datasheet *is* a great tool for reviewing the records in your table, making edits, and inserting new data.

Based on your experience creating the Dolls table (page 32), you probably feel pretty confident breezing around the datasheet. However, most tables are considerably larger than the examples you've seen so far. After all, if you need to keep track of only a dozen bobbleheads, then you really don't need a database—you'll be just as happy jotting the list down in any old spreadsheet, word processor document, or scrap of unused Kleenex.

On the other hand, if you plan to build a small bobblehead empire (suitable for touring in international exhibitions), you need to fill your table with hundreds or thousands of records. In this situation, it's not as easy to scroll through the mass of data to find what you need. All of a sudden, the datasheet seems more than a little overwhelming.

Fortunately, Access is stocked with datasheet goodies that can simplify your life. In this chapter, you'll become a datasheet expert, with tricks like sorting, searching, and filtering at your fingertips. You'll also learn a quick-and-dirty way to print a snapshot of the data in your table.

NOTE
It's entirely up to you how much time you spend using datasheets. Some Access experts prefer to create *forms* for all their tables (as described in Part Three). With forms, you can design a completely customized window for data entry. Designing forms takes more work, but it's a great way to satisfy your inner Picasso.

Datasheet Customization

Getting tired of the drab datasheet, with its boring stretch of columns and plain text? You can do something about it. Access lets you tweak the datasheet's appearance and organization to make it more practical (or suit it to your peculiar sense of style).

Some of these customizations—like modifying the datasheet font—are shameless frills. Other options, like hiding or freezing columns, can genuinely make it easier to work with large tables.

___ NOTE _____

> Access doesn't save formatting changes immediately (unlike record edits, which it stores as soon as you make them). Instead, Access prompts you to save changes the next time you close the datasheet. You can choose Yes to keep your customizations or No to revert to the table's last look and feel (which doesn't affect any edits you've made to the *data* in that table).

Formatting the Datasheet

Access lets you format the datasheet with eye-catching colors and fonts. Do these options make any difference to the way the datasheet works? Not really. But if your computer desktop looks more like a '60s revival party than an office terminal, then you'll enjoy this feature.

To find the formatting features, look at the ribbon's Home → Font section (see Figure 3-1).

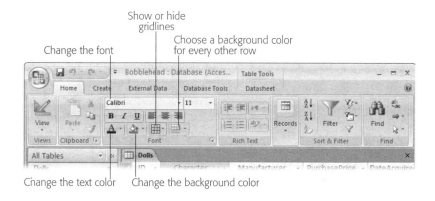

Figure 3-1. The Home → Font section lets you change the text font and colors in the entire datasheet. The most practical frill is the ability to turn off some or all of the gridlines and use alternating row colors to highlight every other row, as shown here.

Every formatting change you make affects the entire table. You may think it's a nifty idea to apply different formatting to different columns, but Access doesn't let you. If this limitation's frustrating you, be sure to check out forms and reports later in this book. Both are more complicated to set up, but give you more formatting power.

> **NOTE**
>
> There's one other way you can use the ribbon's Home → Font section. If you have a field that uses the Memo data type and you've set your field to use rich text (page 72), then you can select some text inside your field, and change its formatting using the ribbon.

GEM IN THE ROUGH

Customizing All Your Datasheets

Access lets you format only one table at a time. So if you find a formatting option you really like, you'll need to apply it separately to every table in your database.

However, you can set formatting options so that they automatically apply to every table in every database by configuring Access itself. To pull this trick off, follow these steps:

1. Choose Office button → Access Options to show the Access Options window.

2. Choose Datasheet from the list on the left.

3. On the right, you see the standard font, color, gridline, and column width options, which you can change to whatever you want.

When you change the datasheet formatting settings in the Access Options window, you change the *defaults* that Access uses. These settings determine the formatting that Access uses for new tables and any tables that aren't customized. When you customize a table, you override the default settings, no matter what they are.

If you set Access to use red text, but you format a specific table to use green text, the green text setting takes precedence. However, if you set a yellow background in the Access Options window, and you don't customize that detail for your table, then it automatically acquires the standard yellow.

Rearranging Columns

The fields in the datasheet are laid out from left to right, in the order you created them. Often, you'll discover that this order isn't the most efficient for data entry.

Imagine you've created a Customers table for a novelty pasta company. When a new customer registration ends up on your desk, you realize that the registration form starts with the name and address information, and then includes the customer's pasta preferences. Unfortunately, the fields on the datasheet are laid out in a completely different order. From right to left, they're arranged like this: ID, FreshPasta-Preference, DriedPastaPreference, FirstName, LastName, Street, City, State, Country. (This organization isn't as crazy as it seems—it actually makes it easier for the people filling pasta orders to quickly find the information *they* want.) Because of this ordering, you need to skip back and forth just to enter the information from a single registration.

Fortunately, you can solve this problem without redesigning the table. Drag the columns you want to move to new positions, as shown in Figure 3-2.

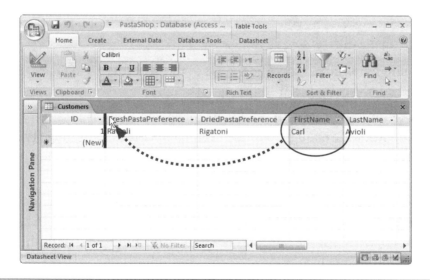

Figure 3-2. To move a column, click the column header once to select that column. Then, drag the column header to its new location. In this example, the FirstName field is about to be relocated so that it's just before the FreshPastaPreference field.

The best part of this approach is that you don't need to modify the database's actual structure. If you switch to Design view after moving a few columns, you'll see that the field order hasn't changed. In other words, you can keep the exact same physical order of fields (in your database file) but organize them differently in Datasheet view.

TIP

Rearranging columns is a relatively minor change. Don't worry about shifting columns around to suit a specific editing job and then switching them back later on. Your changes don't affect the data in the database. If you want to use a particular column order for a one-time job, simply refrain from saving your changes when you close the datasheet.

Resizing Rows and Columns

As you cram more and more information into a table, your datasheet becomes wider and wider. In many cases, you'll be frustrated with some columns hogging more space than they need and others being impossibly narrow.

As you'd expect, Access lets you tweak column widths. But you probably haven't realized how many different ways you can do it:

- ▶ **Resize a single column.** Move the mouse to the column's right edge. Drag to the left (to shrink the column) or to the right (to make it larger).

- ▶ **Resize a column to fit its content.** Double-click the column edge. Access makes the column just wide enough to fit the field name or the largest value (whichever's larger). However, it doesn't make the column so wide that it stretches beyond the bounds of the window.

- ▶ **Resize several adjacent columns.** Drag the first column's header across the columns until you've selected them all. Then, drag the right edge of your selection to the left or the right. All the selected columns shrink or expand to fit the available space, sharing it equally.

- ▶ **Resize a column with pinpoint accuracy.** Right-click the column header, and then choose Column Width. You'll see the Column Width dialog that lets you set an exact width as a number (Figure 3-3).

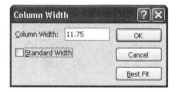

Figure 3-3. The Column Width dialog box lets you set an exact width as a number. (The number doesn't actually have a concrete meaning—it's supposed to be a width in characters, but because modern Access uses proportional fonts, different characters are different sizes.) You can also turn on the Standard Width checkbox to reset the width to the standard narrow size, or click Best Fit to expand the column to fit its content (just as when you double-click the edge of the column).

--- **NOTE** ---

Remember, a column doesn't need to be wide enough to show all its data at once. You can scroll through a lengthy text field using the arrow keys, and if that's too awkward, use the Shift+F2 shortcut to show the full contents of the current field in a Zoom box.

Just as you can resize columns, you can also resize rows. The difference is that Access makes sure all rows have the same size. So when you make one row taller or shorter, Access adjusts all the other rows to match.

You'll mainly want to shrink a row to cram more rows into view at once. You'll want to enlarge a row mostly to show more than one line of text in each text field (see Figure 3-4).

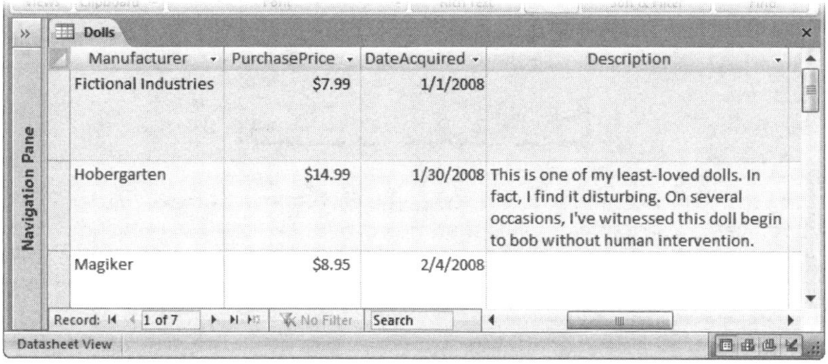

Figure 3-4. If a row's large enough, Access wraps the text inside it over multiple lines, as shown here with the Description column.

Hiding Columns

Many tables contain so many columns that you can't possibly fit them all into view at the same time. This quality's one of the drawbacks to the datasheet, and often you have no choice but to scroll from side to side.

However, in some situations, you may not need to see all the fields at once. In this case, you can temporarily hide the columns that don't interest you, thereby homing in on the important details without distraction. Initially, every field you add to a table is out in the open.

To hide a column, select the column by clicking the column header. (You can also select several adjacent columns by clicking the column header of the first, and then dragging the mouse across the rest.) Then, right-click your selection, and then choose Hide Columns. The column instantly vanishes from the datasheet. (This sudden disappearance can be a little traumatic for Access newbies.)

Fortunately, the field and all its data remain just out of sight. To pop the column back into view, right-click any column header and choose Unhide Columns. Access then shows the Unhide Columns dialog box (Figure 3-5).

Figure 3-5. Using the Unhide Columns dialog box, you can choose to make hidden columns reappear, and (paradoxically) you can hide ones that are currently visible. Every column that has a checkmark next to it is visible—every column that doesn't is hidden. As you change the visibility, Access updates the datasheet immediately. When you're happy with the results, click Close to get back to the datasheet.

___ NOTE ___

At the bottom of the field list, you'll see an entry named Add New Field. This "field" isn't really a field—it's the placeholder that appears just to the right of your last field in datasheet view, which you can use to add new fields (page 62). If you're in the habit of adding fields using Design view (page 59), then you can hide this placeholder to free up some extra space.

If you add a new record while columns are hidden, you can't supply a value for that field. The value starts out either empty or with the default value (if you've defined one for that field, as described on page 134). If you've hidden a required field (page 131), you receive an error message when you try to insert the record. All you can do is unhide the appropriate column, and then fill in the missing information.

Freezing Columns

Even with the ability to hide and resize columns, you'll probably need to scroll from side to side in a typical datasheet. In this situation, you can easily lose your place. You might scroll to see more information in the Contacts table, but then forget exactly which person you're looking at. Access has one more feature that can help you by making sure important information is always visible—*frozen* columns.

A frozen column remains fixed in place at the Access window's left side at all times. Even as you scroll to the right, all your frozen columns remain visible (Figure 3-6). To freeze a column (or columns), select them, right-click the column header, and then choose Freeze Columns.

___ TIP ___

If you want to freeze several columns that aren't next to each other, start by freezing the column that you want to appear at the very left. Then, repeat the process to freeze the column that you want to appear just to the right of the first column, and so on.

Frozen columns must always be positioned at the left size of the datasheet. If you freeze a column that's somewhere else, Access moves it to the left side and then freezes it. You can move it back after you unfreeze the column using the column

Figure 3-6. Top: In this example, the FirstName and LastName field are frozen. They appear initially at the left. (The ribbon's collapsed in this figure to make more room, as described on page 55.)

Bottom: When you scroll to the side to see more information, the FirstName and LastName columns stay put.

reordering trick on page 105. Keep in mind that while a column's frozen, you can't drag it to a different place.

To unfreeze columns, right-click a column header, and then choose Unfreeze All Columns.

___ NOTE _____

Eventually, you'll discover that the customizations provided by the datasheet aren't enough, or you'll need to customize the same table different ways for different people. These signs tell you that you need to step up to forms, a more advanced data display option described in Part Three.

_____

Datasheet Navigation

In Chapter 1, you learned the basics of moving around the datasheet. Using your mouse and a few select keystrokes, you can cover a lot of ground. (Flip back to page 41 for a review of the different keys you can use to jump from place to place and perform edits.)

However, you haven't seen a few tricks yet. One's the timesaving record navigation buttons at the bottom of the datasheet (Figure 3-7).

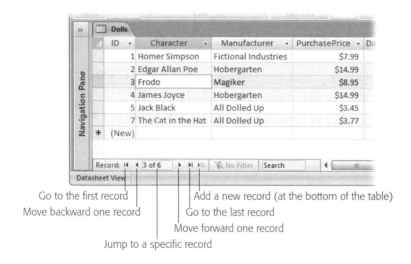

Go to the first record
Move backward one record
Add a new record (at the bottom of the table)
Go to the last record
Move forward one record
Jump to a specific record

Figure 3-7. You could easily overlook the navigation buttons at the bottom of the datasheet. These buttons let you jump to the beginning and end of the table, or, more interestingly, head straight to a record at a specific position. To do this, type the record number (like "4") into the box (where it says "3 of 6" in this example), and then hit Enter. Of course, this trick works only if you have an approximate idea of where in the list your record's positioned.

Several more datasheet features help you orient yourself when dealing with large amounts of data, including *sorting* (which orders the records so you can see what you want), *filtering* (which cuts down the data display to include only the records you're interested in), and *searching* (which digs specific records out of an avalanche of data). You'll try all these features out in the following sections.

Sorting

In some cases, you can most easily make sense of a lot of data by putting it in order. You can organize a customer list by last name, a product catalog by price, a list of wedding guests by age, and so on.

To sort your records, pick a column you want to use to order the records. Click the drop-down arrow at the right edge of the column header, and then choose one of the sort options at the top of the menu (see Figure 3-8).

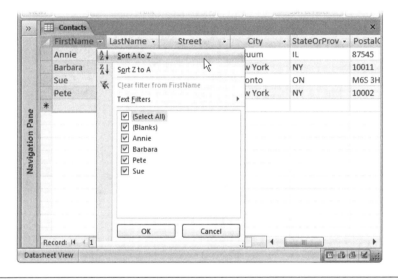

Figure 3-8. This text field gives you the choice of sorting alphabetically from the beginning of the alphabet (A to Z) or backward from the end (Z to A). The menu also provides filtering options, which are described on page 115.

Depending on the data type of field, you'll see different sorting options, as explained in Table 3-1. (You can also apply the same types of sort using the commands in the ribbon's Home → Sort & Filter section.)

In an unsorted table, records are ordered according to when they were created, so that the oldest records are at the top of the datasheet, and the newest at the bottom. Sorting doesn't change how Access stores records, but it does change the way they're displayed.

Table 3-1. Sorting Options for Different Data Types

Data Type	Sort Options	Description
Text, Memo, and Hyperlink	Sort A to Z Sort Z to A	Performs an alphabetic sort (like the dictionary), ordering letter by letter. The sort isn't case-sensitive, so it treats "baloney" and "Baloney" the same.
Number, Currency, and AutoNumber	Sort Smallest to Largest Sort Largest to Smallest	Performs a numeric sort, putting smaller numbers at the top or bottom.
Date/Time	Sort Oldest to Newest Sort Newest to Oldest	Performs a date sort, distinguishing between older dates (those that occur first) and more recent dates.
Yes/No	Sort Selected to Cleared Sort Cleared to Selected	Separates the selected from the unselected values.

> **TIP**
>
> Use the Home → Sort & Filter → Clear All Sorts command to return your table to its original, unsorted order.

Sorting is a one-time affair. If you edit values in a sorted column, then Access doesn't reapply the sort. Imagine you sort a list of people by FirstName. If you then edit the FirstName value for one of the records, changing "Frankie" to "Chen," Access *doesn't* relocate the row to the C section. Instead, the changed row remains in its original place until you resort the table. Similarly, any new records you add stay at the end of the table until the next sort (or the next time the table is opened). This behavior makes sense. If Access relocated rows whenever you made a change, you'd quickly become disoriented.

> **NOTE**
>
> The sorting order's one of the details that Access stores in the database file. The next time you open the table in Datasheet view, Access automatically applies your sort settings.

Sorting on multiple fields

If a sort finds two duplicate values, there's no way to know what order they'll have (relative to one another). If you sort a customer list with two "Van Hauser" entries in it, then you can guarantee that sorting by last name will bring them together, but you don't know who'll be on top.

If you want more say in how Access treats duplicates, then you can choose to sort based on more than one column. The traditional phone book, which sorts people by last name and *then* by first name, is a perfect example of this. People who share the same last name are thus grouped together and ordered according to their first name, like this:

```
...
Smith, Star
Smith, Susan
Smith, Sy
Smith, Tanis
...
```

In the datasheet, sorts are *cumulative*, which means you can sort based on several columns at the same time. The only trick's getting the order right. The following steps take you through the process:

1. **Choose Home → Sort & Filter → Clear All Sorts.**

   Access reverts your table to its original, unsorted order.

2. **Use the drop-down column menu to apply the sub-sort that you want for duplicates.**

   If you want to perform the phone book sort (names are organized by last name, then first name), you need to turn on sorting for the FirstName field. Page 113 explains the sorting options you'll see, depending on the data type.

3. **Use the drop-down column menu to apply the first level sort.**

   In the phone book sort, this is the LastName field.

You can extend these steps to create sorts on more fields. Imagine you have a ridiculously large compendium of names that includes some people with the same last *and* first name. In this case, you could add a third sort—by middle initial. To apply this sort, you'd switch sorting on in this order: MiddleInitial, FirstName, LastName. You'll get this result:

```
...
Smith, Star
Smith, Susan K
Smith, Susan P
Smith, Sy
...
```

Filtering

In a table with hundreds or thousands of records, scrolling back and forth in the datasheet is about as relaxing as a pneumatic drill at 3:00 a.m. Sometimes, you don't even need to see all the records at once—they're just a finger-tiring distraction from the data you're really interested in. In this case, you should cut the datasheet down to just the records that interest you, with *filtering*.

In order to filter records, you specify a condition that record must meet in order to be included in the datasheet. For example, an online store might pick out food items from a full product catalog, a shipping company might look for orders made last week, and a dating service might hunt down bachelors who don't live with their parents. When you apply a filter condition, you end up hiding all the records that don't match your requirements. They're still in the table—they're just tucked neatly out of sight.

Access has several different ways to apply filters. In the following sections, you'll start with the simplest, and then move on to the more advanced options.

Quick filters

A *quick filter* lets you choose what values you want to include and which ones you want to hide, based on the current contents of your table. To apply a quick filter, choose the column you want to use, and then click the drop-down arrow at the column header's right edge. You'll see a list of all the distinct values in that column.

Initially, each value has a checkmark next to it. Clear the checkmark to hide records with that value. Figure 3-9 shows an example where a sort and filter are being used at the same time.

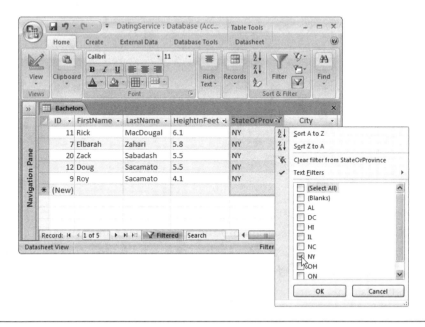

Figure 3-9. This list of eligible bachelors is sorted first by height (in descending largest-to-smallest order), and then filtered to include only those hopefuls who live in the state of New York. A checkmark indicates that records that have this value are included in the datasheet. Others are hidden from view.

___ NOTE ___

To remove all the filters on a column (and show every record in the datasheet), click the drop-down button at the right edge of the column header, and then choose "Clear filter."

Not all data types support filtering. Data types that do include Number, Currency, AutoNumber, Text, Hyperlink, Date/Time, and Yes/No. Memo fields don't support quick filters (because their values are typically too large to fit in the drop-down list), but they do support other types of filters.

You can apply quick filters to more than one column. The order in which you apply the filters doesn't matter, as all filters are *cumulative*, which means you see only records that match all the filters you've set. You can even use quick filters in combination with the other filtering techniques described in the following sections. To remove your filters, choose Home → Sort & Filter → Remove Filter.

___ TIP _____

Quick filters work best if you have a relatively small number of distinct values. Limiting people based on the state they live in is a great choice, as is the political party they support or their favorite color. It wouldn't work as well if you wanted to cut down the list based on birth date, height, or weight, because there's a huge range of different possible values. (You don't need to give up on filtering altogether—rather, you just need to use a different type of filter.)

Filter by selection

Filter by selection lets you apply a filter based on any value in your table. This choice is handy if you've found exactly the type of record you want to include or exclude. Using filter by selection, you can turn the current value into a filter without hunting through the filter list.

Here's how it works. First, find the value you want to use for filtering in the datasheet. Right-click the value, and then choose one of the filter options at the end of the menu (see Figure 3-10).

All data types that support filtering allow you to filter out exact matches. But many also give you some additional filtering options in the right-click menu. Here's what you'll see for different data types:

▶ **Text-based data types.** You can filter values that match exactly, or values that contain a piece of text.

▶ **Numeric data types.** You can filter values that match exactly, or numbers that are smaller or larger than the current number.

▶ **Date data types.** You can filter values that match exactly, or dates that are older or newer than the current date.

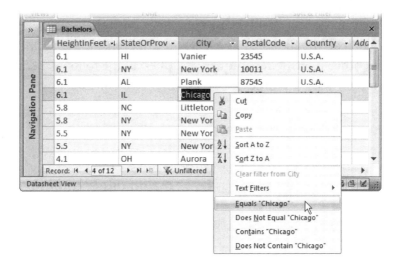

Figure 3-10. *Depending on the data type, you see slightly different filtering options. For a text field (like the City field shown here), you have the option to include only the records that match the current value (Equals "Chicago"), or those that don't (Does Not Equal "Chicago"). You also have some extra filtering options that go beyond what a quick filter can do—namely, you can include or exclude fields that simply contain the text "Chicago." That filter condition applies to values like "Chicagoland" and "Little Chicago."*

Finally, to get even fancier, you can create a filter condition using only *part* of a value. If you have the value "Great at darts" in the Description field in your table of hopeful bachelors, you can select the text "darts," and then right-click just that text. Now you can find other fields that contain the word "darts." This utility is what gives the filter "by selection" feature its name.

Access makes it easy to switch filtering on and off at a moment's notice. Figure 3-11 shows how.

Figure 3-11. *Right next to the navigation controls at the bottom of your datasheet is a Filtered/Unfiltered indicator that tells you when filtering's applied. You can also use this box to quickly switch your filter on and off—clicking it once removes all filters, and clicking it again reapplies the most recent set of filters.*

Filter by condition

So far, the filters you use have taken the current values in your table as a starting point. But if you're feeling confident with filters, you may be ready to try a more advanced approach: *filtering by condition*. When you use a filter by condition, you can define exactly the filter you want.

Imagine you want to find all the rare wine vintages in your cellar with a value of more than $85. Using the filter-by-selection approach, you need to start by finding a wine with a value of $85, which you can use to build your condition. But what if there isn't any wine in your list that has a price of exactly $85, or what if you just can't seem to find it? A quicker approach is defining the filter condition by hand.

Here's how it works. First, click the drop-down arrow at the right edge of the column header. But instead of choosing one of the quick filter options, look for a submenu with filtering options. This menu's named according to the data, so text fields include a Text Filters option, number fields have a Number Filters option, and so on. Figure 3-12 shows an example.

Here's a quick overview that describes the extra options you get using filter by condition, depending on your data type:

▶ **Text-based data types.** All the same options as filter by selection, plus you can find values that start with specific text, or values that end with certain text.

▶ **Numeric data types.** All the same options as filter by selection, plus you can find values that are in a range, meaning they're greater than a set minimum but smaller than a set maximum.

▶ **Date data types.** All the same options as filter by selection, plus you can find dates that fall in a range, *and* you can chose from a huge list of built-in options, like Yesterday, Last Week, Next Month, Year to Date, First Quarter, and so on.

Searching

Access also provides a *quick search* feature that lets you scan your datasheet for specific information. Whereas filtering helps you pull out a batch of important records, searching's better if you need to find a single detail that's lost in the mountains of data. And while filtering changes the datasheet view by hiding some records, searching leaves everything as is. It just takes you to the data you want to see.

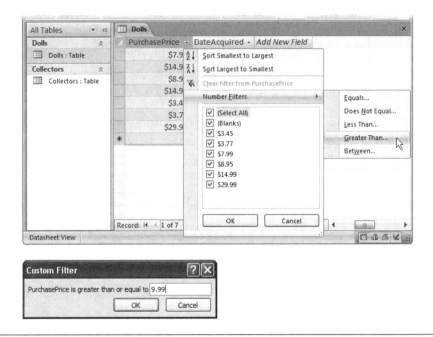

Figure 3-12. Top: With a numeric field like this PurchasePrice field, filtering by condition lets you look at values that fall above a certain minimum.

Bottom: Once you've chosen the type of filter you want, you need to supply the information for that filter. If you choose Greater Than, then you need to supply the minimum number. Records that are equal to or larger than this value are shown in the datasheet.

The quickest way to search is through the search box next to the record navigation controls (see Figure 3-13). Just type in the text you want to find. As you type, the first match in the table is highlighted automatically. You can press Enter to search for subsequent matches.

When performing a search, Access scans the table starting from the first field in the first record. It then goes left to right, examining every field in the current record. If it reaches the end without a match, then it continues to the next record and checks all of its values, and so on. When it reaches the end of the table, it stops.

If you want to change the way Access performs a search, you'll need to use the Find feature instead:

1. **Choose Home → Sort & Filter → Find. (Or, just use the shortcut Ctrl+F.)**

    The Find and Replace dialog box appears (Figure 3-14).

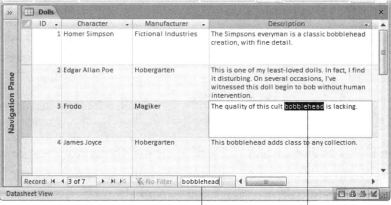

Enter your search term here   The matching text

Figure 3-13. Here, a search is being performed for the word "bobblehead." If you find a match, you can keep searching—just press Enter again to jump to the next match. In this example, pressing Enter sends Access to the next record's Description field.

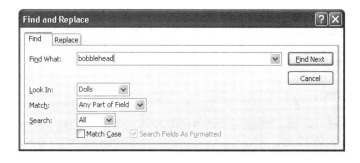

Figure 3-14. The Find and Replace dialog box is the perfect tool for hunting for lost information.

2. **Specify the text you're searching for in the Find What box, and then set any other search options you want to use:**

 ▶ **Find What.** The text you're looking for.

 ▶ **Look In.** Allows you to choose between searching the entire table or just a single field.

 ▶ **Match.** lets you specify whether values need to match exactly. Use Whole Field to require exact matches. Use Start of Field if you want to match beginnings (so "bowl" matches "bowling"), or Any Part of Field if you want to match text anywhere in a field (so "bowl" matches "League of extraordinary bowlers").

▶ **Search.** Sets the direction Access looks: Up, Down, or All (which loops from the end of the table to beginning, and keeps going until it has traversed the entire table).

▶ **Match Case.** If selected, finds only matches that have identical capitalization. So "banana" doesn't match "BANANA."

▶ **Search Fields as Formatted.** If selected, means Access searches the value as it appears on the datasheet. For example, the number 44 may appear in a Currency field as $44.00. If you search for 44, you always find what you're looking for. But if you search for the formatted representation $44.00, you get a match only if you have Search Fields as Formatted switched on. In extremely large tables (with thousands of records), searches may be faster if you switch off Search Fields as Formatted.

NOTE

In order to turn off Search Fields as Formatted, you must choose to search a single field in the Look In box. If you are searching the entire table, then you must search the formatted values.

---

3. **Click Find Next.**

   Access starts searching from the current position. If you're using the standard search direction (Down), Access moves from left to right in the current record, and then down from record to record until it finds a match.

   When Access finds a match, it highlights the value. You can then click Find Next to look for the next match, or Cancel to stop searching.

Printing the Datasheet

If you want to study your data at the dinner table (and aren't concerned about potential conflicts with non-Access-lovers), nothing beats a hard copy of your data. You can dash off a quick printout by choosing File → Print from the menu while your datasheet's visible. However, the results you get will probably disappoint you, particularly if you have a large table.

Find and Replace

The search feature doubles as a powerful (but somewhat dangerous) way to modify records.

Initially, when the Find and Replace dialog box appears, it shows the Find tab. However, you can click the Replace tab to be able to find specific values and replace them with different text. All the settings for a replace operation are the same as for a find operation, except you have an additional text box, called Replace With, to supply the replacement text.

The safest way to perform a replace operation is to click the Find Next button to jump to the next match. At this point, you can look at the match, check that you really *do* want to modify it, and then click Replace to change the value and jump to the next match. Repeat this procedure to move cautiously through the entire table.

If you're a wild and crazy skydiving sort who prefers to live life on the edge, you can use the Replace All button to change every matching value in the entire table in a single step. Although this procedure's ridiculously fast, it's also a little risky. Replace operations can't be reversed (the Undo feature's no help here because it can reverse only a single record change), so if you end up changing more than you intend, there's no easy way back. If you're still seduced by the ease of a Replace All, consider creating a backup of your database file (page 44) before going any further.

The key problem's that Access isn't bothered about tables that are too wide to fit on a printed page. It deals with them by splitting the printout into separate pages. If you have a large table and you print it out using the standard Access settings, you could easily end up with a printout that's four pages wide and three pages long. Assembling this jigsaw is not for the faint of heart. To get a better printout, it's absolutely crucial that you *preview* your table before you print it, as described in the next section.

Print Preview

The print preview feature in Access gives you the chance to tweak your margins, paper orientation, and so on, before you send your table to the printer. This way, you can make sure the final printout's genuinely usable. To preview a table, open it (or select it in the navigation pane), and then choose Office button → Print → Print Preview.

The print preview shows a picture of what your data will look like once it's committed to paper. Unlike the datasheet view, the print preview *paginates* your data (Figure 3-15). You see exactly what fits on each page and how many pages your printout requires (and what content shows up on each page).

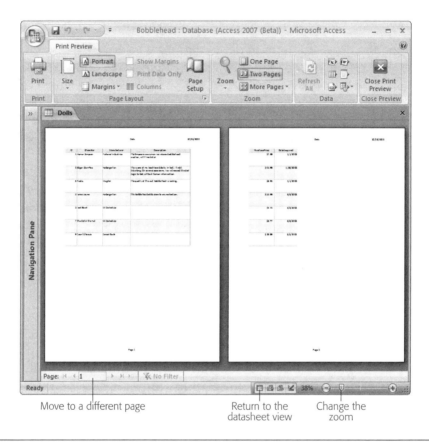

Move to a different page   Return to the   Change the
                               datasheet view   zoom

Figure 3-15. This table's too wide to fit on one sheet of paper, so some of the columns are relocated to a second page.

If you decide you're happy with what you see, then you can fire off your printout by choosing Print Preview → Print → Print from the ribbon. This opens the familiar Windows Print dialog box, where you can pick a printer and seal the deal.

When you're finished looking at the print preview window, choose Print Preview →
Close Preview → Close Print Preview, or click one of the view buttons at the Access
window's bottom-right corner to switch to Datasheet view or Design view.

Moving around the print preview

You can't change anything in the print preview window. However, you can browse
through the pages of your virtual printout and see if it meets your approval.

Here's how you can get around in the preview window:

▶ Use the scroll buttons to move from one page to another. These buttons look the
same as the scroll buttons in the datasheet, but they move from page to page, not
record to record.

▶ To move from page to page, you can use the scroll bar at the side of the window
or the Page Up and Page Down keys.

▶ To jump in for a closer look, click anywhere on the preview page (you'll notice
that the mouse pointer has become a magnifying glass). This click magnifies the
sheet to 100 percent zoom, so you can more clearly see the text and details. To
switch back to full-page view, click the page or click the mouse pointer again.

▶ To zoom more precisely, use the zoom slider that's in the status bar's bottom-
right corner. Slide it to the left to reduce your zoom (and see more at once), or
slide it to the right to increase your zoom (and focus on a smaller portion of your
page).

▶ To see two pages at once, choose Print Preview → Zoom → Two Pages. To see
more, choose Print Preview → Zoom → More Pages, and then pick the number
of pages you want to see at once from the list.

Changing the page layout

Access provides a small set of page layout options that you can tweak using the ribbon's Print Preview → Page Layout section in the print preview window. Here are
your options:

▶ **Size.** Lets you use different paper sizes. If you're fed up with tables that don't fit,
you might want to invest in some larger stock (like legal-sized paper).

▶ **Portrait** and **Landscape.** Let you choose how the page is oriented. Access, like all Office programs, assumes you want to print out text using standard *portrait* orientation. In portrait orientation, pages are turned upright so that the long edge is along the side and the short edge is along the top. It makes perfect sense for résumés and memos, but it's pure madness for a wide table, because it guarantees at least some columns will be rudely chopped off and relocated to different pages. *Landscape* orientation makes more sense in this case, because it turns the page on its side, fitting fewer rows per page but many more columns.

▶ **Margins.** Lets you choose the breathing space between your table and the edges of the page. Margins is a drop-down button, and when you click it, you see a menu with several common margin choices (Normal, Narrow, and Wide). If none of those fit the bill, then click the Page Setup button, which opens a Page Setup dialog box where you can set the exact width of the margin on each side of the page.

Fine-Tuning a Printout

Based on the limited page layout options, you might assume that there's not much you can do customize a printout. However, you actually have more control than you realize. Many of the formatting options that you've learned about in this chapter also have an effect on your printout. By applying the right formatting, you can create a better printout.

Here are some pro printing tips that explain how different formatting choices influence your printouts:

▶ **Font.** Printouts use your datasheet font and font size. Scale this down, and you can fit more in less space.

▶ **Column order and column hiding.** Reorder your columns before printing out to suit what you want to see on the page. Even better, use column hiding (page 108) to conceal fields that aren't important.

▶ **Column widths and row height.** Access uses the exact widths and heights that you've set on your datasheet. Squeeze some columns down to fit more, and expand rows if you have fields with large amounts of text and you want them to wrap over multiple lines.

- **Frozen columns.** If a table's too wide to fit on your printout, then the frozen column is printed on each part. For example, if you freeze the FirstName field, you'll see it on every separate page, so you don't need to line the pages up to find up who's who.

- **Sort options.** They help you breeze through data in a datasheet—and they can do the same for a printout. Apply them before printing.

- **Filter options.** These are the unsung heroes of Access printing. Use them to get just the important rows. That way, your printout has exactly what you need.

The only challenge you face when using these settings is the fact that you can't set them from the print preview window. Instead, you have to set them in the datasheet, jump to the print preview window to see the result, jump back to the datasheet to change them a little bit more, jump back to the print preview window, and so on. This process can quickly get tiring.

--- TIP ---

Don't spend too much time tweaking the formatting options to create the perfect printout. If you have a large table that just can't fit gracefully into a page, you probably want to use reports, which are described in Part Three. They provide much more formatting muscle, including the ability to split fields over several lines, separate records with borders, and allow large values to take up more space by gently bumping other information out of the way.

BLOCKING BAD DATA

- ▶ Data Integrity Basics
- ▶ Input Masks
- ▶ Validation Rules
- ▶ Lookups

EVEN THE BEST DATABASE DESIGNER HAS SPENT A SLEEPLESS NIGHT worrying about the errors that could be lurking in a database. Bad data's a notorious problem—it enters the database, lies dormant for months, and appears only when you discover you've mailed an invoice to customer "Blank Blank" or sold a bag of peanuts for –$4.99.

The best way to prevent these types of problems is to stop bad data from making it into your database in the first place. In other words, you need to set up validation rules that reject suspicious values as soon as someone types them in. Once bad data's entered your database, it's harder to spot than a blueberry in a swimming pool.

This chapter covers the essential set of Access data validation tools:

▶ **The basics** include duplicates, required fields, and default values.

▶ **Input masks** format ordinary text into patterns, like postal codes and phone numbers.

▶ **Validation rules** lay down strict laws for unruly fields.

▶ **Lookups** limit values to a list of preset choices.

Data Integrity Basics

All of Access's data validation features work via the Design view you learned about in Chapter 2. To put them in place, you choose a field and then tweak its properties. The only trick's knowing what properties are most useful. You've already seen some in Chapter 2, but the following sections fill in a few more details.

___ TIP _____

Remember, Access gives you three ways to switch to Design view. You can right-click the table tab title and then choose Design View from the menu, use the Home → View button on the ribbon, or use the tiny view buttons at the Access window's bottom-right corner. And if you're really impatient, then you don't even need to open your table first—just find it in the navigation pane, right-click it there, and then choose Design View.

Preventing Blank Fields

Every record needs a bare minimum of information to make sense. However, without your help, Access can't distinguish between critical information and optional details. For that reason, every field in a new table is optional, except for the primary-key field (which is usually the ID value). Try this out with the Dolls table from Chapter 1; you'll quickly discover that you can add records that have virtually no information in them.

You can easily remedy this problem. Just select the field that you want to make mandatory in Design view, and then set the Required field property to Yes (Figure 4-1).

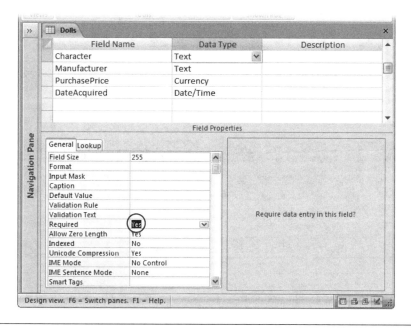

Figure 4-1. The Required field property tells Access not to allow empty values (called nulls in tech-speak).

Access checks the Required field property whenever you add a new record or modify a field in an existing record. However, if your table already contains data, there's no guarantee that it follows the rules.

Imagine you fill the Dolls table with a few bobbleheads before you decide that every record requires a value for the Character field. You switch to Design view, choose the Character field, and then flip the Required field property to Yes. When you save the table (by switching back to Datasheet view or closing the table), Access gives you the option of verifying the bobblehead records that are already in the table (Figure 4-2). If you choose to perform the test and Access finds the problem, it gives you the option of reversing your changes (Figure 4-3).

Figure 4-2. It's a good idea to test the data in your table to make sure it meets the new requirements you put into place. Otherwise, invalid data could still remain. Don't let the message scare you—unless you have tens of thousands of records, this check doesn't take long.

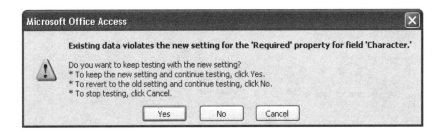

Figure 4-3. If Access finds an empty value, then it stops the search and asks you what to do about it. You can keep your changes (even though they conflict with at least one record)—after all, at least new records won't suffer from the same problem. Your other option is to reset your field to its more lenient previous self. Either way, you can track down the missing data by performing a sort on the field in question (page 112), which brings empty values to the top.

Blank values and empty text

Access supports this Required property for every data type. However, with some data types you might want to add extra checks. That's because the Required property prevents only blank fields—fields that don't have any information in them at all. However, Access makes a slightly bizarre distinction between blank values and something called *empty text*.

Don't Require Too Much

You'll need to think very carefully about what set of values you need, at a minimum, to create a record.

For example, a company selling Elvis costumes might not want to accept a new outfit into their Products table unless they have every detail in place. The Required field property's a great help here, because it prevents half-baked products from showing up in the catalogue.

On the other hand, the same strictness is out of place in the same company's Customers table. The sales staff needs the flexibility to add a new prospect with only partial information. A potential customer may phone and leave only a mailing address (with no billing address, phone number, email information, and so on). Even though you don't have all the information about this customer, you'll still need to place that customer in the Customers table so that he or she can receive the monthly newsletter.

As a general rule, make a field optional if the information for it isn't necessary or might not be available at the time the record is entered.

A blank (null) value indicates that no information was supplied. Empty text indicates that a field value was supplied, but it just happens to be empty. Confused yet? The distinction exists because databases like Access need to recognize when information's missing. A blank value could indicate an oversight—someone might just have forgotten to enter the value. On the other hand, empty text indicates a conscious decision to leave that information out.

NOTE

To try this out in your datasheet, create a text field that has Required set to Yes. Try inserting a new record, and leaving the record blank. (Access stops you cold.) Now, try adding a new record, but place a single space in the field. Here's the strange part: Access automatically trims out the spaces, and by doing so, it converts your single space to empty text. However, you don't receive an error message because empty text isn't the same as a blank value.

The good news is that if you find this whole distinction confusing, then you can prevent both blank values *and* empty text. Just set Required to Yes to stop the blank values, and set Allow Zero Length to No to prevent empty text.

— NOTE

A similar distinction exists for numeric data types. Even if you set Required to Yes, you can still supply a number of 0. If you want to prevent that action, then you'll need to use the validation rules described later in this chapter (page 147).

Setting Default Values

So far, the fields in your tables are either filled in explicitly by the person who adds the record or left blank. But there's another option—you can supply a *default value*. Now, if someone inserts a record and leaves the field blank, Access applies the default value instead.

You set a default value using the Default Value field property. For a numeric Added-Cost field, you could set this to be the number 0. For a text Country field, you may use the text "U.S.A." as a default value. (All text values must be wrapped in quotations marks when you use them for a default value.)

Access shows all your default values in the new-row slot at the bottom of the datasheet (Figure 4-4). It also automatically inserts default values into any hidden columns (page 108).

Access inserts the default value when you create a new record. (You're then free to change that value.) You can also switch a field back to its default value using the Ctrl+Alt+Space shortcut while you're editing it.

— TIP

One nice feature is that you can use the default value as a starting point for a new record. For example, when you create a new record in the datasheet, you can edit the default value, rather than replacing it with a completely new value.

You can also create more intelligent *dynamic* default values. Access evaluates dynamic default values whenever you insert a new record, which means that the

Four default values

Figure 4-4. This dating service uses four default values: a default height (5.9), a default city (New York), a default state (also New York), and a default country (U.S.A.). This system makes sense, because most of their new entries have this information. On the other hand, there's no point in supplying a default value for the name fields.

default value can vary based on other information. Dynamic default values use *expressions* (specialized database formulas) that can perform calculations or retrieve other details. One useful expression, *Date( )*, grabs the current date that's set on your computer. If you use Date( ) as the default value for a date field (as shown in Figure 4-5), then Access automatically inserts the current date whenever you add a new record.

Preventing Duplicate Values with Indexes

Any table's first rule is that each record it contains must be unique. To enforce this restriction, you need to choose a primary key (page 90), which is one or more fields that won't ever be duplicated in different records.

Here's the catch. As you learned in Chapter 2, the safest option's to create an ID field for the primary key. So far, all the tables you've seen have included this detail. But what if you need to make sure *other* fields are unique? Imagine you create an Employees table. You follow good database design principles and identify every

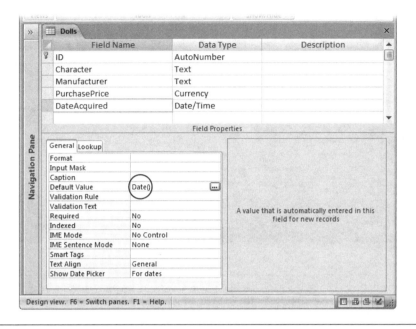

Figure 4-5. *If you use the Date( ) function as the default value for the DateAcquired field in the bob-blehead table, then every time you add a new bobblehead record, Access fills in the current date. You decide whether you want to keep that date or replace it with a different value.*

record with an automatically generated ID number. However, you also want to make sure that no two employees have the same Social Security number (SSN) to prevent possible errors—like accidentally entering the same employee twice.

NOTE

For a quick refresher about why ID fields are such a good idea, refer to page 90. In the Employees table, you certainly could choose to make the SSN the primary key, but it's not the ideal situation when you start linking tables together (Chapter 5), and it causes problems if you need to change the SSN later on (in the case of an error), or if you enter employee information before you've received the SSN.

You can force a field to require unique values with an *index*. A database index is analogous to the index in a book—it's a list of values (from a field) with a cross-reference that points to the corresponding section (the full record). If you index the

SocialSecurityNumber field, Access creates a list like this and stores it behind the scenes in your database file:

SocialSecurityNumber	Location Of Full Record
001-01-3455	...
001-02-0434	...
001-02-9558	...
002-40-3200	...

Using this list, Access can quickly determine whether a new record duplicates an existing SSN. If it does, then Access doesn't let you insert it.

How Indexes Work

It's important that the list of SSNs is *sorted*. Sorting means the number 001-01-3455 always occurs before 002-40-3200 in the index, regardless of where the record's physically stored in the database. This sorting's important, because it lets Access quickly check for duplicates. If you enter the number 001-02-4300, then Access needs to read only the first part of the list. Once it finds the next "larger" SSN (one that falls later in the sort, like 001-02-501), it knows the remainder of the index doesn't contain a duplicate.

In practice, all databases use many more optimizations to make this process blazingly fast. But there's one key principle—without an index, Access would need to check the entire table. Tables aren't stored in sorted order, so there's no way Access can be sure a given SSN isn't in there unless it checks every record.

So how do you apply an index to a field? The trick's the Indexed field property, which is available for every data type except Attachment and OLE Object. When you add a field, the Indexed property's set to No, which means Access doesn't create a field. To add an index and prevent duplicates, you can change the Indexed property in Design view to Yes [No Duplicates]. The third option, Yes [Duplicates OK], creates an index but lets more than one record have the same value. This option doesn't help you catch repeated records, but you can use it to speed up searches.

> **NOTE**
>
> As you know from Chapter 2 (page 91), primary keys also disallow duplicates, using the same technique. When you define a primary key, Access automatically creates an index on that field.

When you close Design view after changing the Indexed field property, Access prompts you to save your changes. At this point, it creates any new indexes it needs. You can't create a no-duplicates index if you already have duplicate information in your table. In this situation, Access gives you an error message when you close the Design window and it attempts to add the index.

Multifield indexes

You can also use indexes to prevent a *combination* of values from being repeated. Imagine you create a People table to track your friends and their contact information. You're likely to have entries with the same first or last name. However, you may want to prevent two records from having the same first *and* last name. This limitation prevents you from inadvertently adding the same person twice.

> **NOTE**
>
> This example could cause endless headaches if you honestly *do* have two friends who share the same first and last names. In that case, you'll need to remove the index before you're allowed to add the name. You should think carefully about legitimate reasons for duplication before you create any indexes.

To ensure that a combination of fields is unique, you need to create a *compound index*, which combines the information from more than one field. Here's how to do it:

1. **In Design view, choose Table Tools | Design → Show/Hide → Indexes.**

   The Indexes window appears (Figure 4-6). Using the Indexes window, you can see your current indexes and add new ones.

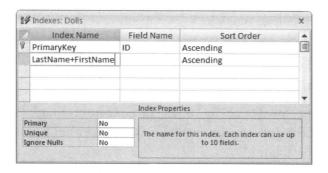

Figure 4-6. The Indexes window shows all the indexes that are defined for a table. Here, there's a single index for the ID field (which Access created automatically) and a compound index that's in the process of being created.

2. **Choose a name for your index. Type this name into the first blank row in the Index Name column.**

   The index name has no real importance—Access uses it to store the index in the database, but you don't see the index name when you work with the table. Usually, you'll use the name of one or both of the fields you're indexing (like Last-Name+FirstName).

3. **Choose the first field in the Field Name column in the same row (like Last-Name).**

   It doesn't matter which field name you use first. Either way, the index can prevent duplicate values. However, the order does affect how searches use the index to boost performance.

4. **In the area at the bottom of the window, set the Unique box to Yes.**

   This creates an index that prevents duplicates (as opposed to one that's used only for boosting search speeds).

   You can also set the Ignore Nulls box to Yes, if you want Access to allow duplicate blank values. Imagine you want to make the SSN field optional. However, if an SSN number *is* entered, then you want to make sure it doesn't duplicate any other value. In this case, you should Ignore Nulls to Yes. If you set Ignore Nulls to No, then Access lets only one record have a blank SSN field, which probably isn't the behavior you want.

NOTE

You can also disallow blank values altogether using the Required property, as described on page 131.

Ignore the Primary box (which identifies the index used for the primary key).

5. **Move down one row. Leave the Index Name column blank (which tells Access it's still part of the previous index), but choose another field in the Field Name column (like FirstName).**

   If you want to create a compound index with more than two fields, then just repeat this step until you've added all the fields you need. Figure 4-7 shows what a finished index looks like.

   You can now close the Indexes window.

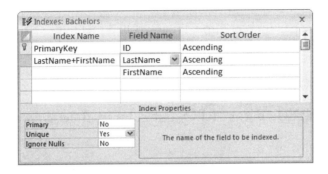

Figure 4-7. Here's a compound index that prevents two people from sharing the same first and last names.

Input Masks

As you've already learned, databases prize *consistency*. If you have a field named Height, you better be sure every value in that field uses the same type of measure-ments; otherwise, your data's not worth its weight in sock lint. Similarly, if you have a PhoneNumber field, you better make sure every phone number has the same for-mat. If some phone numbers are written with dashes, spaces, and parentheses (like *(844) 547-1123*), while others are a bit different (say *847-547-1123*), and a few leave out the area code information altogether (*547-1123*), then you've got a small problem on your hands. Because of the lack of consistency, you'll have a hard time working with this information (say, searching for a specific phone number or sorting the phone numbers into different categories based on area code).

To help you manage values that have a fixed pattern—like phone numbers—you can use an *input mask*. Essentially, an input mask (or just *mask* for short) gives you a way to tell Access what pattern your data should use. Based on this pattern, Access changes the way values are entered and edited to make them easier to understand and less error-prone. Figure 4-8 shows how a mask lets Access format a series of characters as they're being typed into a field.

You can add a mask to any field that uses the Text data type. Masks give you several advantages over ordinary text:

▶ **Masks guide data entry.** When empty, a masked edit control shows the placeholders where values need to go. A phone number mask shows the text (_ _ _) _ _ _-_ _ _ _ when it's empty, clearly indicating what type of information it needs.

▶ **Masks make data easier to understand.** You can read many values more easily when they're presented a certain way. Most people can pick out the numbers in this formatted Social Security number (012-86-7180) faster than this unformatted one (012867180).

▶ **Masks prevent errors.** Masks reject characters that don't fit the mold. If you're using the telephone mask, you can't use letters.

▶ **Masks prevent confusion.** With many types of data, you have several ways to present the same information. You can enter phone numbers both with and without area codes. By presenting the mask with the area code placeholder, you're saying that this information's required (and where it goes). It's also obvious that you don't need to type in parentheses or a dash to separate numbers, because those details are already there. You'll see the same benefit if you use masks with dates, which can be entered in all sorts of different combinations (Year/Month/Day, Month-Day-Year, and so on).

Masks are best suited for when you're storing numeric information in a text field. This scenario occurs with all sorts of data, including credit card numbers, postal codes, and phone numbers. These types of information shouldn't be stored in

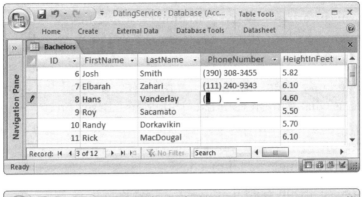

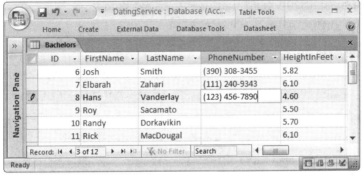

Figure 4-8. Top: Here's a PhoneNumber field with a mask that's ready to go. So far, the person entering the record hasn't typed anything. The PhoneNumber field automatically starts out with this placeholder text.

Bottom: The mask formats the numbers as you type. If you type 1234567890 into this phone number mask, then you see the text (123) 456-7890. Behind the scenes, the databases stores 1234567890, but the information's presented in the datasheet using a nicely formatted package. That package is the mask.

number fields, because they aren't meant to be interpreted as a single number. Instead, they're meant to be understood as a series of digits. (If you do make the mistake of storing a phone number in a number field, you'll find out that people can type in perfectly nonsensical phone numbers like 0 and –14 because these are valid numbers, even if they aren't valid phone numbers. But an input mask on a text field catches these errors easily.)

Masks can't help you with more sophisticated challenges, like data values that have varying lengths or subtle patterns. For instance, a mask doesn't help you spot an incorrect email address.

___ **NOTE** _____

Text and Date/Time are the only data types that support masks.

_____

Using a Ready-Made Mask

The easiest way to get started with masks is to use one of the many attractive options that Access has ready for you. This method's great, because it means you don't need to learn the arcane art of mask creation.

Here's what you need to do to pick out a prebuilt mask:

1. **In Design view, select the text field where you want to apply the mask.**

   For this test, try a PhoneNumber field.

2. **Look for the Input Mask field property. Click inside the field.**

   When you do, a small ellipsis (…) button appears at the left edge, as shown in Figure 4-9.

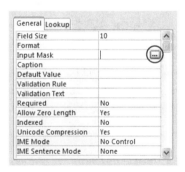

Figure 4-9. The ellipsis (…) button (circled) is just the way Access tells you that you don't need to fill in this value by hand. Instead, you can click the ellipsis and pop up a wizard (like the Input Mask wizard) or some sort of helpful dialog box.

3. Click the ellipsis button.

The Input Mask wizard starts (see Figure 4-10).

Figure 4-10. The Input Mask wizard starts with a short list of commonly used masks. Next to every mask, Access shows you what a sample formatted value looks like. Once you select a mask, you can try using it in the Try It text box. The Try It text box gives you the same behavior that your field will have once you apply the mask.

4. Choose the mask you want from the list of options.

In this case, choose the first item in the list (Phone Number).

__ **NOTE** _____

Don't see what you want? You'll need to create your own (an advanced topic covered in *Access 2007: The Missing Manual*). If you see one that's close but not perfect, select it. You can tweak the mask in the wizard's second step.

5. Click Next.

The wizard's second step appears (see Figure 4-11).

6. If you want, you can change the mask or the placeholder character.

To change the mask, you'll need to learn what every mask character means (see *Access 2007: The Missing Manual* for details).

Figure 4-11. The phone number mask is !(999) 000-000. Each 9 represents an optional number from 0 to 9. Each 0 represents a required number from 0 to 9. So according to this mask, (123) 456-7890 is a valid phone number, as is 123-4567, but (123) 456 isn't.

You use the placeholder to show the empty slots where you enter information. The standard choice is the underscore. Optionally, you can use a space, dash, asterisk, or any other character by typing it in the "Placeholder character" box.

7. **Click Next.**

   If you're adding a mask to a text field, then the wizard's final step appears (see Figure 4-12).

   If you're adding a mask to a date field, then Access doesn't need to ask you how to store the information—it already knows. In this case, you can jump to step 9 and click Finish.

8. **Choose how you want to store the value in this field.**

   The standard choice is to store just the characters you've typed in (in other words, everything you type into the field). If you use this option, the placeholders aren't included. For example, the phone number (416) 123-4567 is stored as *4161234567*. This option saves a little space, and it also lets you change the mask later on to present the information in a slightly different way.

Figure 4-12. The final step lets you choose how the data in your field is chosen—with or without the mask symbols.

You could also store the mask complete with all the extra characters. Then a phone number's stored complete with hyphens, dashes, and spaces, like *(416) 123-4567*. This approach isn't nearly as flexible because you can't change the mask later.

9. **Click Finish.**

   The final mask appears in the Input Mask field property.

   Before going any further, you may want to make sure that the length you've reserved for your field matches the mask. In the phone number example, you need a Field Size of 10 if you've chosen to store unformatted values (because there are 10 digits), or a Field Size of 14 for the whole shebang, complete with placeholders (one dash, one space, and two parentheses).

10. **Switch back to the Datasheet view, and click Yes when Access asks you to save changes.**

   Your input mask is now in place.

Access uses the input mask information to control how you enter information in the datasheet. However, it's possible to circumvent the mask by entering the information in other ways. You could, for instance, create a form (as described in Part Three), and switch off the mask. A mask's not an absolute guarantee against invalid data—if you want such a guarantee, then you need a validation rule instead.

POWER USERS' CLINIC

Adding Your Mask to the Mask List

Sometimes you may create a mask that's so useful you want to use it in many different tables in your database (and maybe even in different databases). While you can certainly copy your mask to every field that needs to use it, Access has a nicer option—you can store your mask in its *mask list*. That way, the mask shows up whenever you run the Input Mask wizard, right alongside all Access's other standard masks.

To add your mask to the list, head to the Input Mask field property (for any field), and then click the ellipsis button to fire up the Input Mask wizard. Then, click the Edit List button, which pops up a handy window where you can edit the masks that Access provides, and add your own (Figure 4-13).

Validation Rules

Input masks are a great tool, but they apply to only a few specific types of information—usually fixed-length text that has a single, unchanging pattern. To create a truly bulletproof table, you need to use more sophisticated restrictions, like making sure a number falls in a certain range, checking that a date hasn't yet occurred, or verifying that a text value starts with a certain letter. *Validation rules* can help you create all these restrictions.

A validation rule's premise is simple. You set up a restriction that tells Access which values to allow in a field and which ones are no good. Whenever someone adds a

Figure 4-13. To add your own mask, use the record scrolling buttons (at the bottom of the window) to scroll to the end. Or you can use this window to change a mask. For example, the prebuilt telephone mask doesn't require an area code. If that's a liberty you're not willing to take, then replace it with the more restrictive version (000) 000-0000.

new record or edits a record, Access makes sure the data lives up to your validation rules. If it doesn't, then Access presents an error message and forces you to edit the offending data and try again.

Applying a Field Validation Rule

Each field can have a single validation rule. The following set of steps show you how to set one up. You'll start out easy, with a validation rule that prevents a numeric field from accepting 0 or any negative number (and in the following sections you'll hone your rule-writing abilities so you can tackle other data types).

Here's how to add your validation rule:

1. **In Design view, select the field to which you want to apply the rule.**

   All data types—except Memo, AutoNumber, and OLE Object—support validation. The validation rule in this example works with any numeric data type (like Number or Currency).

2. **In the Validation Rule field property, type a validation expression** (Figure 4-14).

   An expression's a bit of SQL that performs a check on the data you've entered. Access performs its validation check when you finish entering a piece of data, and try to navigate to another field or another record. For example, *>0* is a validation rule that forces the value in a Number field to be larger than 0. You'll learn more validation rules in the following sections.

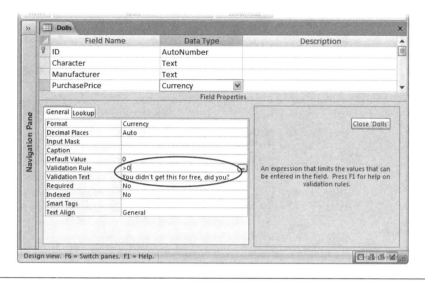

Figure 4-14. Here, the Validation Rule property prevents impossible prices, and the Validation Text provides an error message.

3. **Type some error-message text in the Validation Text field property.**

   If you enter a value that fails the validation check, then Access rejects the value and displays this error text in a dialog box. If you don't supply any text, then Access shows the validation rule for the field (whatever you entered in step 2), which is more than a little confusing for most mere mortals.

4. **Right-click the tab title, and then choose Datasheet View.**

   If your table has existing records, Access gives you the option of checking them to make sure they meet the requirements of your validation rule. You decide whether you want to perform this check, or skip it altogether.

   Once you're in Datasheet view, you're ready to try out your validation rule (Figure 4-15).

___ **NOTE** _____

Just because your table has validation rules doesn't mean the data inside *follows* these rules. A discrepancy can occur if you added records before the validation rules came into effect. (You learned about the same potential problem with required fields on page 131.) To avoid these headaches, set up your validation rules before you start adding data.

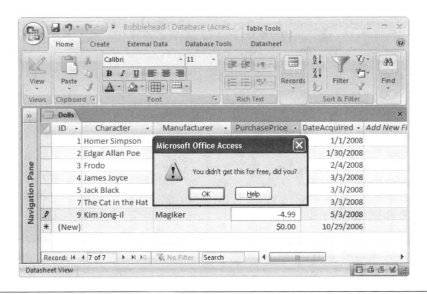

Figure 4-15. Here, a validation rule of >0 prevents negative numbers in the Price field. When you enter a negative number, Access pops up a message box with the validation text you defined, as shown here. Once you click OK, you return to your field, which remains in edit mode. You can change the value to a positive number, or press Esc to cancel the record edit or insertion.

Writing a Field Validation Rule

As you can see, it's easy enough to apply a validation rule to a field. But *creating* the right validation rule takes more thought.

Although validation's limited only by your imagination, Access pros turn to a few basic patterns again and again. The following sections give you some quick and easy starting points for validating different data types.

> **NOTE**
>
> Access uses your validation rule only if a field contains some content. If you leave it blank, then Access accepts if without any checks. If this isn't the behavior you want, then just set the Required property to Yes to make the field mandatory, as described on page 131.

Validating numbers

For numbers, the most common technique's to check that the value falls in a certain range. In other words, you want to check that a number's less than or greater than another value. Your tools are the comparison signs < and >. Table 4-1 shows some common examples.

Table 4-1. Expressions for Numbers

Comparison	Sample Expression	Description
Less than	<100	The value must be less than 100.
Greater than	>0	The value must be greater than 0.
Not equal to	<>42	The value can be anything except 42.
Less than or equal to	<=100	The value must be less than or equal to 100.
Greater than or equal to	>=0	The value must be greater than or equal to 0.
Equal to	=42	The value must be 42. (Not much point in asking anyone to type it in, is there?)
Between	Between 0 and 100	The value must be 0, 100, or somewhere in between.

Validating dates

As with numbers, date validation usually involves checking to see if the value falls within a specified range. Here, your challenge is making sure that your date's in the right format for an expression. If you use the validation rule *>Jan 30, 2007*, Access is utterly confused, because it doesn't realize that the text (Jan 30, 2007) is supposed to represent a date. Similarly, if you try *>1/30/07*, then Access assumes the numbers on the right are part of a division calculation.

To solve this problem, use Access universal date syntax, which looks like this:

```
#1/30/2007#
```

A universal date always has the date components in the order month/day/year, and it's always bracketed by the # symbol on either side. Using this syntax, you can craft a condition like >#1/30/2007#, which states that a given date must be larger than (fall after) the date January 30, 2007. January 31, 2007 fits the bill, but a date in 2006 is out.

The universal date syntax can also include a time component, like this:

```
#1/30/2007 5:30PM#
```

> **NOTE**
>
> When comparing two dates, Access takes the time information into consideration. The date #1/30/2007# doesn't include any time information, so it's treated as though it occurs on the very first second of the day. As a result, Access considers the date value #1/30/2007 8:00 AM# larger, because it occurs eight hours later.

Once you've learned the universal date syntax, you can use any of the comparison operators you used with numbers. You can also use these handy *functions* to get information about the current date and time:

▶ **Date( )** gets the current date (without any time information, so it counts as the first second of the day).

▶ **Now( )** gets the current instant in time, including the date and time information.

> **NOTE**
>
> A function's a built-in code routine that performs some task, like fetching the current date from the computer clock.

Table 4-2 has some examples.

Table 4-2. Expressions for Dates

Comparison	Sample Expression	Description
Less than	<#1/30/2007#	The date occurs before January 30, 2007.
Greater than	>#1/30/2007 5:30 PM#	The date occurs after January 30, 2007, or on January 30, 2007, after 5:30 p.m.
Less than or equal to	<=#1/30/2007#	The date occurs before January 30, 2007, or on the first second of January 30, 2007.
Greater than or equal to	>=#1/30/2007#	The date occurs on or after January 30, 2007.
Greater than the current date	>Date( )	The date occurs today or after.
Less than the current date	<Date( )	The date occurs yesterday or before.
Greater than the current date (and time)	>Now( )	The date occurs today after the current time, or any day in the future.
Less than the current date (and time)	<Now( )	The date occurs today before the current time, or any day in the past.

Validating text

With text, validation lets you verify that a value starts with, ends with, or contains specific characters. You perform all these tasks with the *Like* operator, which compares text to a pattern.

This condition forces a field to start with the letter R:

```
Like "R*"
```

The asterisk (*) represents zero or more characters. Thus, the complete expression asks Access to check that the value starts with R (or r), followed by a series of zero or more characters.

You can use a similar expression to make sure a piece of text ends with specific characters:

```
Like "*ed"
```

This expression allows the values *talked*, *walked*, and *34z%($)#ed*, but not *talking*, *walkable*, or *34z%($)#*.

For a slightly less common trick, you can use more than one asterisk. The following expression requires that the letter *a* and *b* appear (in that order but not necessarily next to each other) somewhere in a text field:

```
Like "*a*b*"
```

Along with the asterisk, the Like operator also supports a few more characters. You can use ? to match a single character, which is handy if you know how long text should be or where a certain letter should appear. Here's the validation rule for an eight-character product code that ends in 0ZB:

```
Like "?????0ZB"
```

The # character plays a similar role, but it represents a number. Thus, the following validation rule defines a product code that ends in 0ZB and is preceded by five numbers:

```
Like "#####0ZB"
```

And finally, you can restrict any character to certain letters or symbols. The trick's to put the allowed characters inside square brackets.

Suppose your company uses an eight-character product code that always begins with A or E. Here's the validation rule you need:

```
Like "[AE]???????"
```

Note that the [AE] part represents one character, which can be either A or E. If you wanted to allow A, B, C, D, you'd write [ABCD] instead, or you'd use the handy shortcut [A-D], which means "allow any character from A to D, including A and D."

Here's one more validation expression, which allows a seven-letter word, and doesn't allow numbers or symbols. It works by repeating the [A-Z] code (which allows any letter) seven times:

```
Like [A-Z][A-Z][A-Z][A-Z][A-Z][A-Z][A-Z]
```

As you can see, text validation expressions aren't always pretty. Not only can they grow to ridiculous sizes, but there are lots of restrictions they can't apply. You can't, for instance, let the length of the text vary between a minimum and maximum that you set. And you can't distinguish between capitalized and lowercase letters.

Combining validation conditions

No matter what the data type, you can also *combine* your conditions in two different ways. Using the *And* keyword, you can create a validation rule that enforces two requirements. This trick's handy, because each field can have at most a single validation rule.

To use the And keyword, just write two validation rules and put the word And in between. It doesn't matter which validation rule's first. Here's a validation rule that forces a date to be before today but later than January 1, 2000:

```
<Date( ) And >#1/1/2000#
```

You can also use the Or keyword to accept a value if it meets either one of two conditions. Here's a validation rule that allows numbers greater than 1000 or less than −1000:

```
>1000 Or <-1000
```

Creating a Table Validation Rule

Field validation rules always apply to a single field. However, database designers often need a way to compare the values in different fields. Suppose you have an Orders table that logs purchases from your monogrammed sock store. In your Orders table, you use two date fields: DateOrdered and DateShipped. To keep everything kosher, you need a validation rule that makes sure DateOrdered falls *before* DateShipped. After all, how can you ship a product out before someone orders it?

Because this validation rule involves two fields, the only way to put it in place is to create a validation rule for the whole table. Table validation rules can use all the tricks you've learned about so far, *and* they can pull the values out of any field in the current record.

Here's how to create a table validation rule:

1. **In Design view, choose Table Tools | Design → Show/Hide → Property Sheet.**

   A box with extra settings appears on the right side of the window (Figure 4-16).

NOTE

You can create only a single validation rule for a table. This limit might sound like a problem, but you can get around it by using the And keyword (page 155) to yoke together as many conditions as you want. The validation rule may be a little difficult to read, but it still works without a hitch.

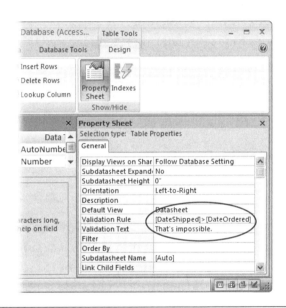

Figure 4-16. The Property Sheet shows some information about the entire table, including the sorting (page 112) and filtering settings (page 115) you've applied to the datasheet, and the table validation rule. Here, the validation rule prevents orders from being shipped before they're ordered.

2. **In the Property Sheet tab, set the Validation Rule.**

   A table validation rule can use all the same keywords you learned about earlier. However, table validation rules usually compare two or more fields. The validation rule *[DateOrdered] < [DateShipped]* ensures that the value for the DateOrdered field is older than that used for the DateShipped.

When referring to a field in a table validation rule, you need to include square brackets around your field names. That way, Access can tell the difference between fields and functions (like the Date( ) function you learned about on page 135).

3. **Set the Validation Text.**

   This message is the error message that's shown if the validation fails. It works the same as the validation text for a field rule.

   When you insert a new record, Access checks the field validation rules first. If your data passes the test (and has the right data types), then Access checks the table validation rule.

— TIP

Once you set the table validation rule, you might want to close the Property Sheet to get more room in your design window. To do so, choose Table Tools | Design → Show/Hide → Property Sheet.

Lookups

In a database, minor variations can add up to big trouble. Suppose you're running International Cinnamon, a multinational cinnamon bun bakery with hundreds of orders a day. In your Orders table, you have entries like this:

```
Quantity   Product
10         Frosted Cinnamon Buns
24         Cinnamon Buns with Icing
16         Buns, Cinnamon (Frosted)
120        FCBs
...
```

(Other fields, like the ID column and the information about the client making the order, are left out of this example.)

All the orders shown here amount to the same thing: different quantities of tasty cinnamon and icing confections. But the text in the Product column's slightly different. This difference doesn't pose a problem for ordinary human beings (for example, you'll have no trouble filling these orders), but it does create a small disaster if you want to analyze your sales performance later. Since Access has no way to tell that a Frosted Cinnamon Bun and an FCB are the same thing, it treats them differently. If you try to total up the top-selling products or look at long-range cinnamon sales trends, then you're out of luck.

Lookups are one more tool to help standardize your data. Essentially, a lookup lets you fill a value in a field by choosing from a ready-made list of choices. Used properly, this tool solves the problem in the Orders table—you simply need a lookup that includes all the products you sell. That way, instead of typing the product name in by hand, you can choose Frosted Cinnamon Buns from the list. Not only do you save some time, but you also avoid variants like FCBs, thereby ensuring that the orders list is consistent.

Access has two basic types of lookup lists: lists with a set of fixed values that you specify, and lists that are drawn from a linked table. In the next section, you'll learn how to create the first type. Then, in Chapter 5, you'll graduate to the second.

Creating a Simple Lookup with Fixed Values

Simple lookups make sense if you have a simple, short list that's unlikely to change. The state prefix in an address is a perfect example. In this case, there's a set of just 50 two-letter abbreviations (AL, AK, AZ, and so on).

To try out the process in the following list of steps, you can use the Bachelors table included with the online examples for this chapter (look for the DatingService.accdb database file). Or, you can jump straight to the completed lookup by checking out the DatingServiceLookup.accdb file:

1. **Open the table in Design view.**

   If you're using the DatingService.accdb example, then open the Bachelors table.

2. **Find the field where you want to add the lookup.**

   In the Bachelors table, it's the State field.

3. **Make sure your field has the correct data type.**

   Text and Number are the most common data types that you'll use in conjunction with the lookup feature.

4. **Choose Lookup Wizard from the data type list.**

   This action doesn't actually change your data type. Instead, it tells Access you want to run the Lookup wizard based on the current data type. When you select this option, the first step of the Lookup wizard appears (Figure 4-17).

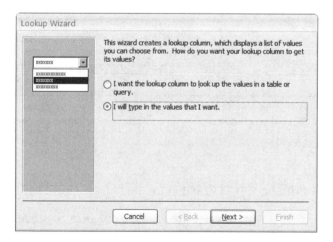

Figure 4-17. First you choose the source of your lookup: fixed values or data from another table.

5. **Choose "I will type in the values that I need".**

   Page 187 describes your other choice: drawing the lookup list from another table.

6. **Click Next.**

   The second step of the wizard gives you the chance to supply the list of values that should be used, one per row (Figure 4-18). In this case, it's a list of abbreviations for the 50 U.S. states.

   You may notice that you can supply multiple columns of information. For now, stick to one column. You'll learn why you may use more on page 187.

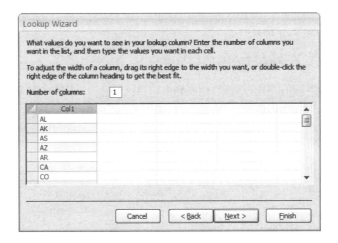

Figure 4-18. *This lookup includes the abbreviations for all the American states. This list's unlikely to change in the near future, so it's safe to hard-code this rather than store it in another table.*

7. **Click Next.**

   The final step of the Lookup wizard appears.

8. **Choose whether or not you want the lookup column to store multiple values.**

   If you allow multiple values, then the lookup list displays a checkbox next to each item. You can select several values for a single record by checking more than one item.

In the State field, it doesn't make sense to allow multiple values—after all, a person can physically inhabit only one state (discounting the effects of quantum teleportation). However, you can probably think of examples where multiple selection does make sense. For example, in the Products table used by International Cinnamon, a multiple-value lookup would let you create an order for more than one product. (You'll learn more about multiple value selections and table relationships in Chapter 5.)

9. **Click Finish.**

   Switch to Datasheet view (right-click the tab title, and then choose Datasheet View), and then save the table changes. Figure 4-19 shows the lookup in action.

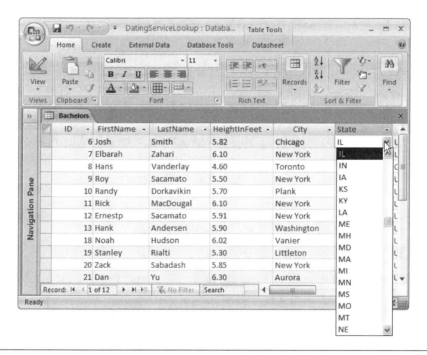

Figure 4-19. When you move to a field that has a lookup, you'll see a down-pointing arrow on the right side. Click this arrow, and a drop-down list appears with all your possibilities. Choose one to insert it into the field.

Creating a Lookup That Uses Another Table

In the previous example (on page 158), you created a lookup list that's stored as part of your field settings. This is a good approach, but it's not the best solution. A much more flexible approach is to store the lookup list in a separate table.

There are several reasons to use a separate table:

* **It allows you to add, edit, and remove items,** all by simply editing the lookup table. Even if you think you have a set of fixed, unchanging values, it's a good idea to consider a separate table. For example, the set of state abbreviations in the previous section seem unlikely to change—but what if the dating service goes international, and you need to add Canadian provinces to the list?

* **It allows you to reuse the same lookup list in several different fields** (either in the same table, or in different tables). That beats endless copy-and-paste operations.

* **It allows you to store extra information.** For example, maybe you want to keep track of the state abbreviation (for mailing purposes) but show the full state name (to make data entry easier). You'll learn how to perform this trick on page 187.

Table-based lookups are a little trickier, however, because they involve a table *relationship*: a link that binds two tables together and (optionally) enforces new restrictions. Chapter 5 is all about relationships, which are a key ingredient in any practical database.

Adding New Values to Your Lookup List

When you create a lookup that uses fixed values, the lookup list provides a list of *suggestions.* You can choose to ignore the lookup list and type in a completely different value (like a state prefix of ZI), even if it isn't on the list. This design lets you use the lookup list as a timesaving convenience without limiting your flexibility.

In many cases, you don't want this behavior. In the Bachelors table, you probably want to prevent people from entering something different in the State field. In this case, you want the lookup to be an error-checking and validation tool that actually stops entries that don't belong.

Fortunately, even though this option's mysteriously absent in the Lookup wizard, it's easy enough to add after the fact. Here's what you need to do:

1. **In Design view, go to the field that has the lookup.**

2. **In the Field Properties section, click the Lookup tab.**

   The Lookup tab provides options for fine-tuning your lookup, most of which you can configure more easily in the Lookup wizard. In the Row Source box, for example, you can edit the list of values you supplied. (Each value's on the same line, in quotation marks, separated from the next value with a semicolon.)

3. **Set the Limit to List property to Yes.**

   This action prevents you from entering values that aren't in the list.

4. **Optionally, set Value List Edits to Yes.**

   This action lets people modify the list of values at any time. This way, if something's missing from the lookup list, you can add it on the fly (Figure 4-20).

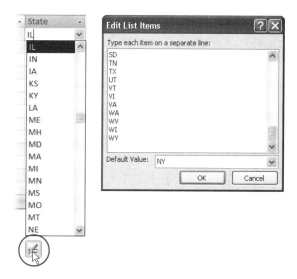

Figure 4-20. If you set Value List Edits to Yes, an icon appears under the lookup list when you use it (left). Click this icon to open an Edit List Items dialog box (right) where you can edit the items in the lookup list and change the default value.

LINKING TABLES WITH RELATIONSHIPS

- ▶ Relationship Basics
- ▶ Using a Relationship
- ▶ More Exotic Relationships
- ▶ Relationship Practice

THE TABLES YOU'VE SEEN SO FAR lead lonely, independent lives. You don't find this isolation with real-world databases. Real databases have their tables linked together in a web of *relationships*.

Suppose you set out to build a database that can manage the sales of your custom beadwork shop. The first ingredient's simple enough—a Products table that lists your merchandise—but before long you'll need to pull together a lot more information. The wares in your Products table are sold in your Orders table. The goods in your Orders table are mailed out and recorded in a Shipments table. The people in your Customers table are billed in your Invoices table. All these tables—Products, Orders, Shipments, Customers, and Invoices—have bits of related information. As a result, if you want to find out the answer to a common question (like, "How much does Jane Malone owe?" or "How many beaded wigs did we sell last week?"), you'll need to consult several tables.

Based on what you've learned so far, you already know enough to nail down the design for a database like this one. But relationships introduce the possibility of inconsistent information. And once a discrepancy creeps in, you'll never trust your database the same way again.

In this chapter, you'll learn how to *explicitly* define the relationships between tables. This process lets you prevent common errors, like data in different tables that doesn't sync up. It also gives you a powerful tool for browsing through related information in several tables.

Relationship Basics

One of any database's key goals is to break information down into distinct, manageable pieces. In a well-designed database, you'll end up with many tables. Although each table records something different, you'll often need to travel from one table to another to get all the information you want.

To better understand relationships (of the non-romantic kind, anyway), consider an example. The following section demonstrates two ways to add information to the bobblehead database: one that risks redundant data, and one that avoids the problem by properly using a relationship.

Redundant Data vs. Related Data

Think back to the Dolls table you created in Chapter 1 to store a list of bobblehead dolls. One of the Dolls table's pieces of information is the Manufacturer field, which lists the name of the company that created each doll. Although this seems like a simple-enough detail, it turns out that to properly assess the value of a bobblehead, you need to know a fair bit more about the manufacturing process. You may want to know things like where the manufacturing company's located, how long it's been in business, and if it's had to fight off lawsuits from angry customers.

If you're feeling lazy, you could add all this information to the Dolls table, like so (the grayed-out columns are the new ones):

ID	Character	Manufacturer	Manufacturer Location	Manufacturer Opening-Year	Manufacturer Lawsuits	Purchase Price
342	Yoda	MagicPlastic	China	2003	No	$8.99

Your first reaction to this table is probably to worry about the clutter of all these fields. But don't panic—in the real world, tables must include all the important details, so they often grow quite wide. (That's rule #3 of data design, from page 95.) So don't let the clutter bother you. You can use techniques like column hiding (page 108) to filter out the fields that don't interest you.

Although column clutter isn't a problem, another issue lurks under the surface in this example—redundant data. A well-designed table should list only one type of thing. This version of the Dolls table breaks that rule by combining information about the bobblehead *and* the bobblehead manufacturer.

This situation seems innocent enough, but if you add a few more rows, things don't look as pretty:

ID	Character	Manufacturer	Manufacturer Location	Manufacturer Opening-Year	Manufacturer Lawsuits	Purchase Price
342	Yoda	MagicPlastic	China	2003	No	$8.99
343	Dick Cheney	Rebobblicans	Taiwan	2005	No	$28.75
344	Tiger Woods	MagicPlastic	China	2003	No	$2.99

Once you have two bobbleheads that were made by the same company (in this case, MagicPlastic), you've introduced duplicate data, the curse of all bad databases. (You'll recognize this as a violation of rule #4 of good database design, from page 96.) The potential problems are endless:

▶ If MagicPlastic moves its plants from China to South Korea, you'll need to update a whole batch of bobblehead records. If you were using two tables with related data (as you'll see next), you'd have just one record to contend with.

▶ It's all too easy to update the manufacturer information in one bobblehead record but miss it in another. If you make this mistake, you'll wind up with *inconsistent* data in your table, which is even worse than duplicate data. Essentially, your manufacturer information will become worthless because you won't know which record has the correct details, so you won't be able to trust anything.

▶ If you want to track more manufacturer-related information (like a contact number) in your database, you'll have to update your Dolls table and edit *every single record*. Your family may not see you for several few weeks.

▶ If you want to get information about manufacturers (but not dolls), you're out of luck. For example, you can't print out a list of all the bobblehead manufacturers in China (at least not easily).

It's easy to understand the problem. By trying to cram too many details into one spot, this table fuses together information that would best be kept in two separate tables. To fix this design, you need to create two tables that use *related data*. For example, you could create a Dolls table like this:

ID	Character	Manufacturer	PurchasePrice
342	Yoda	MagicPlastic	$8.99
343	Dick Cheney	Rebobblicans	$28.75
344	Tiger Woods	MagicPlastic	$2.99

And a separate Manufacturers table with the manufacturer-specific details:

ID	Manufacturer	Location	OpeningYear	Lawsuits
1	MagicPlastic	China	2003	No
2	Rebobblicans	Taiwan	2005	No

This design gives you the flexibility to work with both types of information (dolls and manufacturers) separately. It also removes the risk of duplication. The savings are small in this simple example, but in a table with hundreds or thousands of bobblehead dolls (and far fewer manufacturers), the difference is dramatic.

Now, if MagicPlastic moves to South Korea, you need to update the Location field for only one record, rather than many instances in an overloaded Dolls table. You'll also have an easier time building queries (Chapter 6) that combine the information in neat and useful ways. (For example, you could find out how much you've spent on all your MagicPlastic dolls and compare that with the amounts you've spent for dolls made by other manufacturers.)

___ **NOTE** _____

Access includes a tool that attempts to spot duplicate data in a table and help you pull the fields apart into related tables. (To try it out, choose Database Tools → Analyze → Analyze Table.) Although it's a good idea in theory, this tool really isn't that useful. You'll do a much better job of spotting duplicate data and creating well designed tables from the start if you understand the duplicate-data problem yourself.

Matching Fields: The Relationship Link

This bobblehead database shows you an example of a *relationship*. The telltale sign of a relationship is two tables with matching fields. In this case, the tip-off's the Manufacturer field, which exists in both the Dolls table and the Manufacturers table.

In this example, the fields that link the two tables have the same name in both tables: Manufacturer. However, you don't have to do it this way. You can give these fields different names, so long as they have the same data type.

Using these linked fields, you can start with a record in one table and look up related information in the other. Here's how it works:

▶ **Starting at the Dolls table,** pick a doll that interests you (let's say Yoda). You can find out more information about the manufacturer of the Yoda doll by looking up "MagicPlastic" in the Manufacturers table.

▶ **Starting at the Manufacturers table,** pick a manufacturer (say, Rebobblicans). You can now search for all the products made by that manufacturer by searching for "Rebobblicans" in the Dolls table.

In other words, a relationship gives you the flexibility to ask more questions about your data, and get better answers.

Linking with the ID Column

In the previous example, the Dolls and Manufacturers tables are linked through the Manufacturer field, which stores the name of the manufacturing company. This seems like a reasonable design—until you spend a couple of minutes thinking about what might go wrong. And databases experts are known for spending entire weeks contemplating inevitable disasters.

Here are two headaches that just may lie in store:

▶ **Two manufacturers have the same company name.** So how do you tell which one made a doll?

▶ **A manufacturer gets bought out by another company and changes its name.** All of a sudden, there's a long list of records to change in the Dolls table.

You might recognize these problems, because they're similar to the challenges you faced when you tackled primary keys (page 90). As you learned, it's difficult to find information that's guaranteed to be unique and unchanging. Rather than risk problems, you're better off just relying instead on an AutoNumber field, which stores an Access-generated ID number.

Interestingly enough, you use the same solution when linking tables. To refer to a record in another table, you shouldn't use just any piece of information—instead, you should use the unique ID number that points to the right record. Here's a redesigned Dolls table that gets it right by changing the Manufacturer field to ManufacturerID:

ID	Character	ManufacturerID	PurchasePrice
342	Yoda	1	$8.99
343	Dick Cheney	2	$28.75
344	Tiger Woods	1	$2.99

If you take a look back at the Manufacturers table (page 169), then you can quickly find out that the manufacturer with the ID value 1 is MagicPlastic.

This design's the universal standard for databases. However, it does have two obvious drawbacks:

▶ The person adding records to the Dolls table probably doesn't know the ID of each manufacturer.

▶ When you look at the Dolls table, you can't tell what manufacturer created each doll.

To solve both these problems, use a *lookup*. Lookups show the corresponding manufacturer information in the Dolls table, and they also let you choose from a list of manufacturers when you add a record or edit the ManufacturerID field. (You saw how to use lookups with value lists on page 162. You'll learn how to use lookups to bring together related tables, like Dolls and Manufacturers, on page 173.)

— TIP

For even more power, you can use a *join query* (page 229). A join query lets you fill in all the manufacturer details alongside the doll information so you can view them side by side.

The Parent-Child Relationship

No, this isn't a detour into feel-good Dr. Phil psychology. Database nerds use the labels *parent* and *child* to identify the two tables in a relationship, and keep track of which one's which.

Here's the analogy. As you no doubt know, in the real world a parent can have any number of children. However, a child has exactly one set of parents. The same rule works for databases. In the bobblehead database, a single manufacturer record can be linked to any number of doll records. However, each doll record refers to a single manufacturer. So according to the database world's strange sociology, Manufacturers is a parent table and Dolls is a child table. They're linked by a *parent-child relationship*.

> **TIP**
>
> Don't think too hard about the parent-child analogy. It's not a perfect match with biological reality. For example, in the bobblehead database, you may create a manufacturer that doesn't link to any dolls (in other words, a parent with no children). You still call that record a parent record, because it's part of the parent table.

It's important to realize that you can't swap the parent and child tables around without changing your relationship. It's *incorrect* to suggest that Dolls is the parent table and Manufacturers is the child table. You can see that such a suggestion would break the parent-child analogy: a single doll can't have more than one manufacturer, and a manufacturer isn't limited to creating a single doll. In order to prevent problems and all-around fuzzy thinking, you need to know exactly which table's the parent and which one's the child.

> **TIP**
>
> If you have trouble identifying which table's the parent, there's a simple rule to steer you right. The child table always contains a piece of identifying information from the parent table. In the bobblehead database, the Dolls table contains the ManufacturerID field. On the other hand, the Manufacturer table doesn't have any doll information.

If you have database-savvy friends, you'll hear the term parent-child relationship quite a bit. The same relationship's also called a *one-to-many* relationship (where *one* is the parent and *many* represents the children, because a single parent record in one table can link to several child records in the other). It's the most common relationship, but not the only one—you'll learn about two other types on pages 193 and 195.

NOTE

Relationships are so common in modern-day databases that software like Access is often described as a *relational database management system* (RDBMS). A database without relationships is about as common as a beachfront resort in Ohio.

Using a Relationship

The relationship between Dolls and Manufacturers is *implicit*, which is a fancy way of saying that you know the relationship exists, but Access doesn't. Database pros aren't satisfied with this arrangement. Instead, they almost always define their relationships *explicitly*. When you create an explicit relationship, you clearly tell Access how two tables are related. Access then stores the information about that relationship in the database file.

You have good reasons to bring your relationships out into the open. Once Access knows about a relationship, it can enforce better error checking. It can also provide handy features for browsing related data and editing linked fields. You'll see all these techniques in the following sections. But first, you need to learn how to define a relationship.

Defining a Relationship

You can try out the following steps with the Bobblehead.accdb file, which is included with the online examples for this chapter. It contains the Dolls and Manufacturers tables, in their original form (with no relationships defined). The BobbleheadRelationships.accdb database file shows the final product: two tables with the right relationship.

Here's what you need to do to set up a relationship:

1. **Every relationship links two fields, each in a different table. Your first step is to identify the field you need to use in the parent table.**

   In a well-designed database, you use the primary-key field (page 90) in the parent table. For example, in the Manufacturers table, you use the ID column, which uniquely identifies each manufacturer.

2. **Open the child table in Design view. (The quickest way is to right-click it in the navigation pane, and then choose Design View.)**

   In this example, the child table is Dolls.

3. **Create the field you need in the child table, if it's not there already.**

   Each child record creates a link by storing a piece of information that points to a record in the parent table. You need to add a new field to store this information, as shown in Figure 5-1.

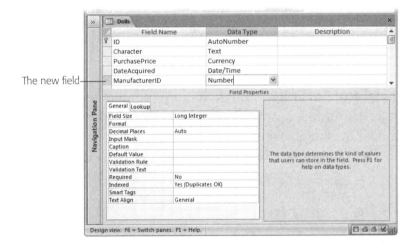

Figure 5-1. In the Dolls table, you need a field that identifies the manufacturer for that doll. It makes sense to add a new field named ManufacturerID. Set the data type to Number, and the Field Size to Long Integer, so it matches the ID field in the Manufacturers table. After you add this field, you need to fill it with the right information. (Each doll record should have the ID number of the corresponding manufacturer.)

The fields that you link in the parent and child tables must have consistent data types. However, there's one minor wrinkle. If the parent field uses the AutoNumber data type, then the child field should use the Number data type instead (with a Field Size of Long Integer). Behind the scenes, an AutoNumber and a Long Integer actually store the same numeric information. But the AutoNumber data type tells Access to fill in the field with a new, automatically-generated value whenever you create a record. You obviously don't want this behavior for the ManufacturerID field in the Dolls table.

4. **Close both tables.**

   Access prompts you to save your changes. Your tables are now relationship-ready.

5. **Choose Database Tools → Show/Hide → Relationships.**

   Access opens a new tab named Relationships. This tab's a dedicated window where you can define the relationships between all the tables in your database. In this example, you'll create a just a single relationship, but you can use the Relationships tab to define many more.

   Before Access lets you get to work in the Relationships tab, it pops up a Show Table dialog box asking what tables you want to work with (see Figure 5-2).

6. **Add both the parent table and child table to your work area.**

   It doesn't matter which one you choose first. To add a table, select it in the list, and then click Add (or just double-click it).

   Access represents each table in the Relationships tab by a small box that lists all the table fields. If relationships are already defined between these tables, they'll appear as connecting lines.

7. **Click Close.**

   You can now arrange the tables in the Relationships tab (see Figure 5-3). The Relationships tab shows a *database diagram*—it's the canvas where you add relationships by "drawing" them on.

Figure 5-2. You can add as many tables as you want to the Relationships tab. Be careful not to add the same table twice (it's unnecessary and confusing).

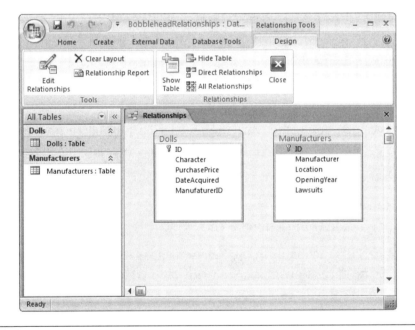

Figure 5-3. You can drag the tables you've added to any place in the window. If you have a database that's thick with relationships, this ability lets you arrange them so that the relationships are clearly visible. To remove a table from the diagram, right-click it, and then choose Hide Table. To add another table, right-click the blank space, and then choose Show Table to pop up the Show Table dialog box.

— TIP

> Access gives you a shortcut if you need to rework the design of a table that's open in the Relationships tab. Just right-click the table box, and choose Design Table.

8. **To define your relationship, find the field you're using in the parent table. Drag this field to the field you want to link it to in the child table.**

In this case, you're linking the ManufacturerID field in the Dolls table (the child) to the ID field in the Manufacturers table (the parent). So drag ManufacturerID (in the Dolls box) over to ID (in the Manufacturers box).

— TIP

> You can drag the other way, too (from the child to the parent). Either way, Access creates the same relationship.

When you release the mouse button, the Edit Relationships dialog box appears (see Figure 5-4).

Figure 5-4. Access is clever enough to correctly identify the parent table (shown in the Table/Query box) and the child table (shown in the Related Table/Query box) when you connect two fields. Access identifies the field in the parent table because it has a primary key (page 90) or a unique index (page 135). If something isn't quite right in the Edit Relationships dialog box, then you can swap the tables or change the fields you're using to create the relationship before continuing.

9. **If you want to prevent potential errors, then put a checkmark in the Enforce Referential Integrity option. (It's always a good idea.)**

   This setting turns on enhanced error checking, which prevents people from making a change that violates the rules of a relationship (like creating a doll that points to a nonexistent manufacturer). You'll learn more about referential integrity and the two settings for cascading changes on page 180. For now, it's best to switch on the Enforce Referential Integrity option and leave the others unchecked.

10. **Click Create.**

    This action creates the relationship that links the two tables. It appears in the diagram as a line (Figure 5-5).

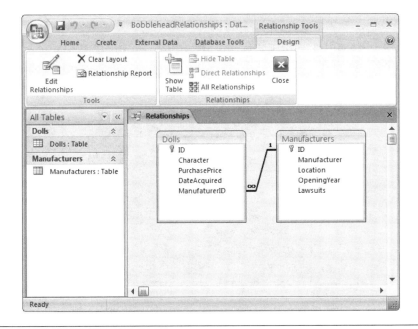

Figure 5-5. Access uses a line to connect related fields in the Relationships tab. The tiny 1 and infinity (∞) symbols let you distinguish between the "one" and the "many" side in this one-to-many relationship. To edit the relationship, double-click the line. To remove it altogether, right-click the line, and then choose Delete.

TIP

If you chose Enforce Referential Integrity (in step 9), Access checks to make sure any existing data in the table follows the relationship rules. If it finds some that doesn't, then it alerts you about the problem and refuses to continue. At this point, the best strategy's to create the relationship without referential integrity, correct the invalid data, and then edit the relationship later to turn on referential integrity.

11. **Close the Relationships tab. (You can click the X in the tab's top-right corner, or choose Relationship Tools | Design → Relationships → Close.)**

Access asks whether or not you want to save the Relationships tab's layout. Access is really asking you whether you want to save the relationship diagram you've created. No matter what you choose, the relationship remains in the database, and you can use it in the same way. The only difference is whether you'll be able to quickly review or edit the relationship in the Relationships tab.

If you choose to keep the relationship diagram, the next time you switch to the Relationships tab (by choosing Database Tools → Show/Hide → Relationships), you see the same arrangement of tables. This feature's handy.

If you choose not to keep the relationship diagram, it's up to you to recreate the diagram next time by adding the tables you want to see and arranging them in the window (although you won't need to redefine the relationships). This process takes a little more work.

TIP

Many database pros choose to save their database diagram, because they want to see all their relationships at once in the Relationships tab, just the way they left them. However, real-world databases often end up with a tangled web of relationships. In this situation, you may choose *not* to save a complete diagram so you can focus on just a few tables at once.

Editing Relationships

The next time you want to change or add relationships, you'll follow the same path to get to the Relationship window (choose Database Tools → Show/Hide → Relationships).

If you choose to save a relationship diagram (in step 11 in the previous section), the tables you added appear automatically, just as you left them. If you want to work with tables that aren't in any relationships yet, you can add them to the diagram by right-clicking anywhere in the blank area, and then choosing Show Table.

If you choose *not* to save your relationship diagram, you can use a few shortcuts to put your tables back on display:

▶ Drag your tables right from the navigation pane, and then drop them in the Relationships tab.

▶ Choose Relationship Tools | Design → Relationships → All Relationships to show all the tables that are involved in *any* relationships you've created previously.

▶ Add a table to the diagram, select it, and then choose Relationship Tools | Design → Relationships → Direct Relationships to show the tables that are linked to *that* table.

As you already know, you can use the Relationships tab to create new relationships. You can also edit the relationships you've already created. To do so, right-click the line that represents the relationship, and then choose Edit Relationship. (This takes some nimble finger-clicking. If you don't see the Edit Relationships option in the menu, you've just missed the line.) To remove a relationship, right-click the relationship line, and then choose Delete.

NOTE

Usually, you edit a relationship to change the options for referential integrity, which you'll learn about in the next section.

Referential Integrity

Now that you've gone to the work of defining your relationship, it's time to see what benefits you've earned. As in the real world, relationships impose certain restrictions. In the database world, these rules are called *referential integrity*. Taken together, they ensure that related data's always consistent.

___ NOTE _____

Referential integrity comes into action only if you switched on the
Enforce Referential Integrity option (page 178) for your relationship.
Without this detail, you're free to run rampant and enter inconsistent
information.

In the bobblehead example, referential integrity requires that every manufacturer
you refer to in the Dolls table must exist in the Manufacturer table. In other words,
there can never be a bobblehead record that points to a nonexistent manufacturer.
That sort of error could throw the hardiest database software out of whack.

To enforce this rule, Access disallows the following three actions:

▶ Adding a bobblehead that points to a nonexistent manufacturer.

▶ Deleting a manufacturer that's linked to one or more bobblehead records. (Once
this record's removed, you're left with a bobblehead that points to a nonexistent
manufacturer.)

▶ Updating a manufacturer by changing its ID number, so that it no longer matches
the manufacturer ID in the linked bobblehead records. (This updating isn't a
problem if you use an AutoNumber field, because you can't change AutoNumber
values once you've created the record.)

___ NOTE _____

If you need to add a new doll made by a new manufacturer, you must
add the manufacturer record first, and *then* add the doll record. There's
no problem if you add manufacturer records that don't have corresponding doll records—after all, it's perfectly reasonable to list a manufacturer even if you don't have any of the dolls they've made.

Along with these restrictions, Access also won't let you remove a table if it's in a relationship. You need to delete the relationship first (using the Relationships window)
and *then* remove the table.

Blank values for unlinked records

It's important to realize that there's one operation you can perform that doesn't violate referential integrity: creating a bobblehead that doesn't point to *any* manufacturer. You do this by leaving the ManufacturerID field blank (which database nerds

refer to as a *null value*). The only reason you'll leave the ManufacturerID field blank is if the manufacturer record doesn't exist in your database, or if the information doesn't apply. Perhaps the bobblehead wasn't created by any manufacturer but was created by an advanced space-faring alien race and left on this planet for you to discover.

If this blank-value back door makes you nervous, then you can stop it. Just set the Required field property (page 131) on the ManufacturerID field in the Dolls table. This setting ensures that every bobblehead in your Dolls table has legitimate manufacturer information. This technique's important when related information isn't optional. A sales company shouldn't be able to place an order or create an invoice without linking to the customer who made the order.

Cascading deletes

The rules of referential integrity stop you cold if you try to delete a parent record (like a manufacturer) that other child records (like dolls) link to. However, there's another option—and it's much more drastic. You can choose to blow away all related child records whenever you delete a parent. For example, this would allow you to remove a manufacturer and wipe out all the dolls that were produced by that manufacturer.

> **WARNING**
>
> Cascading deletes are risky. It's all too easy to wipe out way more records than you intend, and if you do there's no going back. Even worse, the Undo feature can't help you reverse this change. So proceed with caution.

To turn on this option, you need to switch on the Cascade Delete Related Records setting when you create your relationship (Figure 5-4). You can also modify the relationship later on to add this setting.

Once you've switched this option on, you can try it out by deleting a manufacturer, as shown in Figure 5-6.

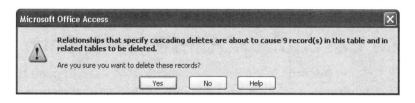

Microsoft Office Access

⚠ Relationships that specify cascading deletes are about to cause 9 record(s) in this table and in related tables to be deleted.

Are you sure you want to delete these records?

[Yes] [No] [Help]

Figure 5-6. In this example, the Dolls-Manufacturers relationship uses the Cascade Delete Related Records setting. When you delete a manufacturer, Access warns you that you'll actually end up deleting every linked doll record, for a total of nine records.

FREQUENTLY ASKED QUESTION

Switching Off Referential Integrity

Are there any situations where you don't want to enforce referential integrity?

In most cases, referential integrity's the ultimate database safety check, and no one wants to do without it—especially if the database includes mission-critical information for your business. Remember, referential integrity prevents only inconsistent data. It still lets you leave a field blank if there's no related record that you want to link to.

The only time you may decide to dodge the rules of referential integrity is when you're using *partial copies* of your database. This situation usually happens in a large business that's using the same database at different sites.

Consider an extremely successful pastry sales company with six locations. When a customer makes an order at your downtown location, you add a new record in the Orders table, and fill in the CustomerID (which links to a full record in the Customers table). But here's the problem. The full customer record may not be in your copy of the database—instead, it's in one of the databases at another site, or at company headquarters. Although the link in the Orders table's valid, Access assumes you've made a mistake because it can't find the matching customer record.

In this situation, you may choose to turn off referential integrity so you can insert the record. If you do, then be sure to enter the linked value (in this case, the CustomerID) very carefully to avoid errors later on.

Use Cascading Deletes with Care

Cascade Delete Related Records is the nuclear option of databases, so think carefully about whether it makes sense for you. This setting makes it all too easy to delete records when you should really be *changing* them.

If you're dropping a customer from your customer database, then it doesn't make sense to remove the customer's payment history, which you need to calculate your total profit. Instead, you're better off modifying the customer record to indicate that this record isn't being used anymore. You could add a Yes/No field named Active to the customer record, and set this field to No to flag customer accounts that aren't currently in use, without removing them.

You should also keep in mind that cascading deletes are just a convenience. They don't add any new features. If you don't switch on Cascade Delete Related Fields, you can still remove linked records, as long as you follow the correct order. If you want to remove a manufacturer, then start by removing any linked bobbleheads, or changing those bobbleheads to point to a different manufacturer (or have no manufacturer at all) by modifying the ManufacturerID values. Once you've taken this step, you can delete the manufacturer record without a problem.

Cascading updates

Access also provides a setting for cascading updates. If you switch on this feature (by going to the Edit Relationships dialog box, and then choosing Cascade Update Related Fields), Access copies any change you make to the linked field in the parent record to all the children.

With the bobblehead database, a cascading update lets you change the ID of one of your manufacturers. When you change the ID, Access automatically inserts the new value into the ManufacturerID field of every linked record in the Dolls table. Without cascading updates, you can't change a manufacturer's ID if there are linked doll records.

Cascading updates are safer than cascading deletes, but you rarely need them. That's because if you're following the rules of good database design, you're linking based on an AutoNumber ID column (page 87). Access doesn't let you edit an AutoNumber value, and you don't ever need to. (Remember, an AutoNumber simply identifies a record uniquely, and it doesn't correspond to anything in the real world.)

On the other hand, cascading updates come in handy if you're working with a table that hasn't been designed to use AutoNumber values for links. If the Dolls and Manufacturers table were linked based on the manufacturer name, then you need cascading updates—it makes sure that child records are synchronized whenever a manufacturer name's changed. Cascading updates are just as useful if you have linked records based on Social Security numbers, part numbers, serial numbers, or other codes that aren't generated automatically and are subject to change.

Navigating a Relationship

Relationships aren't just useful for catching mistakes. Relationships also make it easier for you to browse through related data. In Chapter 6, you'll learn to create search routines that pull together information from related tables (page 229). But even without this technique, Access provides some serious relationship mojo in the datasheet.

Here's how it works. If you're looking at a parent table in the datasheet, then you can find the related child records for any parent record by clicking the plus box that's just at the left of the row (Figure 5-7).

This drops a *subdatasheet* into view, which shows just the related records (Figure 5-8). You can use the subdatasheet to edit the doll records here in exactly the same way as you would in the full Dolls datasheet. You can even add new records.

> **NOTE**
> You can open as many subdatasheets as you want at the same time. The only limitation is that the records in a subdatasheet don't show up if you print the datasheet (page 122).

A parent table may be related to more than one child table. In this case, Access gives you a choice of what table you want to use when you click the plus box. Imagine you've created a Customers table that's linked to a child table of customer orders (Orders), and a child table of billing information (Invoices). When you click the plus box, Access doesn't know which table to choose, so it asks you (see Figure 5-9).

Figure 5-7. Curious to find out what dolls you have from MagicPlastic? Just click the plus box (circled).

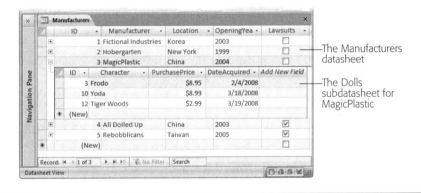

The Manufacturers datasheet

The Dolls subdatasheet for MagicPlastic

Figure 5-8. The subdatasheet's really a filtered version of the ordinary Dolls datasheet. It shows only the records that are linked to the manufacturer you chose. The subdatasheet has all the same view settings (like font, colors, column order) as the datasheet for the related table.

--- NOTE ---

You have to choose the subdatasheet you want to use only once. Access remembers your setting and always uses the same subdatasheet from that point on.

Figure 5-9. When Access doesn't know which table to use as a subdatasheet, it lets you pick from a list of all your tables. In this case, only two choices make sense. Choose Orders to see the customer's orders, or Invoices to see the customer's invoices. When you select the appropriate table in the list, Access automatically fills in the linked fields in the boxes at the bottom of the window. You can then click OK to continue.

As you create more elaborate databases, you'll find that your tables are linked together in a chain of relationships. One parent table might be linked to a child table, which is itself the parent of another table, and so on. This complexity doesn't faze Access—it lets you drill down through all the relationships (see Figure 5-10).

Lookups with Related Tables

So far, you've seen how relationships make it easier to review and edit your records. But what about when you add your records in the first place? Relationships are usually based on an unhelpful AutoNumber value. When you create a new doll, you probably won't know that 3408 stands for Bobelle House O' Dolls. Access stops you from entering a manufacturer ID that isn't linked to anyone at all, but it doesn't help you choose the ID value you want.

Fortunately, Access has a technique to help you out. In the previous chapter, you learned about *lookups* (page 157), a feature that provides you with a list of possible values for a column. When creating a lookup, you can supply a list of fixed values, or

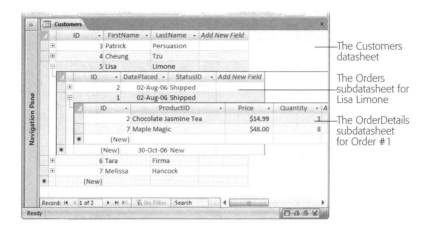

Figure 5-10. There are two relationships at work here. Customers is the parent of Orders (which lists all the orders a customer's placed). Orders is the parent of OrderDetails (which lists the individual items in each order). By digging through the levels, you can see what each customer bought.

you can pull values from another table. You could create a lookup for the ManufacturerID field in the Dolls table that uses a list of ID values drawn from the Manufacturers table. This type of lookup helps a bit—it gives you a list of all the possible values you can use—but it still doesn't solve the central problem. Namely, the befuddled people using your database won't have a clue what ID belongs to what manufacturer. You still need a way to show the manufacturer name in the lookup list.

Happily, *lookup lists* provide just this feature. The trick is to create a lookup that has more than one column. One column holds the information (in this case, the manufacturer name) that you want to display to the person using the database. The other column has the data you want to use when a value's picked (in this case, the manufacturer ID).

NOTE

Access is a bit quirky when it comes to lookups. It expects you to add the lookup, and *then* the relationship. (In fact, when you set up a lookup that uses a table, Access creates a relationship *automatically*.) So if you've been following through with the examples on your own, then you'll need to *delete* the relationship between the Dolls and Manufacturers tables (as described on page 180) before you go any further.

The following steps show how you can create a lookup list that links the Dolls and Manufacturers tables:

1. **Open the child table in Design view.**

   In this example, it's the Dolls table.

2. **Select the field that links to the parent table, and, in the Data Type column, choose the Lookup Wizard option.**

   In this example, the field you want is ManufacturerID.

3. **Choose "I want the lookup column to look up the values in a table or query" and then click Next.**

   The next step shows a list of all the tables in your database, except the current table.

4. **Choose the parent table, and then click Next.**

   In this case, you're after the Manufacturers table. Once you select it and move to the next step, you'll see a list of all the fields in the table.

5. **Add the field you use for the link and another more descriptive field to the list of Selected Fields (Figure 5-11). Click Next to continue.**

   In this case, you need to add the ID field and the Manufacturer field.

   ___ TIP _____

   In some cases, you might want to use more than one field with descriptive information. For example, you might grab both a FirstName and LastName field from a FamilyRelatives table. But don't add too much information, or the lookup list will become really wide in order to fit it all in. This looks a bit bizarre.

   _____

6. **Choose a field to use for sorting the lookup list (Figure 5-12), and then click Next.**

   In this example, the Manufacturer field's the best choice to sort the list.

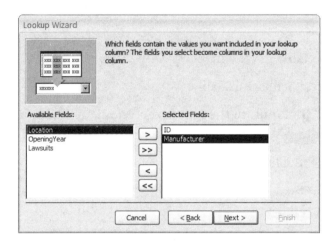

Figure 5-11. The secret to a good lookup is getting two pieces of information: the primary key (in this case, the ID field) and a more descriptive value (in this case, the manufacturer's name). The ID field's the piece of information you need to store in the doll record, while the Manufacturer field's the value you'll show in the lookup list to make it easier to choose the right manufacturer.

Figure 5-12. It's important to sort the lookup list, so that the person using it can find the right item quickly. One links students to classes, and the other links teachers to classes.

7. **The next step shows a preview of your lookup list (Figure 5-13). Make sure the "Hide key column" option's selected, and then click Next.**

   Although the primary-key field has the value that links the two tables together, it doesn't mean much to the person using the database. The other, descriptive field's more important.

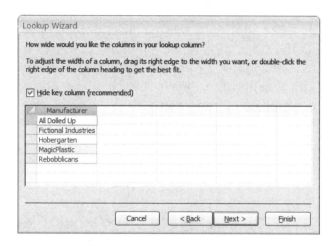

Figure 5-13. Here, the lookup list shows the manufacturer name (the Manufacturer field) and hides the manufacturer ID (the ID field).

8. **Choose a name for the lookup column.**

   Usually, it's clearest if you keep the name of the field that uses the lookup (in this case, ManufacturerID).

   The final step also gives you an option named Allow Multiple Values. If you check this, then the lookup list shows a checkbox next to each item, so that you can pick several at once. (In this example, you can create a doll that has more than one manufacturer.)

9. **Click Finish.**

   Now, Access creates the lookup for the field and prompts you to save the table. Once you do, Access creates a relationship between the two tables you've linked with your lookup column. Here, Access creates a parent-child relationship between Manufacturers and Dolls, just as you did yourself on page 173.

NOTE

The relationships that Access creates don't enforce referential integrity, because Access doesn't know if your records can live up to that strict standard. You can have a doll that points to a nonexistent manufacturer. If this possibility seems dangerously lax, you can edit your relationship using the Relationships tab (as described on page 180). Begin by adding both the Dolls and the Manufacturers table to the relationships diagram. Then, right-click the relationship line in between, and then choose Edit Relationship. Finally, switch on the Enforce Referential Integrity checkbox, and then click OK.

Now, if you switch to the design view of the Dolls table, you can use your lookup when you're editing or adding records (Figure 5-14).

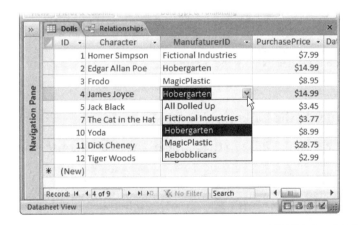

Figure 5-14. Even though the Dolls table stores an ID value in the ManufacturerID field behind the scenes, that's not how it appears on your datasheet. Instead, you see the related manufacturer name. Even better, if you need to add a new record or change the manufacturer that's assigned to an existing one, then you can pick the manufacturer from the list by name.

Refreshing a Lookup

I just added a record, but it doesn't appear in my lookup. Why not?

Access fills in your lookup lists when you first open the table. For example, when you open the Dolls table, Access gets a list of manufacturers ready to go. However, sometimes you might have both the table that *uses* the lookup and the table that *provides* the lookup data open at the same time. In this situation, the changes you make in the table that provides the lookup won't appear in the table that uses the lookup.

To see how this works, open both the Dolls and Manufacturers tables at once. (They'll appear in separate tabs.) In the Manufacturers table, add a new manufacturer. Now, switch back to the Dolls table and try using the ManufacturerID lookup. You'll notice that the lookup list doesn't show the new record.

Fortunately, there's an easy to solution. You can tell Access to refresh the lookup list at any time by choosing Home → Records → Refresh All. Try that out in the Dolls table, and you'll see the updated list of manufacturers appear in the lookup.

More Exotic Relationships

As you learned on page 172, a one-to-many (a.k.a. *parent-child*) relationship that links a single record in one table to zero, one, or more records in another table is the most common relationship. A single manufacturer could be linked to one bobblehead, several bobbleheads, or no bobbleheads at all.

Along with one-to-many relationships, there are two subtly different types of relationships: one-to-one relationships and many-to-many relationships. You'll learn about both in the following sections.

One-to-One Relationship

A *one-to-one relationship* links one record in a table to zero or one record in another table. People sometimes use one-to-one relationships to break down a table with lots of fields into two (or more) smaller tables.

A Products table may include detailed information that describes the product and its price, and additional information that describes how it's built. This information's important only to the people in the engineering department, so you may choose to split it into a separate table (named something like ProductsEngineering). That way, sales folks don't need to think about it when they're making an order. Other times, you might break a table into two pieces because it's simply too big. (Access doesn't let any table have more than 255 fields.)

You create a one-to-one relationship in the same way you create a one-to-many relationship—by dragging the fields in the Relationships tab (Figure 5-15). The only difference is that the linked fields in *both* tables need to be set to prevent duplicates. This way, a record in one table can (at most) be linked to a single record in the other table.

___ NOTE _____

A field prevents duplicates if it's set as the primary key for a table (page 90), or if it has an index that prevent duplicates (page 135).

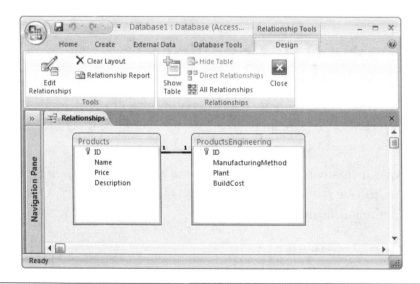

Figure 5-15. When you link two fields that don't allow duplicates (and you have the Enable Referential Integrity option switched on), Access realizes that you're creating a one-to-one relationship. Access places the number 1 at each side of the line to distinguish it from other types of relationships. In this example, the ID column in the Products table and the ID column in the ProductsEngineering table are both primary keys of their respective tables, so there's no way to link more than one record in ProductsEngineering to the same record in Products.

Approach One-to-One Relationships with Caution

One-to-one relationships are extremely rare in Access. Usually, features like column hiding (page 108) and queries (Chapter 6) are better choices if you want to see only some of the fields in a table.

Splitting a table into two pieces complicates the design of your database, and you'd generally do it only if you have other reasons to separate the tables. Some possible examples include:

* The two parts of the table need to be placed in separate databases so that different people can copy them to separate computers and edit them independently.

* You want to stop prying eyes from seeing sensitive data. One way to do this is to put the information that should be secure into a separate table, and put that separate table in a different, more secure database file.

* You have a table that stores huge amounts of data, like an Attachment field (page 84) with large documents. In this case, you might get better performance by splitting the table. You might even choose to put one half of the table in a separate database.

* Some of the data in your table's optional. Rather than include a lot of blank fields, you can pop it into a separate table. If you don't need to include this information, then you don't need to add a record to the linked table.

If you don't have these requirements, then you're better off creating a single large table.

Many-to-Many Relationship

A *many-to-many relationship* links one or more records in one table to one or more records in another table. Consider a database that tracks authors and books in separate tables. Best-selling authors don't stop at one book (so you need to be able to link one author to several books). However, authors sometimes team up on a single title (so you need to be able to link one book to several authors). A similar situation occurs if you need to put students into classes, employees into committees, or ingredients into recipes. You can even imagine a situation where this affects the bobblehead database, if more than one manufacturer can collaborate to create a single bobblehead doll.

Many-to-many relationships are relatively common, and Access gives you two ways to deal with them.

Junction tables

Junction tables are the traditional approach for dealing with many-to-many relationships, and people use them throughout the database world (including in industrial-strength products like Microsoft SQL Server). The basic idea's that you create an extra table that has the sole responsibility of linking together two tables.

Each record in the junction table represents a link that binds together a record from each table in the relationship. In the books and authors database, a single record in the junction table links together one author with one book. If the same author writes three books, then you need to add three records to the junction table. If two authors work on one book, then you need an additional record to link each new author.

Suppose you have these records in your Authors table:

ID	FirstName	LastName
10	Alf	Abet
11	Cody	Pendant
12	Moe	DeLawn

And you have these records in your Books table:

ID	Title	Published
402	Fun with Letters	January 1, 2007
403	How to Save Money by Living with Your Parents	February 24, 2008
404	Unleash Your Guilt	May 5, 2007

Here's the Authors_Books table that binds it all together:

ID	AuthorID	BookID
1	10	402
2	11	403
3	12	403
4	11	404

Authors_Books is a junction table that defines four links. The first record indicates that author #10 (Alf Abet) wrote book #402 (Fun with Letters). As you traverse the rest of the table, you'll discover that Cody Pendant contributed to two books, and two authors worked on the same book (How to Save Money by Living with Your Parents).

— TIP

The junction table often has a name that's composed of the two tables it's linking, like Authors_Books.

The neat thing about a junction table is that it's actually built out of two one-to-many relationships that you define in Access. In other words, the junction table's a child table that has two parents. The Authors table has a one-to-many relationship with the Authors_Books table, where Authors is the parent. The Books table also has a one-to-many relationship with Authors_Books, where Books is the parent. You can define these two relationships in the Relationships tab to make sure referential integrity rules the day (Figure 5-16).

Although junction tables seem a little bizarre at first glance, most database fans find that they quickly become very familiar. As with the one-to-many relationships you used earlier, you can create lookups (page 187) for the AuthorID and BookID fields in the Authors_Books table. However, you'll always need to add the Authors_Books record by hand to link an author to a book.

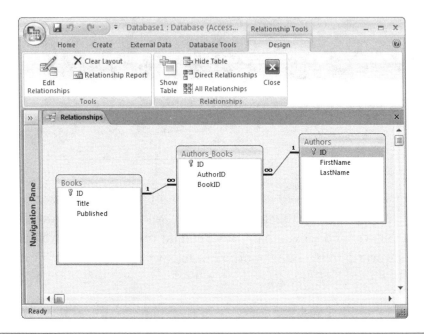

Figure 5-16. The many-to-many relationship between Authors and Books is really two one-to-many relationships that involve the Authors_Books table. Once you've defined these relationships, you can't link to an author or book that doesn't exist, and can't delete an author or book that has a record in the Authors_Books table.

Relationship Practice

Every database designer needs to see the world in terms of tables and relationships. Savvy database designers can quickly assess information and see how it's related. With this ability, they can build just the right database for any situation.

The following sections provide two scenarios that help you practice more realistic relationship building. Both databases used in these scenarios are available with the samples for this chapter, and they'll turn up again in the following chapters, when you start to build more sophisticated database objects like queries, reports, and forms.

The Music School

Cacophoné Studios runs a medium-sized music school. They have a fixed series of courses in mind, and a roster of teachers that can fill in for most of them. They also have a long list of past and potential customers. Last year, a small catastrophe happened when 273 students were crammed into the same class and no teacher was assigned to teach it. (Next door, a class of 14 had somehow ended up with three instructors.) They're hoping that Access can help them avoid the same embarrassment this time around.

Identifying the tables

Every business is a little different, and it would take a long, detailed analysis to get the perfect table structure for Cacophoné Studios. However, even without knowing that much, you can pick out some fairly obvious candidates:

▶ **Teachers.** A table to store a list of all the teachers on their roster, complete with contact information.

▶ **Students.** A table to store all class-goers past, present, and potential. You don't need to distinguish between these different groups of people in the Students table—instead, you can sort out the current students from the others by looking for related data (namely, their class enrollments). So you can keep things simple in the Students table, and just store name and contact information.

▶ **Classes.** A table to store the classes that Cacophoné Studios is running. This table should include the class name, date it starts, date it ends, maximum enrollment number, and any other key information.

Cacophoné Studios will certainly want many more tables before long. But these tables are enough to get started.

Identifying the relationships

It's fairly easy to pick out the relationships you need. Students take classes. Teachers teach classes. This suggests two relationships—one between Students and Classes, and one between Teachers and Classes.

But there's a bit of a hitch. Cacophoné Studios certainly doesn't want to stop a single student from taking more than one class, so you'll need a many-to-many relationship between the two tables. And even though Cacophoné Studios plans to have only one teacher in each class, they want to keep open the possibility that two or more teachers might co-teach. So Teachers and Classes are also locked in a more complex many-to-many relationship. To support these two relationships, you can create two junction tables, named Students_Classes and Teachers_Classes (respectively).

Figure 5-17 shows a snapshot of this arrangement.

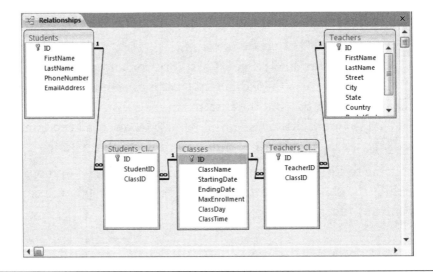

Figure 5-17. Two many-to-many relationships form the basis of the Cacophoné Studios music school.

___ NOTE _____

Each record in the Students_Classes table represents a student enrollment in a class. You may want to add some additional fields to Students_Classes to track information like the enrollment date, an enrollment discount you might have offered for early booking, and so on.

_____

Getting more detailed

Cacophoné Studios is off to the right start, but there's a lot more they still need to think about. First of all, each time they offer a class, they need to create a separate record in the Classes table. This method makes sense, but it causes a potential problem. That's because when a class (like Electro-Acoustic Gamelan) ends, it's usually offered again in a new session, with new students. Although this is a whole new class, it has some information in common with the previous class, like the description, fee, course requirements, and so on.

To deal with this requirement, you need to create another table, named ClassDescriptions. The ClassDescriptions record should have all the descriptive information for a class. The Classes record represents a single, scheduled session of a particular class. That way, the school can offer the same class multiple times without confusion.

To make this design work, each record in Classes links to a single record in ClassDescriptions. There's a one-to-many relationship between ClassDescriptions and Classes (Figure 5-18).

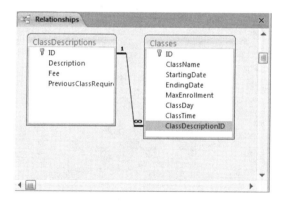

Figure 5-18. Thanks to the ClassDescriptions table, you can use the same description for several classes, thereby avoiding redundant data.

Cacophoné Studios also needs to think about the sticky financial side of things. Each time they put a student in a class, they need to collect a set fee. Each time they assign a teacher to a class, they need to pay up.

Two tables can fill in these details: TeacherPayments and StudentCharges. Obviously, these tables need relationships—but maybe not the ones you expect. You may assume that you should link the StudentCharges record directly to the records in the Students table. That linking makes sense, because you need to know which student owes money. However, it's also important to keep track of what the money's for— namely, the class that the student's paying for. In other words, every record in StudentCharges needs to link to both the Students and the Classes table.

But there's an easier approach. You can save some effort by linking the StudentCharges table directly to the Students_Classes table. Remember, each record in Students_Classes has the student and class information for one enrollment. Every time you add a record in Students_Classes, you need to add a corresponding charge in StudentCharges. One record in the Students_Classes table should link to exactly one record in the StudentCharges table. A similar relationship exists between the Teachers_Classes and TeacherPayments tables. Figure 5-19 shows the whole shebang (not including the ClassDescriptions table shown in Figure 5-18).

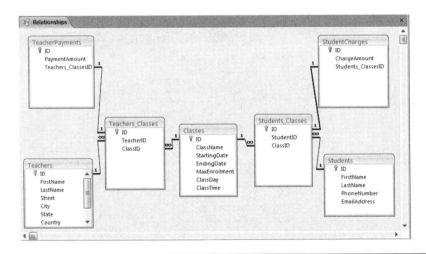

Figure 5-19. Every assigned class results in a payment in the TeacherPayments table (top left). Every enrollment results in a charge in StudentCharges (top right). Although this picture's a bit intimidating at first glance, you should be able to work your way through all the tables and relationships one by one. When building a database, it's easiest to start with a few tables, and then keep adding on.

Remember, to create a one-to-one relationship, you need to use a primary key or an index that doesn't allow duplicates (page 135). In this example, you need to add a no-duplicates index to the Student_ClassesID field in the StudentCharges table, and the Teacher_ClassesID field in the TeacherPayments table. These indexes make sure that students get charged only once for each class they take, and teachers get only a single payment for each class they teach.

This database has quickly become quite sophisticated. And Cacophoné Studios probably isn't done yet. (For example, it'll more than likely want a table to track student payments.) As with most realistic databases, you can keep adding on new tables and relationships endlessly.

FREQUENTLY ASKED QUESTION

Printing Your Relationship

Why is the Office button → Print command disabled when I'm looking at the Relationships tab?

Once you've created your relationships, you might want to have a printed copy at your fingertips. You can't print the contents of the Relationships tab directly, but you *can* convert it into a report, which is a specialized database object that lets you create a printout whenever you want. (You'll learn how to create reports in Part Three.)

To create a report for your relationships, first arrange all the tables to your liking in the Relationships tab. Then, choose Relationship Tools | Design → Tools → Relationship Report. A preview window appears, which looks more

or less the same as the current contents of the Relationships tab. You can then choose Office button → Print to send it to the printer.

When you close the relationship report, Access asks you if you want to save it permanently in your database. Usually, you won't bother, because you can easily regenerate the report whenever you need it. However, if you have a complex database and you want to print several different diagrams (each showing a different group of relationships), you may decide to save your relationship report for later use. You'll learn more about reports in Chapter 8.

The Chocolate Store

A *sales* database that stores the products, customers, and orders for a company that sells something is one of the most common databases. In fact, this pattern turns up so often that it's worth looking at a quick example. As you'll see, there are a few basic principles that apply to every sales-driven business, whether the business is selling collectible books or discount pharmaceuticals.

In this example, you'll meet Boutique Fudge, a mail-order company that serves decadent treats to a large audience of chocolate-crazed customers. Their daring chefs are always innovating, and they need a better way to manage their ever-growing catalog of chocolate goodness. They also need a way to keep track of customers and the orders they make.

The product catalog and customer list

Even though you don't know much about Boutique Fudge, you can already think of a few key tables that it'll need. In order to put anything up for sale, they should have the following tables:

▶ **Products** lists the sinful chocolate delicacies they have for sale. This table records the name, description, and price of each item available. A few optional details also make sense—for example, why not keep track of the current stock using two numeric fields (UnitsInStock and UnitsOnOrder) and a Yes/No field (named Discontinued) to identify products that aren't available any longer?

NOTE

In many databases, you can't delete old information. A company like Boutique Fudge can't simply delete old products from their catalogs, because these products might be linked to old orders. Also, it makes sense to keep historical information to allow data analysis. (Boutique Fudge could use a query to uncover the top selling products in 1999, and check if declining cocoa levels are linked to lessening sales). For this reason, you need tricks like the Discontinued field. When you list the products for sale, you can leave out all the discontinued ones, using the filtering skills you picked up on page 115.

- **ProductCategories** splits products into a few descriptive groups. That way, customers can browse just the products in the category they want (whether it's Beverages, Candies, Chocolate, or Personalized Choco-wear.)

- **Customers** holds the list of chocoholics that have signed up to make an order. You need all the customary information here, like customer names, shipping information, and billing information.

NOTE

Many companies let customers supply multiple shipping addresses and credit cards. If you allow this flexibility, then you'll need (surprise) more tables. You could create a table of CustomerCreditCards. Every record in Customers could then link to one or more records in CustomerCreditCards. BoutiqueFudge takes the easy way out, and stores a customer credit card and address directly in the Customers table.

So far, there's only one relationship at work: a one-to-many relationship between ProductCategories and Products. Figure 5-20 shows this design.

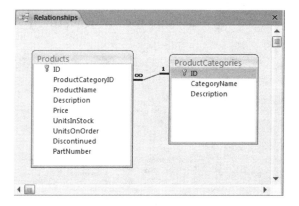

Figure 5-20. A product (like Chocolate Jasmine Tea) can be placed in one category (like Beverages), but a single category holds many products.

Ordering products

It doesn't matter how fancy your sales database is—if it doesn't have a way for customers to *order* the items they're interested in, then Boutique Fudge will run out of money fast.

Database newbies often make the mistake of assuming that they can use one table to store order information. In truth, you need two:

▶ **Orders** records each order a customer places. It links to the customer who made the order, and adds information like the date the order was placed.

▶ **OrderDetails** lists the individual items in an order. Each record in the OrderDetails table includes the ID of the product that was ordered, the number of units ordered, and the price at which they were ordered.

Because the average order includes more than one item, a single record in the Orders table is usually linked to multiple records in the OrderDetails table (as shown in Figure 5-21). This setup may sound a bit awkward (because it means you'll need to create a batch of new records for just one order), but the process doesn't have to be that difficult. Access has two features that help out: the subdatasheet feature you've already seen (Figure 5-22) and the forms feature (Chapter 9).

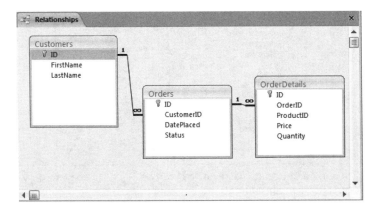

Figure 5-21. Every order can hold an unlimited number of order items. This ability makes Boutique Fudge happy.

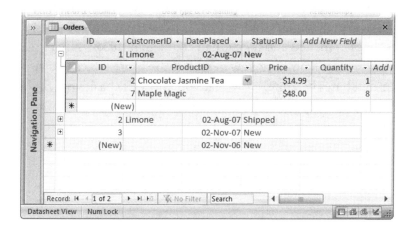

Figure 5-22. Thanks to the subdatasheet feature (page 185), you can add an order record and the linked order items in the same place.

Notice that the OrderDetails record stores the price of each ordered item. This system may seem to violate the redundant data rule. After all, the product prices are always available in the Products table. However, product prices change, and companies offer discounts. For those reasons, it's absolutely essential that you keep track of the price of an item when it was ordered. Otherwise, you'll have to guess how much each customer owes you.

___ NOTE ___

Database nerds call this sort of information *point-in-time data*, because it varies over time.

You should also notice that the Order record doesn't store the total cost of the order. That's because the total cost is simply the sum of all the ordered items. If you stored a total cost, you'd open up the possibility of inconsistent data—in other words, you've got a problem if the order total you store doesn't match the cost of all the items.

You still have more work to do before Boutique Fudge can become a true database-driven company. For example, you'll probably need to create a Shipments table that tracks orders that it's mailed and a Payments table that makes sure customers pay up. Conceptually, there's nothing new here, but the more tables you add, the more complex your databases become. Now that you know the basics of relationships and good table design, you can stay cool under the pressure.

PART TWO: MANIPULATING DATA WITH QUERIES

QUERIES THAT SELECT RECORDS

▶ Query Basics

▶ Creating Queries

▶ Queries and Related Tables

▶ Query Power: Calculated Fields and Text Expressions

▶ Calculated Fields

IN A TYPICAL DATABASE, WITH THOUSANDS OR MILLIONS OF RECORDS, you may find it quite a chore finding the information you need. In Chapter 3, you learned how to go on the hunt using the tools of the datasheet, including filtering, searching, and sorting. At first glance, these tools seem like the perfect solution for digging up bits of hard-to-find information. However, there's a problem: The datasheet features are *temporary*.

To understand the problem, imagine you're creating an Access database for a mail-order food company named Boutique Fudge. Using datasheet filtering, sorting, and column hiding, you can pare down the Orders table so it shows only the most expensive orders placed in the past month. (This information's perfect for targeting big spenders or crafting a hot marketing campaign.) Next, you can apply a different set of settings to find out which customers order more than five pounds of fudge every Sunday. (You could use this information for more detailed market research, or just pass it along to the Department of Health.) But every time you apply new datasheet settings, you lose your previous settings. If you want to jump back from one view to another, then you need to painstakingly reapply all your settings. If you've spent some time crafting the perfect view of your data, this process adds up to a lot of unnecessary extra work.

The solution to this problem's to use *queries*: ready-made search routines that you store in your database. Even though the Boutique Fudge company has only one Orders table, it may have dozens (or more) queries, each with different sorting and filtering options. If you want to find the most expensive orders, then you don't need to apply the filtering, sorting, and column hiding settings by hand—instead, you can just fire up the MostExpensiveOrdersLastMonth query, which pulls out just the information you need. Similarly, if you want to find the fudge-a-holics, then you can run the LargeRepeatFudgeOrders query.

Queries are a staple of database design. In this chapter, you'll learn all you need to design and fine-tune basic queries.

Query Basics

As the name suggests, queries are a way to ask *questions* about your data, like what products net the most cash, where do most customers live, and who ordered the embroidered toothbrush? Access saves each query in your database, like any other database object (page 24). Once you've saved a query, you can run it any time you want to take a look at the live data that meets your criteria.

Queries' key feature is their amazing ability to reuse your hard work. Queries also introduce some new features that you don't have with the datasheet alone:

▶ **Queries can combine related tables.** This feature's insanely useful because it lets you craft searches that take related data into account. In the Boutique Fudge example, you can use this feature to create queries that find orders with specific product items, or orders made by customers living in specific cities. Both these searches need relationships, because they branch out past the Orders table to take in information from other tables (like Products and Customers). You'll see how this works on page 229.

▶ **Queries can perform calculations.** The Products table in the Boutique Fudge database lists price information, along with the quantity in stock. A query can multiply these details, and then add a column that lists the calculated value of the product you have on hand. You'll try out this trick on page 241.

▶ **Queries can automatically apply changes.** If you want to find all the orders made by a specific person and reduce the cost of each one by 10 percent, then a query can apply the entire batch of changes in one step. This action requires a different type of query, an *action query*, which you'll consider in Chapter 7.

In this chapter, you'll consider the simplest and most common type of query: the *select query*, which retrieves a subset of information from a table. Once you've retrieved this information, you print or edit it using a datasheet, in the same way you interact with a table.

Creating Queries

Access gives you three ways to create a query:

▶ **The Query wizard** gives you a quick-and-dirty way to build a simple query. However, this option also gives you the least control.

___ NOTE _____

If you decide to use the Query wizard to create your query, then you'll probably want to refine your query later on using Design view.

_____

▶ **Design view** offers the most common approach to query building. It provides a handy graphical tool that you can use to perfect any query.

▶ **SQL view** gives you a behind-the-scenes look at the actual query *command*, which is a piece of text (ranging from one line to more than a dozen) that tells Access exactly what to do. The SQL view's where many Access experts hang out; for more information on the world of SQL, see *Access 2007: The Missing Manual*.

Creating a Query in Design View

The best starting point for query creation's the Design view. The following steps show you how it works. (To try this out yourself, you can use the BoutiqueFudge.accdb database that's included with the downloadable samples for this chapter.) The final result—a query that gets the results that fall in the first quarter of 2007—is shown in Figure 6-6.

Here's what you need to do:

1. **Choose Create → Other → Query Design.**

   A new design window appears, where you can craft your query. But before you get started, Access pops open the Show Table dialog box, where you can choose the tables that you want to work with (Figure 6-1).

2. **Select the table that has the data you want, and then click Add (or just double-click the table).**

   In the Boutique Fudge example, you need the Orders table.

   Access adds a box that represents the table to the design window. You can repeat this step to add several related tables, but for now stick with just one.

3. **Click Close.**

   The Show Table dialog disappears, giving you access to the Design view for the query.

4. **Select the fields you want to include in your query.**

   To select a field, double-click it in the table box (Figure 6-2). Take care not to add the same field more than once, or that column shows up twice in the results. If you're using the Boutique Fudge example, then make sure you choose at least the ID, DatePlaced, and CustomerID fields.

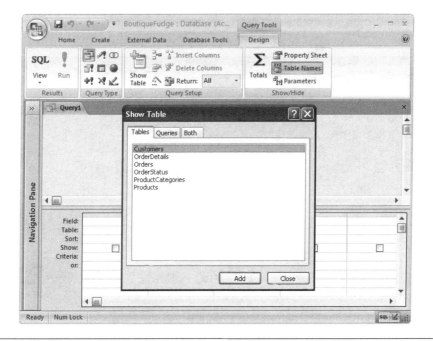

Figure 6-1. You've seen the Show Table dialog box before—it's the same way you added tables to the relationships window in Chapter 5.

You can double-click the asterisk (*) to choose to include *all* the columns from a table. However, in most cases, it's better to add each column separately. Not only does this help you more easily see at a glance what's in your query, it also lets you choose the column order, and use the field for sorting and filtering.

NOTE

A good query includes only the fields you absolutely need. Keeping your query lean ensures it's easier to focus on the important information (and easier to fit your printout on a page).

5. **Arrange the fields from left to right in the order you want them to appear in the query results.**

When you run the query, the columns appear in the same order as they're listed in the column list in Design view. (Ordinarily, this system means the columns appear from left to right in the order you added them.) If you want to change the order, then all you need to do is drag (as shown in Figure 6-3).

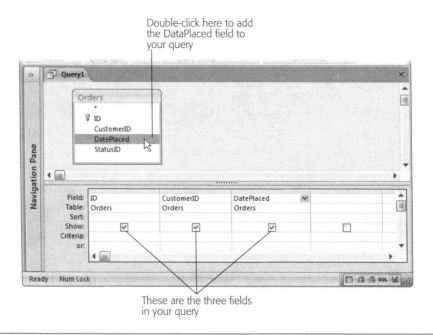

Double-click here to add the DataPlaced field to your query

These are the three fields in your query

Figure 6-2. Each time you double-click a field in the table box, Access adds it to the field list at the bottom of the window. You can then configure various settings to control filtering criteria and sorting for that column. If you don't want to keep mousing back to the table box, then you can add a field directly to the column list by choosing its name from the drop-down Field box.

6. **If you want to hide one or more columns, then clear the Show checkbox for those columns.**

   Ordinarily, Access shows every column you've added to the column list. However, in some situations you want to work with a column in your query, but not actually display its data. Usually, it's because you want to use the column values for sorting or filtering.

7. **Choose a sort order.**

   If you don't supply a sort order, then you'll get the records right from the database in whatever order they happen to be. This convention usually (but not always) means the oldest records appear first, at the top of the table. To sort your table explicitly, choose the field you want to use to sort the results, and then, in the corresponding Sort box, choose a sorting option. In the current example, the

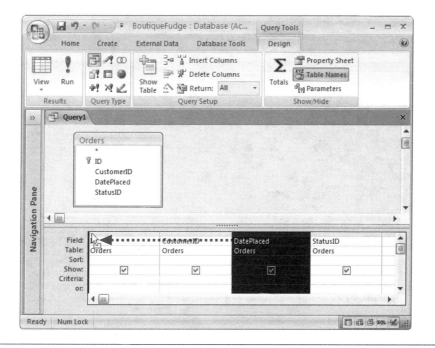

Figure 6-3. To reorder your columns, drag the gray bar at the top of the column you want to move to its new home. This technique's similar to the technique you use to arrange columns in the datasheet (page 105). In this example, the DatePlaced field's being moved to the far left side.

table's sorted by date in descending order, so that the most recent orders are first in the list (Figure 6-4).

--- TIP --

You can sort based on several fields. The only trick's that your columns need to be ordered so that the first sorting criteria appears first (to the left) in the column list. Use the column rearranging trick from step 5 to make sure you've got it right.

---

8. Set your filtering criteria.

Filtering (page 115) is a tool that lets you focus on the records that interest you and ignore all the rest. Filtering cuts a large swath of data down to the information you need, and it's the heart of many a query. (You'll learn much more about building a filter expression in the next section.)

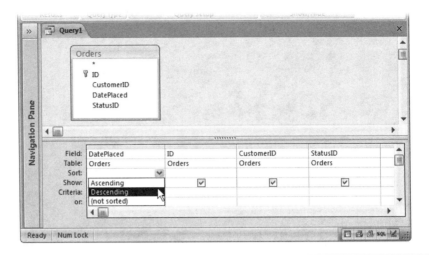

Figure 6-4. Choose Ascending if you want to sort a text field from A-Z, a numeric field from lowest to highest, or a date field from oldest to most recent. Choose Descending to use the reverse order. Page 112 has more information about sorting and how it applies to different data types.

Once you have the filter expression you need, place it into the Criteria box for the appropriate field (Figure 6-5). In the current example, you can put this filter expression in the Criteria box for the DatePlaced field to get the orders placed in the first three months of the year:

```
>=#1/1/2007# And <=#3/31/2007#
```

You aren't limited to a single filter—in fact, you can add a separate filter expression to each field. If you want to use a field for filtering but not display it in the results, then clear the Show checkbox for that field.

9. **Choose Query Tools | Design → Results → Run.**

   Now that you've finished the query, you're ready to put it into action. When you run the query, you'll see the results presented in a datasheet (complete with lookups on linked fields), just like when you edit a table. (Figure 6-6 shows the result of the query on the Orders table).

   You can switch back to Design view by right-clicking the tab title and then choosing Design View.

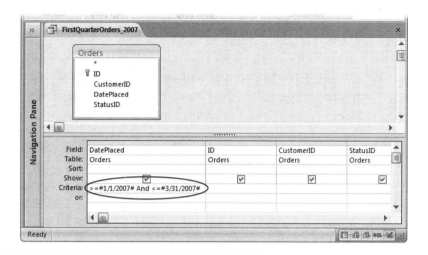

Figure 6-5. Here's a filter that finds orders made in a date range (from January 1 to March 31, in the year 2007). Notice that when you use an actual hard-coded date as part of a condition (like January 1, 2007 in this example), you need to bracket the date with the # symbols. For a refresher about date syntax, refer to page 151.

Figure 6-6. Here are the results of a query that shows orders placed within a specific date range. You can use the datasheet window to review or print your results, or you can edit information just as you would in a table datasheet.

___ **NOTE** _____

The datasheet for your query acquires any formatting you applied to the datasheet of the underlying table. If you applied a hot-pink background and cursive font to the datasheet for the Orders table, then the same settings apply to any queries that use the Orders table. However, you can change the datasheet formatting for your query just as you would with a table.

10. Save the query.

You can save your query at any time using the keyboard shortcut Ctrl+S. If you don't, then Access automatically saves your query when you close the query tab (or your entire database). Of course, you don't *need* to save your query. Sometimes you might create a query for a specific, one-time-only task. If you don't plan to reuse the query, then there's no point in cluttering up your database with extra objects.

The first time you save your query, Access asks for a name. Use the same naming rules that you follow for tables—refrain from using spaces or special characters, and capitalize the first letter in each word. A good query describes the view of data that it presents. One good choice for the example shown in Figure 6-6 is FirstQuarterOrders_2007.

> **NOTE**
>
> Remember, when you save a query, you aren't saving the query *results*—you're just saving the query *design*, with all its settings. That way, you can run the query any time to get the live results that match your criteria.

Once you've created a query, you'll see it in your database's navigation pane (Figure 6-7). If you're using the standard All Tables view, then the query appears under the table that it uses. If a query uses more than one table, then the same query appears in more than one group in the navigation pane.

You can launch the query at any time by double-clicking it. Suppose you've created a query named TopProducts that grabs all the expensive products in the Products table (using the filter criteria >50 on the Price field). Every time you need to review, print, or edit information about expensive products, you run the TopProducts query. To fine-tune the query settings, right-click it in the navigation pane, and then choose Design View.

Access lets you open your table and any queries that use it at the same time. (They all appear in separate tabs.) However, you can't modify the design of your table until you close all the queries that use it.

If you add new records to a table while a query's open, then the new records don't automatically appear in the query. Instead, you'll need to run your query again. The

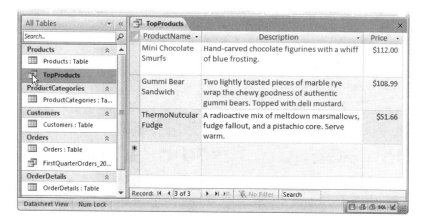

Figure 6-7. By default, the navigation pane organizes your queries so they appear right underneath the table they use. For example, the TopProducts query (shown here) appears under the Products table.

quickest way is to choose Home → Records → Refresh → Refresh All. You can also close your query and open it again, because Access runs your query every time you open it in Datasheet view.

— **NOTE** —

Remember, a query's a *view* of some of the data in your table. When you edit your query results, Access changes the data in the underlying table. On the other hand, it's perfectly safe to rename, modify, and delete queries—after all, they're there to make your life simpler.

Building filter expressions

The secret to a good query's getting the information you want, and nothing more. To tell Access what records it should get (and which ones it should ignore), you need a *filter expression*.

The filter expression defines the records you're interested in. If you want to find all the orders that were placed by a customer with the ID 1032, you could use this filter expression:

```
=1032
```

To put this filter expression into action, you need to put it in the Criteria box under the CustomerID field.

Technically, you could just write *1032* instead of *=1032*, but it's better to stick to the second form, because that's the pattern you'll use for more advanced filter expressions. It starts with the *operator* (in this case, the equals sign) that defines how Access should compare the information, followed by the *value* (in this case, 1032) you want to use to make the comparison.

WORD TO THE WISE

Don't Get Confused by Lookups

As you know, lookups change the way values appear on the datasheet. If you add a lookup on the CustomerID field in the Orders table, then you don't see a cryptic number like 1032. Instead, you see some descriptive information, like the name *Hancock, John*.

However, when you write your filter expression, you need to remember what information's actually stored in the field. So the CustomerID filter expression *=1032* works fine, but *=Hancock, John* doesn't, because the name information's actually stored separately. (It's in the Customers table, not the Orders table.)

Sometimes, you really *do* want to create a filter expression that uses linked information. You may want to find records in the Orders table using a customer name instead of a customer ID, because you don't have the ID value handy. In this situation, you have two choices:

* You can look up the ID value you need in the Customers table before you start. Then, you can use that value when you build your query for the Orders table.

* You can use a *join query* to get the name information from the Customers table, and display it alongside the rest of your order details. You'll learn how to perform this trick on page 229.

If you're matching text, then you need to include quotation marks around your value. Otherwise, Access wonders where the text starts and stops:

```
="Harrington Red"
```

Instead of using an exact match, you can use a range. Add this filter expression to the OrderTotal field to find all the orders worth between $10 and $50:

```
<50 And >10
```

This condition's actually two conditions (less than 50 and greater than 10), which are yoked together by the powerful *And* keyword (page 155). Alternatively, you can use the *Or* keyword if you want to see results that meet any one of the conditions you've included (page 155).

Date expressions are particularly useful. Just remember to bracket any hardcoded dates with the # character (page 151). If you add this filter condition to the DatePlaced field, then it finds all the orders that were placed in 2007:

```
<#1/1/2008# And >#12/31/2006#
```

This expression works by requiring that dates are earlier than January 1, 2008, but later than December 31, 2006.

— **TIP** _____

> With a little more work, you could craft a filter expression that gets the orders from the first three months of the *current* year, no matter what year it is. This trick requires the use of the functions Access provides for dates. See page 134 for more details.

_____

UP TO SPEED

Filter Syntax

If filters seem uncannily familiar, there's a reason. Filters have exactly the same syntax as the validation rules you used to protect a table from bad data (page 147). The only difference is the way Access interprets the condition. A validation rule like *<50 And >10* tells Access a value shouldn't be allowed unless it falls in the desired range (10 to 50). But if you pop the same rule into a filter condition, it tells Access you aren't interested in seeing the record unless it fits the range. Thanks to this similarity, you can use all the validation rules you saw on pages 150 to 157 as filter conditions.

Getting the top records

When you run an ordinary query, you see *all* the results that match your filter conditions. If that's more than you bargained for, you can use filter expressions to cut down the list.

However, in some cases, filters are a bit more work than they should be. Imagine a situation where you want to see the top 10 most expensive products. Using a filter condition, you can easily get the products that have prices above a certain threshold. Using sorting, you can arrange the results so the most expensive items turn up at the top. However, you can't as easily tell Access to get just 10 records and then stop.

In this situation, the query Design view has a shortcut that can help you out. Here's how it works:

1. **Open your query in Design view (or create a new query and add the fields you want to use).**

   This example uses the Products table, and includes the ProductName and Price fields.

2. **Sort your table so that the records you're most interested in are at the top.**

   If you want to find the most expensive products, then add a descending sort (page 112) on the Price field.

3. **In the Query Tools | Design → Query Setup → Return box, choose a different option (Figure 6-8).**

   The standard option's All, which gets all the matching records. However, you can choose 5, 25, or 100 to get the top 5, 25, or 100 matching records, respectively. Or, you can use a percentage value like 25 percent to get the top quarter of matching records.

   > **NOTE**
   >
   > For the Query Tools | Design → Query Setup → Return box to work, you must choose the right sort order. To understand why, you need to know a little more about how this feature works. If you tell Access to get just five records, it actually performs the normal query, gets all the records, and arranges them according to your sort order. It then throws everything away except for the first five records in the list. If you've sorted your list so that the most expensive products are first (as in this example), you're left with the top five budget-busting products in your results.

4. **Run your query to see the results (Figure 6-9).**

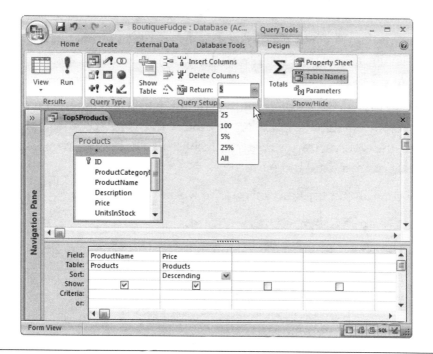

Figure 6-8. If you don't see the number you want in the list, just type it into the Return box on your own. There's no reason you can't grab the top 27 most expensive products.

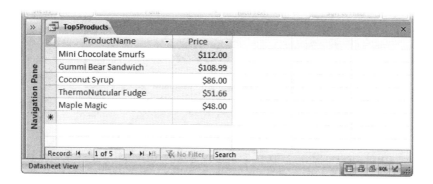

Figure 6-9. Here are the top five most expensive products.

Creating a Simple Query with the Query Wizard

Design view's usually the best place to start constructing queries, but it's not the only option. You can use the Query wizard to give you an initial boost, and then refine your query in Design view.

The Query wizard works by asking you a series of questions, and then creating the query that fits the bill. Unlike many of the other wizards in Access and other Office applications, the Query wizard's relatively feeble. It's a good starting point for query newbies, but not an end-to-end performer.

Here's how you can put the Query wizard to work:

1. **Choose Create → Other → Query Wizard.**

   Access gives you a choice of several different wizards (Figure 6-10).

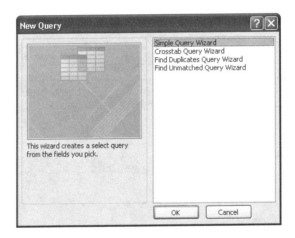

Figure 6-10. In the first step of the Query wizard, you choose from a small set of basic query types.

2. **Choose a query type. The Simple Query wizard's the best starting point for now.**

   The Query wizard includes a few common kinds of queries. With the exception of the crosstab query, there's nothing really unique about any of these choices. You'll learn to create them all using Design view:

- **Simple Query Wizard** gets you started with an ordinary query, which displays a subset of data from a table. This query's the kind you created in the previous section.

- **Crosstab Query Wizard** generates a crosstab query, which lets you summarize large amounts of data using different calculations. You can find more on this advanced topic in *Access 2007: The Missing Manual*.

- **Find Duplicates Query Wizard** is similar to the Simple Query wizard, except it adds a filter expression that shows only records that share duplicated values. If you forgot to set a primary key or create a unique index for your table (page 135), then this can help you clean up the mess.

- **Find Unmatched Query Wizard** is similar to the Simple Query wizard, except it adds a filter expression that finds unlinked records in related tables. You could use this to find an order that isn't associated with any particular customer. You'll learn how this works on page 237.

3. **Click OK.**

   The first step of the Query wizard appears.

4. **In the Tables/Queries box, choose the table that has the data you want. Then, add the fields you want to see in the query results, as shown in Figure 6-11.**

   For the best control, add the fields one at a time. Add them in the order you want them to appear in the query results, from left to right.

   You can add fields from more than one table. To do so, start by choosing one of the tables, add the fields you want, and then choose the second table and repeat the process. This process really makes sense only if the tables are related. You'll learn more on page 229.

5. **Click Next.**

   If your query includes a numeric field, the Query wizard gives you the choice of creating a summary query that arranges rows into groups, and calculates information like totals and averages. If you get this choice, pick Detail and then click Next.

   The final step of the Query wizard appears (Figure 6-12).

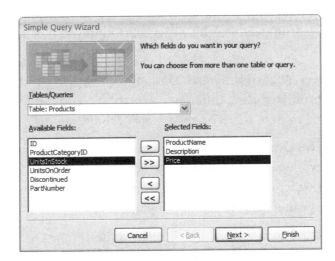

Figure 6-11. To add a field, select it in the Available Fields list, and then click the > arrow button (or just double-click it). You can add all fields at once by clicking the >> arrow button, and you can remove fields by selecting them in the Selected Fields list and then clicking <. In this example, three fields are included in the query.

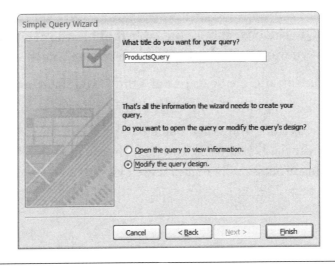

Figure 6-12. In the last step, you choose the name for your query, and decide whether you want to see the results right away or refine it further in Design view.

6. Supply a query name in the "What title do you want for your query?" box.

7. **If you want to fine-tune your query, then choose "Modify the query design". If you're happy with what you've got, then choose "Open the query to view information" to run the query.**

   One reason you may want to open your query in Design view is to add filter conditions (page 115) to pick out specific rows. Unfortunately, you can't set filter conditions in the Query wizard.

8. **Click Finish.**

   Your query opens in Design view or Datasheet view, depending on the choice you made in step 7. You can run it by choosing Query Tools | Design → Results → Run.

Queries and Related Tables

In Chapter 5, you learned how to split data down into fundamental pieces and store it in distinct, well-organized tables. This sort of design's only problem's that it's more difficult to get the full picture when you have related data stored in separate places. Fortunately, Access has the perfect solution—you can bring the tables back together for display using a *join*.

A join's a query operation that pulls columns from two tables and fuses them together in one grid of results. You use joins to amplify child tables by adding information from the parent table. Here are some examples:

▶ In the bobblehead database, you can show a list of bobblehead dolls (drawn from the child table Dolls) along with the manufacturer information for each doll (from the parent table Manufacturers).

▶ In the Cacophoné music school database, you can get a list of available classes, with instructor information.

▶ In the Boutique Fudge database, you can get a list of orders, complete with the details for the customer who placed the order.

You've already learned how to create lookup tables to show just a bit of information from a linked table. A lookup can show the name of a product category in place of the ID number in the ProductID field. However, a join query's far more powerful. It can grab oodles of information from the linked table—far more than you could fit in a single field.

Figure 6-13 shows how a table join works.

ClassName	StartingDate	EndingDate
Electro-Acoustic Gamelan	1/1/2008	6/3/2008
Disharmony	1/3/2008	6/5/2008
Funk 101	1/1/2008	6/3/2008
Classic Djembe	1/1/2008	6/3/2008
Funk 201	1/4/2008	9/12/2008
Trombone Soul	1/4/2008	9/12/2008
Funk 301	1/4/2008	9/12/2008

Classes (table)

ID	FirstName	LastName
1	Sander	Klaus
2	Faria	MacDonald
3	Donald	Liu

Teachers (table)

Join query

ClassName	StartingDate	EndingDate	FirstName	LastName
Electro-Acoustic Gamelan	1/1/2008	6/3/2008	Sander	Klaus
Disharmony	1/3/2008	6/5/2008	Sander	Klaus
Funk 101	1/1/2008	6/3/2008	Donald	Liu
Classic Djembe	1/1/2008	6/3/2008	Faria	MacDonald
Funk 201	1/4/2008	9/12/2008	Donald	Liu
Trombone Soul	1/4/2008	9/12/2008	Donald	Liu
Funk 301	1/4/2008	9/12/2008	Donald	Liu

ClassesWithTeachersInfo (query)

Figure 6-13. On its own, the Classes table tells you about each class, but it gives you only the ID of the assigned instructor. But join this table to the Teachers table, and you can get any other details from the linked teacher record—including the first and last name. You'll see how to build this example on page 241.

Joining Tables in a Query

Access makes it remarkably easy to join two tables. The first step's adding both tables to your query, using the Show Table dialog box. If you're creating a new query in Design view, then the Show Table dialog appears right away. If you're working with a query you've already created, then make sure you're in Design view, right-click the window, and then choose Show Table.

If you've already defined a relationship between the two tables (using the relation-ships window, as described on page 173), then Access uses that relationship to auto-matically create a query join. You'll see a line on the diagram that connects the appropriate fields, as shown in Figure 6-14.

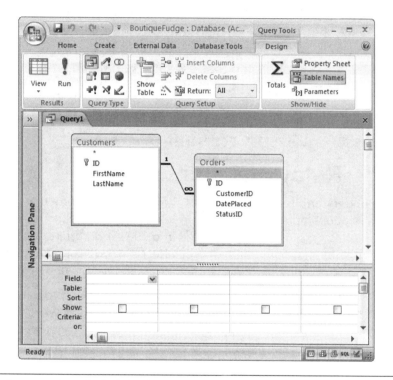

Figure 6-14. Access automatically joins the CustomerID field in the Orders table to the ID field in the Customers table, based on the relationship that's defined in the database.

If you *haven't* already defined a relationship between the two related tables, then you probably should, before you create your query (see Chapter 5 for full instructions). But if for some cryptic reason you've decided not to create the relationship (perhaps the database design was set in stone by another, less savvy Access designer), then you can manually define the join in the query window. To do so, just drag the linked field in one table to the matching field in the other table. You can also remove a join by right-clicking the line between the tables, and then choosing Delete.

> If you add two unrelated tables, then Access tries to help you out by guessing a relationship. If it spots a field with the same data type and the same name in both tables, then it adds a join on this field. This action often isn't what you want—for example, many tables share a common ID field. Also, if you're following the database design rules from page 92, then your linked fields have slightly different names in each table, like ID and CustomerID. If you run into a problem where Access assumes a relationship that doesn't exist, then just remove it before adding the join you really want.

UP TO SPEED

Relationships vs. Joins

It's important to understand the differences between a relationship and a query join.

* **Relationship.** A permanent link between two tables, which is stored in your database. When creating a relationship in the database, you have the option of switching on referential integrity: a set of rules that prevents inconsistent data in related tables (page 180).

* **Join.** A query feature that lets you combine related data from two tables into one set of results. The join doesn't affect how you enter or edit that information in the underlying tables.

If you have a relationship in place, then Access assumes you'll want to use a join to link those tables together in a query, which only makes sense.

Once you have your two tables in the query design window and you've defined the join, then you're ready to choose the fields you want. You can pick fields from both tables. You can also add filter conditions and supply a sort order, as you would with any other query. Figure 6-15 shows an example of a query that uses a join, and Figure 6-16 shows that same query in action.

When you have two linked tables, it's easy to forget what you're show-ing. If you join the Orders and Customers tables, and then select fields from each, then what do you you end up with: a list of classes or a list of instructors? Easy, you get a list of orders, complete with customer information. Queries with linked tables always act on the *child* table and bring in additional information from the parent.

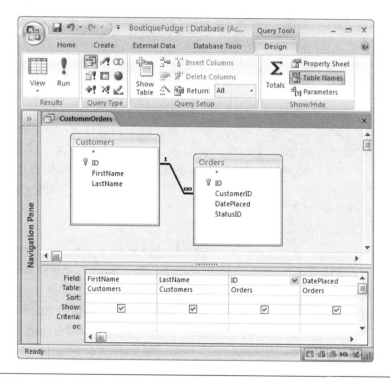

Figure 6-15. This query shows information from the Orders and Customers tables. It doesn't matter whether the first field's from the Orders or Customers table—either way, you're creating a list of orders with added customer information. Notice how the Table box (under the Field box) shows which table each field comes from.

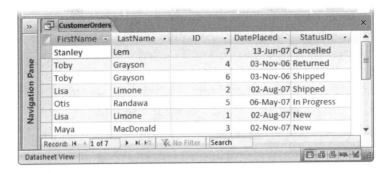

Figure 6-16. You can easily see at a glance who ordered what. The ID column's the order ID (although you could display the IDs from both the Customers and Orders tables).

___ NOTE _____

When you perform a join, you see repeated information. If you join the Customers and Orders tables, you see the first and last name of a shopaholic customer appear next to several orders. However, this doesn't violate the database rule against duplicate data. Even though the customer details *appear* in more than one place in the query results, they're *stored* only once in the Customers table.

Remember, when you link a parent and child table with a join query, you're really performing a query that gets all the records from the child table, and then adds extra information from the parent table. For example, you can use a join query to get a list of orders (from the child table) and supplement each record with information about the customer that made the order. No matter how you create the join, you won't ever get a list of customers with order information tacked on—that wouldn't make sense, because every customer can make multiple orders.

Joins are one of the most useful features in any query writer's toolkit. They let you display one table that has all the information you need.

___ WARNING _____

When using more than one table, there's always a risk that two tables have a field with the same name. This possibility isn't a problem if you don't plan to show these fields in your query, but it can cause confusion if you do.

Modifying Information Using a Join Query

You need to be careful when modifying the data in a query that uses a join. There's never a problem if you want to modify the details from the child table. In the example in Figure 6-16, it's easy enough to change the DatePlaced or StatusID fields to change the order record.

However, consider what happens if you change one of the values in the *parent* table, like the customer's first or last name. Obviously, the same customer information may appear several times in the query. (For example, the query in Figure 6-16 shows two orders by a customer named Toby.) If you modify the customer name in one place, then Access automatically changes the information in the Customers table, and then refreshes the entire query. So, if you

change "Toby" to "Tony" in Figure 6-16, then Access refreshes the second and third rows of the datasheet.

A potential problem occurs if you want to change the *link* between the order record and the customer record. You may want to edit an order that's assigned to Toby so that the database says Lisa made the order. However, you *can't* make this change by editing the FirstName and LastName fields in the query. (If you do, you'll simply wind up changing Toby's record in the Customers table.) Instead, you need to change the CustomerID field in the Orders table so that it points to the right person. In the query shown in Figure 6-16, the CustomerID field isn't included, so there's no way to change the link.

Outer Joins

The queries you saw in the previous example use what database nerds call an *inner join*. Inner joins show only linked records—in other words, records that appear in both tables. If you perform a query on the Customers and Orders tables, then you don't see customers that haven't placed an order. You also don't see orders that aren't linked to any particular customer (the CustomerID value's blank) or aren't linked to a valid record (they contain a CustomerID value that doesn't match up to any record in the Customers table).

Outer joins are more accommodating—these joins include all the same results you'd see in an inner join, *plus* the leftover unlinked records from one of the two tables (it's your choice). Obviously, these unlinked records show up in the query results with some blank values, which correspond to the missing information that the other table would supply.

Suppose you perform an outer join between the Orders and Customers tables, and then configure it so that all the order records are shown. Any orders that aren't linked to a customer record appear at the bottom of the list, and have blank values in all the customer-related fields (like FirstName and LastName):

FirstName	LastName	ID	DatePlaced	StatusID
Stanley	Lem	7	13-Jun-07	Cancelled
Toby	Grayson	4	03-Nov-06	Returned
Toby	Grayson	6	03-Nov-06	Shipped
		18	01-Jan-08	In Progress
		19	01-Jan-08	In Progress

In this particular example, it doesn't make sense for orders that aren't linked to a customer to exist. (In fact, it probably indicates an order that was entered incorrectly.) However, if you suspect a problem, an outer join can help you track down the problem.

--- TIP
> You can prevent orphaned order records altogether by making CustomerID a required value (page 131) and enforcing referential integrity (page 180).

You can also perform an outer join between the Orders and Customers tables that shows all the *customer* records. In this case, at the end of the query results, you'll see every unlinked customer record, with the corresponding order fields left blank:

FirstName	LastName	ID	DatePlaced	StatusID
Stanley	Lem	7	13-Jun-07	Cancelled
Toby	Grayson	4	03-Nov-06	Returned
Toby	Grayson	6	03-Nov-06	Shipped

FirstName	LastName	ID	DatePlaced	StatusID
Ben	Samatara			
Goosey	Mason			
Tabasoum	Khan			

In this case, the outer join query picks up three stragglers.

So how do you add an outer join to your query? Your start with an inner join (which Access usually adds automatically; see page 230), and then *convert* it to an outer join. To do so, just right-click the join line that links the two tables in the design window, and then choose Join Properties (or just double-click the line). The Join Properties dialog box (Figure 6-17) appears, and lets you change the type of join you're using.

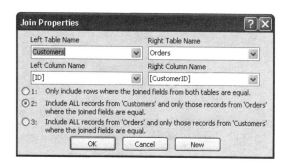

Figure 6-17. The first option, "Only include rows where the joined fields from both tables are equal", performs the standard inner join. The other two options let you create an outer join that incorporates all the unlinked rows from one of the two tables.

Finding unmatched records

Inner joins are by far the most common joins. However, outer joins let you create at least one valuable type of query: a query that can track down unmatched records.

You've already seen how an outer join lets you see a list of all your orders, *plus* the customers that haven't made any orders. That combination isn't terribly useful. However, the marketing department's already salivating over the second part of this equation—the list of people who haven't bought anything. This information could help them target a first-time-buyer promotion.

To craft this query, you start with the outer-join query that includes all the customer records. Then, you simply add one more ingredient: a filter condition that matches records that don't have an order ID. Technically, these are considered *null* (empty) values.

Here's the filter condition you need, which you must place in the Criteria box for the ID field of the Orders table:

```
Is Null
```

Now, when Access performs the query, it includes only the customer records that aren't linked to anything in the orders table. Figure 6-18 shows the query in Design view.

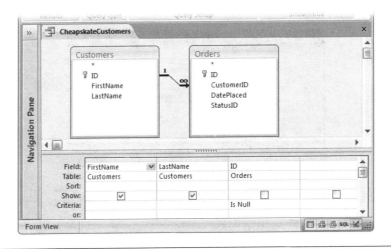

Figure 6-18. This query combines an outer join with a filter condition that matches only unlinked customer records. Notice the Show checkbox isn't checked. That's because the ID field's used for a filter condition, but there's no point in displaying it in the results datasheet.

Multiple Joins

Just as you're getting comfortable with inner and outer joins, Access has another feature to throw your way. Many queries don't stop at a single join. Instead, they use three, four, or more to bring multiple related tables into the mix.

Although this sounds complicated at first, it really isn't. Multiple joins are simply ways of bringing more related information into your query. Each join works the same in a multiple-join situation as it does when you use it on its own. To use multiple joins, just add all the tables you want from the Show Table dialog box, make sure the join lines appear, and then choose the fields you want. Access is almost always intelligent enough to figure out what you're trying to do.

Figure 6-19 shows an example where a child table has two parents that can both contribute some extra information.

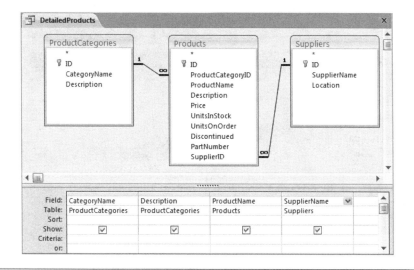

Figure 6-19. In this example, a list of products is amplified with product category information and supplier information. The Products table's a child of both the ProductCategories and Suppliers tables, so this query uses both tables effortlessly.

Sometimes, the information you want's more than one table away. Consider the OrderDetails table Boutique Fudge uses to list each item in a customer's order. On its own, the OrderDetails doesn't provide a link to the customer who ordered the item, but it does provide a link to the related order record. (See page 206 for a discussion of this design.) If you want to get the information about who ordered each item, you need to add the OrderDetails, Orders, and Customers table to your query, as shown in Figure 6-20.

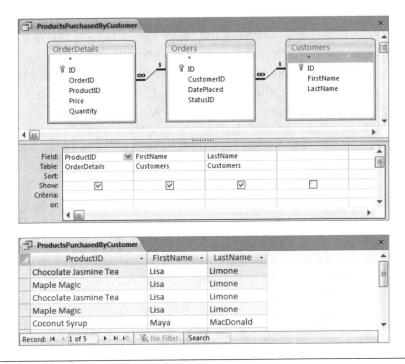

Figure 6-20. If you want to find out who ordered each item, then you need to find the linked Orders table, and then continue to the linked Customers table. Even if you don't want to show any data from the Orders table, you still need to follow this two-step process. The top figure shows the query that does this, and the bottom figure shows the result you'll get when you run the query.

Multiple joins are also the ticket if you have a many-to-many relationship with a junction table (page 195), like the one between teachers and classes. As you'll remember from Chapter 5 (page 198), the Cacophoné Studios music school uses an intermediary table to track teacher class assignment. If you want to get a list of classes, complete with instructor names, then you need to create a query with three tables: Classes, Teachers, and Teachers_Classes (see Figure 6-21).

Query Power: Calculated Fields and Text Expressions

Every Access expert stocks his or her database with a few (or a few dozen) useful queries that simplify day-to-day tasks. Earlier in this chapter, you learned how to create queries that chew through avalanches of information and present exactly

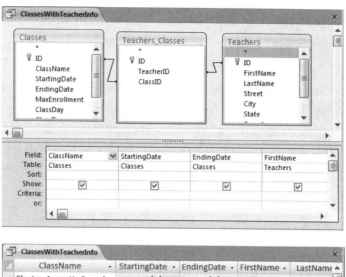

Figure 6-21. Here's how you define a list of classes that includes the name of the assigned teacher next to each class. The top query shows the design you need, and the bottom figure shows the result.

what you need to see. But as Access masters know, there's much more power lurking just beneath the surface of the query design window.

In this section, you'll delve into some query magic that's sure to impress your boss, co-workers, and romantic partners. You'll learn how to carry out calculations in a query and perform some basic text manipulation (joining together first and last names, for example).

Calculated Fields

When you started designing tables, you learned that it's a database crime to add information that's based on the data in another field or another table. An example of this mistake is creating a Products table that has both a Price and a PriceWithTax field. The fact that the PriceWithTax field is calculated based on the Price field is a problem. Storing both is a redundant waste of space. Even worse, if the tax rate changes, then you're left with a lot of records to update and the potential for inconsistent information (like a with-tax price that's lower than a no-tax price).

Even though you know not to create fields like PriceWithTax, sometimes you *will* want to see calculated information in Access. Before Boutique Fudge prints a product list for one of its least-loved retailers, it likes to apply a 10 percent price markup. To do this, it needs a way to adjust the price information before printing the data. If the retailer spots the lower price without the markup, they're sure to demand it.

Queries provide the perfect solution for these kinds of problems, because they include an all-purpose way to mathematically manipulate information. The trick's to add a *calculated field*: a field that's defined in your query, but doesn't actually exist in the table. Instead, Access calculates the value of a calculated field based on one or more other fields in your table. The values in the calculated field are never stored anywhere—instead, Access generates them each time you run the query.

Defining a Calculated Field

To create a calculated field, you need to supply two details: a name for the field, and an *expression* that tells Access what calculation it must perform. Calculated fields are defined using this two-part form:

```
CalculatedFieldName: Expression
```

For example, here's how you can define the PriceWithTax calculated field:

```
PriceWithTax: [Price] * 1.10
```

Essentially, this expression tells Access to take the value from the Price field, and then multiply it by 1.10 (which is equivalent to raising the price by 10 percent). Access repeats this calculation for each record in the query results. For this expression to work, the Price field *must* exist in the table. However, you don't need to show the Price field separately in the query results.

You can also refer to the Price field using its *full name*, which is made up of the table name, followed by a period, followed by the field name, as shown here:

```
PriceWithTax: [Products].[Price] * 1.10
```

This syntax is sometimes necessary if your query involves more than one table (using a query join, as described on page 229), and the same field appears in both tables. In this situation, you must use the full name to avoid ambiguity. (If you don't, Access gives you an error message when you try to run the query.)

To add the PriceWithTax calculated field to a query, you need to use Design view. First, find the column where you want to insert your field. (Usually, you'll just tack it onto the end in the first blank column, although you can drag the other fields around to make space.) Next, type the full definition for the field into the Field box (see Figure 6-22).

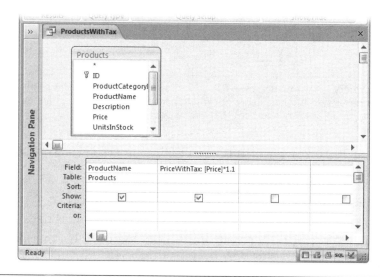

Figure 6-22. This query shows two fields straight from the database (ID and Name), and adds the calculated PriceWithTax field. The ordinary Price field, which Access uses to calculate PriceWithTax, isn't shown at all.

Now you're ready to run the query. When you do, the calculated information appears alongside your other columns (Figure 6-23).

Calculated fields do have one limitation—since the information isn't stored in your table, you can't edit it. If you want to make a price change, you'll need to edit the underlying Price field—trying to change PriceWithTax would leave Access thoroughly confused.

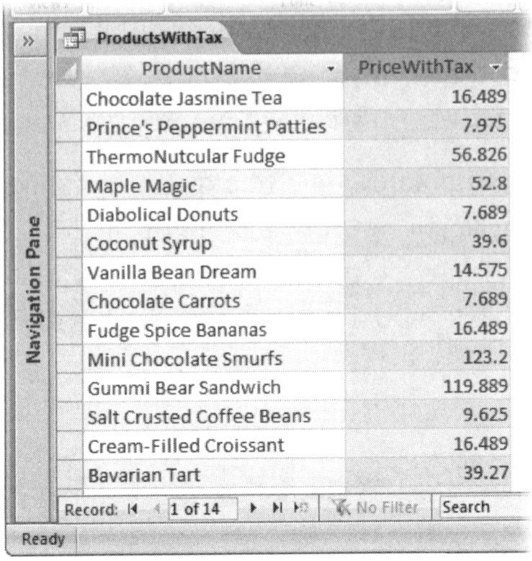

Figure 6-23. The query results now show a PriceWithTax field, with the result of the 10 percent markup. The neat part's that this calculated information's now available instantaneously, even though it isn't stored in the database. Try and beat that with a pocket calculator.

Before going any further, it's worth reviewing the rules of calculated fields. Here are some pointers:

▶ **Always choose a unique name.** An expression like *Price: [Price] * 1.10* creates a *circular reference*, because the name of the field you're using is the same as the name of the field you're trying to create. Access doesn't allow this sleight of hand.

▶ **Build expressions out of fields, numbers, and math operations.** The most common calculated fields take one or more existing fields or hard-coded numbers and combine them using familiar math symbols like addition (+), subtraction (-), multiplication (*), or division (/).

▶ **Expect to see square brackets.** The expression *PriceWithTax: [Price] * 1.10* is equivalent to *PriceWithTax: Price * 1.10* (the only difference is the square brackets around the field name Price). Technically, you need the brackets only if your field name contains spaces or special characters. However, when you type in expressions that don't use brackets in the query Design view, then Access automatically adds them, just to be on the safe side.

Query Synchronization

Here's an interesting trick to try. Run the ProductsWithTax query and leave it open, displaying its results. Now, open the Products table that has the actual data, and then change the price of any product. Switch back to the Prod-uctsWithTax query. Has the PriceWith-Tax value changed?

If you can't stand the suspense, fear not—the PriceWithTax is automatically refreshed to reflect the new price. Access automatically keeps query views synchronized with the live data in your table. When you change a record, Access notices—and it instantly refreshes the query window.

It's worth noting a few exceptions to this rule:

* Access doesn't notice if you insert a new record after you launch a query—to get that to appear in your query results, you need to refresh the results.

* If you change a record so it no longer appears in your query, it doesn't automatically disappear from view. If you have a query showing all products over $100, and you cut the price of one down to $50, then it still appears in your query result list (with the new price) until you refresh the results.

* Similarly, if you change a record that currently appears in your query so it no longer fits one of your filter criteria, it doesn't disappear from view until you rerun the query.

To get the latest results, you can refresh individual records or the entire query. To refresh a single record, choose Home → Records → Refresh → Refresh Record. To rerun the query and refresh everything, choose Home → Records → Refresh → Refresh All. This action also shows any new records and hides any that have been changed so that they no longer satisfy your filter conditions.

Simple Math with Numeric Fields

Many calculated fields rely entirely on ordinary high school math. Table 6-1 gives a quick overview of your basic options for combining numbers.

Table 6-1. Arithmetic Operators

Operator	Name	Example	Result
+	Addition	1+1	2
-	Subtraction	1-1	0
*	Multiplication	2*2	4
^	Exponentiation	2^3	8
/	Division	5/2	2.5
\	Integer division (returns the lowest whole number and discards the remainder)	5\2	2
Mod	Modulus (returns the remainder left after division)	5 Mod 2	1

You're free to use as many fields and operators as you need to create your expression. Consider a Products table with a QuantityInStock field that records the number of units in your warehouse. To determine the value you have on hand for a given product, you can write this expression that uses two fields:

```
ValueInStock: [UnitsInStock] * [Price]
```

— **WARNING** —————————————————————————————

When performing a mathematical operation with a field, you'll run into trouble if the field contains a blank value.

Date fields

You can also use the addition and subtraction operators with date fields. (You can use multiplication, division, and everything else, but it doesn't have any realistic meaning.)

Using addition, you can add an ordinary number to a date field. This number moves the date forward by that many days. Here's an example that adds two weeks of headroom to a company deadline:

```
ExtendedDeadline: [DueDate] + 14
```

If you use this calculation with the date January 10, 2007, the new date becomes January 24, 2007.

Using subtraction, you can find the number of days between any two dates. Here's how you calculate how long it was between the time an order was placed and when it was shipped:

```
ShippingLag: [ShipDate] - [OrderDate]
```

If the ship date occurred 12 days after the order date, you'd see a value of 12.

NOTE

Date fields can include time information. In calculations, the time information's represented as the fractional part of the value. If you subtract two dates and wind up with the number 12.25, that represents 12 days and six hours (because six hours is 25 percent of a full day).

Remember, if you want to include *literal* dates in your queries (specific dates you supply), you need to bracket them with the # character and use Month/Day/Year format. Here's an example that uses that approach to count the number of days between the date students were expected to submit an assignment (March 20, 2007) and the date they actually did:

```
LateDays: [DateSubmitted] - #03/20/07#
```

A positive value indicates that the value in DateSubmitted is larger (more recent) than the deadline date—in other words, the student was late. A value of 4 indicates a student that's four days off the mark, while –4 indicates a student that handed the work in four days ahead of schedule.

Order of operations

If you have a long string of calculations, Access follows the standard rules for *order of operations*: mathematician-speak for deciding which calculation to perform first when there's more than one calculation in an expression. So if you have a lengthy expression, Access doesn't just carry on from left to right. Instead, it evaluates the expression piece by piece in this order:

1. **Parentheses (Access always performs any calculations within parentheses first)**

2. **Percent**

3. **Exponents**

4. **Division and multiplication**

5. **Addition and subtraction**

Suppose you want to take the QuantityInStock and the QuantityOnOrder fields into consideration to determine the value of all the product you have available and on the way. If you're not aware of the order of operation rules, then you might try this expression:

```
TotalValue: [UnitsInStock] + [UnitsOnOrder] * [Price]
```

The problem here is that Access multiplies QuantityOnOrder and Price together, and *then* adds it to the QuantityInStock. To correct this oversight, you need parentheses like so:

```
TotalValue: ([UnitsInStock] + [UnitsOnOrder]) * [Price]
```

Now the QuantityInStock and QuantityOnOrder fields are totaled together, and then multiplied with the Price to get a grand total.

> **TIP**
>
> Need some more space to write a really long expression? You can widen any column in the query designer to see more at once, but you'll still have trouble with complex calculations. Better to click in the Field box, and then press Shift+F2. This action pops open a dialog box named Zoom, which shows the full content in a large text box, wrapped over as many lines as necessary. When you've finished reviewing or editing your expression, click OK to close the Zoom box and keep any changes you've made, or Cancel to discard them.

Expressions with Text

Although calculated fields usually deal with numeric information, they don't always. You have genuinely useful ways to manipulate text as well.

If you have text information, then you obviously can't use addition, subtraction, and other mathematical operations. However, you can join text together. You can, for instance, link several fields of address information together and show them all in one field, conserving space (and possibly making it easier to export the information to another program).

To join text, you use the ampersand (&) operator. For example, here's how to create a FullName field that draws information from the FirstName and LastName fields:

```
FullName: [FirstName] & [LastName]
```

This expression looks reasonable enough, but it's actually got a flaw. Since you haven't added any spaces, the first and last name end up crammed together, like this: *BenJenks*. A better approach is to join together *three* pieces of text: the first name, a space, and the last name. Here's the revised expression:

```
FullName: [FirstName] & " " & [LastName]
```

This produces values like *Ben Jenks*. You can also swap the order and add a comma, if you prefer to have the last name first (like *Jenks, Ben*) for better sorting:

```
FullName: [LastName] & ", " & [FirstName]
```

___ **NOTE** _____

Access has two types of text values: those you draw from other fields, and those you enter directly (or *hard-code*). When you hard-code a piece of text (such as the comma and space in the previous example), you need to wrap it in quotation marks so Access knows where it starts and stops.

_____

You can even use the ampersand to tack text alongside numeric values. If you want the slightly useless text "The price is" to appear before each price value, use this calculated field:

```
Price: "The price is: " & [Price]
```

QUERIES THAT UPDATE RECORDS

- ▶ Understanding Action Queries
- ▶ Update Queries
- ▶ Append Queries
- ▶ Delete Queries

QUERIES ARE MOST FAMOUSLY KNOWN for their ability to show small subsets of huge amounts of information. This type of query's called a *select query*, and it's the variety you learned about in Chapter 6.

Many Access fans don't realize that queries have another identity. Not only can you use them to search for information, but you can also use them to *change* data. Queries that take this more drastic step—whether it's deleting, updating, or adding records—are known collectively as *action queries*.

Understanding Action Queries

Action queries aren't quite as useful as select queries, because they tend to be less flexible. You create an ideal query once, and reuse it over and over. Select queries fit the bill, because you'll often want to review the same sort of information (last week's orders, top-selling products, class sizes, and so on). But action queries are trickier, because they make *permanent* changes.

In most cases, a change is a one-time-only affair, so you don't have any reason to hang onto an action query that just applies the same change all over again. And even if you do need to modify some details regularly (like product prices or warehouse stocking levels), the actual values you set aren't the same each time. As a result, you can't create an action query that can apply your change in an automated fashion.

But before you skip this chapter for greener pastures, it's important to consider some cases where action queries are surprisingly handy. Action queries shine if you have:

▶ **Batch tasks that you want to repeatedly apply.** Some tasks *can* be repeated exactly. You may need to copy a large number of records from one table to another, delete a batch of old information, or update a status field across a group of records. If you need to perform this kind of task over and over again, action queries are a perfect timesaver.

▶ **Complex or tedious tasks that affect a large number of records.** Every once in a while, a table needs a minor realignment. You may decide that it's time to increase selling prices by 15 percent, or you may discover that all orders linked to customer 403 really should point to customer 404. These are one-off tasks, but they affect a large number of records. To polish them off, you need to spend some serious time in the datasheet—or you can craft a new action query that makes the change more efficiently. When you're done, you decide whether you delete the action query, or save it in case you want to modify and reuse your work later on.

Testing Action Queries (Carefully)

In the wrong hands, action queries are nothing but a high-tech way to shoot yourself in the foot. They commit changes (usually to multiple records), and once you've applied the changes, you can't reverse them. Some database fans avoid action queries completely.

If you do decide to use action queries (and there are plenty of handy tricks you can accomplish with them), then you need to take the right precautions. Most importantly, before you use an action query, make a database backup! This step's especially crucial when you're creating a new action query, because it may not always generate the result you expect. To make a backup, you can copy your .accdb database file (just like you would any other file; one way is to right-click it, and then select Copy). If you don't want to mess with Windows Explorer, then you can create a backup without leaving Access by selecting the Office button → Manage → Back Up Database (page 44).

TIP

It's always easier to make a backup than to clean up the wake of changes left by a rampaging action query.

Backups are great for disaster recovery, but it's still a good idea to avoid making a mistake in the first place. One safe approach is to start by creating a select query. You can then make sure your query's selecting the correct records before taking the next step and converting it into an action query (by choosing one of the action query types in the Query Tools | Design → Query Type section of the ribbon).

The Action Query Family

Access has four types of action queries:

▶ **An update query** changes the values in one or more records.

▶ **An append query** selects one or more records, and then adds them to an existing table.

- ▶ **A make-table query** selects one or more records, and then creates a new table for them.

- ▶ **A delete query** deletes one or more records.

In the following sections, you'll try out all of these queries.

Update Queries

An update query searches for some records, and then modifies them. Usually, you'll limit your modifications to a single field, but Access lets you change as many fields as you want. You also have a fair bit of flexibility in *how* you apply the update. The simplest option's to stuff an entirely new value into a field. You could create a query that moves all the products in one category into another by entering a new value in the CategoryID field. Alternatively, you could take the current values in a field and change them, using an expression (a specialized database formula that can perform a variety of different calculations). You could increase all your product prices by 10 percent, or add a week to the due date of every outstanding project.

TIP

If you have a relatively straightforward, one-time-only update to make, you may prefer to use the datasheet's find-and-replace feature (page 120). This approach gives you the chance to review the matches and choose whether or not to apply the change for each value.

The example that follows uses the Products and ProductsCategories tables from the Boutique Fudge database (which is described on page 204). The query updates all the products in the Beverages category, increasing their prices by 10 percent. You can try this example for yourself by downloading the examples for this chapter from the "Missing CD" page at *www.missingmanuals.com*.

Here's how you can create the update query:

1. **Create a new query by choosing Create → Other → Query Design.**

   The Show Table dialog box appears.

2. **Add each table you want to include in your query by selecting it and then clicking Add (just as you did when creating a select query). Click Close when you're finished.**

Usually, an update query will use a single table. However, if you need information from more than one related table, then add them all. Adding multiple tables creates a join (page 229). Joins work the same in an action query as they do in a select query—they pull information from a parent table, and then display it alongside the records from the child table.

In this example, you need the Products and ProductCategories tables.

3. **Change your query to an update query by choosing Query Tools | Design → Query Type → Update.**

The column list at the bottom of the window changes to reflect your new type of query. The Sort and Show boxes disappear (because they have no meaning in the world of update queries), and a new Update To box appears for every field that's included in the query.

4. **Add the field (or fields) you want to use for filtering, and then set the Criteria box for each one.**

Your filter conditions determine what records Access selects. Since this query's an update query, the records you select are the records you'll end up changing.

In this example, you need to use the CategoryID field or CategoryName field. If you use the CategoryID field, you need to supply the ID value for your category. If you use the CategoryName field, you can match records using the descriptive name.

To add a field, double-click it in the table box, just as you would with a select query. Then set the criteria to the value you want to match, as in Figure 7-1. If you want to apply an update to all the records in a table, then you don't need to set any filter criteria.

5. **Add the field (or fields) you want to change.**

In this example, you need to add the Price field so you can modify the product prices.

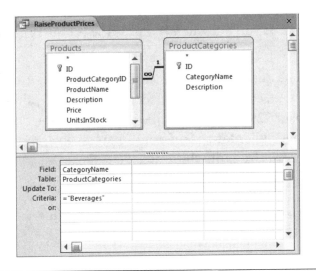

Figure 7-1. This query matches products in the Beverages category.

6. **In the Update To box, supply the new value that your query will apply to each field.**

   You have two options for updating a field. You can apply a fixed value by typing it into the Update To box. If you take this approach, Access updates every record you select with the exact same value.

   You can also use an expression that takes one or more existing fields values, and uses them to calculate a new value. You can use all the operations and functions described in this chapter to manipulate text, numbers, and dates. You can, for instance, use the following expression on the Price field to ratchet up product prices by 10 percent:

   `[Price]*1.10`

7. **Add any other fields that you want to inspect to confirm that you're selecting the correct records.**

   Before you run your query and apply your changes, you perform a preview that displays all the rows your update query will select (and thus, all the records it'll change when you run it). In order to confirm that your query's grabbing the right records, you may need to see some other identifying information in the datasheet grid, like the ProductName.

However, there's one bit of bureaucratic trickery you need to perform to make this preview work. Access ignores fields that you don't plan to update. So if you want to make sure the ProductName field appears in the datasheet preview, then you need to supply something in the Update To box. In this case, use the value [ProductName]. This step tells Access to update the ProductName field with the current value of the ProductName field. In other words, Access doesn't actually change anything, but it shows the ProductName field in the datasheet preview.

Figure 7-2 shows the finished update query.

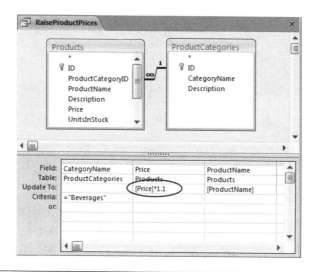

Figure 7-2. This query matches all the products in a specific category and raises the price 10 percent.

8. **Right-click the query's tab title, and choose Datasheet View to see the rows that your query affects (Figure 7-3).**

This step lets you preview the rows you're about to change, before you actually pull the trigger. In the datasheet, you see all the records that match your query's filters—in other words, all the records you'll change when you run the query. However, you won't see the changes you want to make.

In a basic select query, viewing the datasheet and running the query are equivalent actions. In an action query, viewing the datasheet shows you the rows that'll be affected, but doesn't actually change them. Running the query performs the modification, but doesn't show you the changed records.

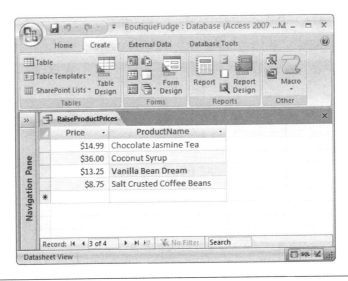

Figure 7-3. Here's the datasheet preview. It shows all the products in the Beverages category, with the current prices. When you run this query, these are the records that will be changed.

9. **Now switch back to Design view (right-click the tab title, and then choose Design View.) If you're confident you've got your query right, choose Query Tools | Design → Results → Run to run your update query and have Access apply your changes.**

Remember, it's always a good idea to back up your database (page 44) before you take this step.

When you run an action query, Access warns you about the change it's about to make (Figure 7-4). Click Yes to make the change.

Sadly, Access doesn't show you the updated records—in fact, it doesn't show you anything. If you're wondering what happened, you may want to review the records you just changed. One way to do this is to show the preview for your update query again (by right-clicking the tab title, and then choosing Datasheet View). This method works as long as you haven't changed the records in such a way that they no longer match your filtering conditions. (If you have, you'll need to create a new query or browse the table to double-check your data.)

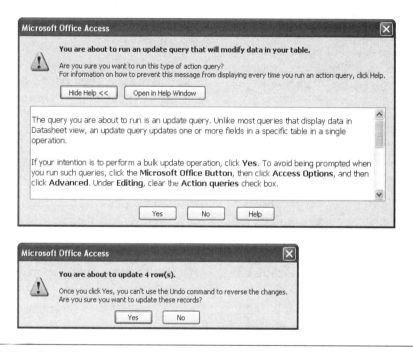

Figure 7-4. Top: Every time you run an action query, Access warns you that the query will change your database. If you don't need this reminder, follow the steps in this window to open the Access Options dialog box and turn off this warning. (You'll need to click No to close the dialog box first.)

Bottom: Next, Access tells you how many records will be affected and gives you a last-minute chance to back out. Access always gives you this information, even if you turn off the standard warning. If you click Yes now, then Access updates your table.

When Access Blocks Your Update

Consider this bit of Access existential philosophy: What happens if you click Run (as described in step 9 on page 258), and nothing happens? There's no warning, no message box, and no error to explain what went wrong. All you get is a cryptic message in the Status bar at the bottom of the Access window, which blandly advises you, "The action or event has been blocked by Disabled Mode". What does it all mean?

Access is a truly paranoid program. It's just not ready to let you perform some actions unless you explicitly say it's OK.

As you learned on page 48, every time you open your database, Access shows a message bar with a security warning. It's up to you what you do about that security warning. You can click the X in the top-right corner to hide the message bar altogether. In this case, your database remains in a slightly disabled state. You can still create, modify, and delete database objects on your own.

However, you can't run any code or action queries. (To get the message bar back and see the security warning again, choose Database Tools → Show/Hide → Message Bar.)

Your other choice is to click the Options button in the message bar to show the Microsoft Office Security Options dialog box. Then, choose "Enable this content", and then click OK. This action gives Access your ironclad guarantee that the database is safe—in other words, it hasn't been created by some Cheeto-munching hacker in his parents' basement. Once you take this step, Access allows you to run action queries (at least until you close the database and open it again, at which point the security warning reappears).

10. **If you want to save your query, then hit Ctrl+S (or close the query tab). You'll need to supply a name for your query.**

Consider using a query name that clearly indicates that this is an action query. You may want to use a name like UpdateProductPrices. Action queries show up with an exclamation-mark icon in the navigation bar. Each type of action query has a slightly different icon—for update queries, you'll see a pencil with an exclamation mark beside it (Figure 7-5).

If you don't plan to use your query again, then consider deleting it. Deleting it prevents you (or someone else) from accidentally rerunning the query and applying changes you don't want.

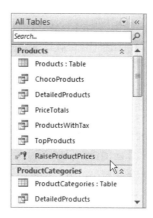

Figure 7-5. Remember, every time you double-click a query in the navigation pane, you run it. If the query you click is an action query, like the one highlighted here, you may have just updated or deleted some important data. (To open an action query without running it, right-click it, and then choose Design View instead.)

Append Queries

An append query selects records from a table, and then inserts them into another table. (Technically speaking, *appending* is the process of adding records to the end of a table.)

You may create an append query for a number of reasons, but usually you do it to transfer records from one table to another. You may want to use an append query to transfer records from one database to another. This trick's handy if you have duplicate tables in different databases (perhaps because different people need to use the database on different computers).

> **NOTE**
>
> Once you've finished copying records to a new table, you may want to follow up with a delete query (page 266) to remove the old versions.

Append queries also make sense if you're working with a super-sensitive database. In this case, you might enter new records in a temporary table so someone else can look them over. When the inspection's finished, you can then use an append query to transfer the records to the real table.

Append queries are a bit stricter than other types of action queries. In order to transfer the records, you need to make sure the two tables line up. Here are some guidelines:

▶ **Data types must match.** The fields you select (from the source table) and the fields you're heading towards (in the target table) must have matching data types. However, the names don't need to match. You can configure your query so that information drawn from a field named FirstName is placed into a field name F_Name, provided they're both text fields.

▶ **You can ignore some fields.** If the source has fields that aren't in the destination table, just don't include them in your query. If the destination table has fields that aren't in the source, then Access leaves them blank, or uses the default values (page 134). However, if you leave out a required field (one that has the Required field property set to Yes, as explained on page 131), then you'll get an error.

▶ **Access enforces all the normal rules for adding a record.** You can't do things like insert data that violates a validation rule (page 147), and you can't insert duplicate values into a field that has a primary key or a unique index (page 135).

▶ **If the destination table has an AutoNumber field, then don't supply a value for that field.** Access automatically generates one for each record you insert.

___ NOTE _____

You can't copy AutoNumber values in an append query. If you use AutoNumber fields for your ID fields, then the new copied records have different ID numbers from the originals.

_____

Access gives you another choice that's similar to the append query: the *make-table query,* which is the same in all ways but one. The make-table query *creates* the destination table, and then copies the records to it.

Creating an Append (or Make-Table) Query

The following steps show you how to create an append or make-table query. You'll transfer records from the Contacts table in the Marketing.accdb database to the PotentialClients table in the Sales.accdb database. (You can find both these databases on the "Missing CD" page at *www.missingmanuals.com.*)

1. **Open the source database.**

   In this example, that's the Marketing.accdb database that has the contact information.

2. **Create a new query by choosing Create → Other → Query Design.**

   The Show Table dialog box appears.

3. **Using the Show Table dialog box, add the source table that has the records you want to copy. Then click Close to close it.**

   This example uses the Contacts table.

4. **Change your query to an append query by choosing Query Tools | Design → Query Type → Append (or choose Query Tools | Design → Query Type → Make Table to convert it to a make-table query).**

   The destination table (the PotentialClients table in the Sales.accdb database) already exists. For that reason, you use an append query instead of a make-table query.

   When you change your query to an append or make-table query, Access asks you to supply the destination table (the place where you'll copy the records), as shown in Figure 7-6.

5. **If you want to transfer the records to another database, then choose Another Database, and then click Browse. Browse to your database file, and then click OK to select it.**

   You're transferring records to the Sales.accdb database.

   Especially if you plan to keep using this new query, be sure to keep the destination database in the same spot. If you move the destination file to another location (or rename it), Access can't find it when you run the query and gives you an error.

Figure 7-6. Access wants to know where you plan to transfer the records you're copying. You can choose a table from the handy drop-down list. If you're copying data from one database to another, then choose the Another Database option, click the Browse button to specify the database file, and then click OK.

6. **In the Table Name box, enter the name of the table to which you want to transfer the records.**

   If you're creating an append query, then the table you choose must already exist somewhere—either in the database file or another one you have on hand. You can pick it out of the Table Name drop-down list.

   If you're creating a make-table query, then you need to type in the name for a brand-new table. Access will create this table when you run the query.

   Here, you're transferring records to the PotentialClients table.

7. **Click OK to close the Append or Make Table dialog box.**

8. **Now, add the field (or fields) you want to copy from the source table.**

   Remember, you don't have to copy *all* the fields. In this example, all you need is the FirstName and LastName fields.

9. **If you're creating an append query, then fill in the names of the destination fields in the Append To boxes.**

   In this example, set the Append To box for the FirstName field to F_Name. That way, Access copies the information from the FirstName field in the source table to the F_Name field in the destination table (Figure 7-7). Similarly, set Last-Name so it appends to L_Name.

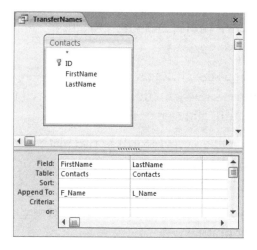

Figure 7-7. This append query transfers the information from the Contacts table in the Marketing database to the PotentialClients list in the Sales database. Since both these tables use ID fields with the AutoNumber data type, the ID numbers in the copied records will be different from the ID numbers in the original records. (If this isn't the behavior you want, then you need to copy the AutoNumber ID from the Contacts table to a normal numeric column in the PotentialClients table—one that doesn't use the AutoNumber feature.)

10. **If you want to copy only *some* of the records in the source table, then set the filter conditions you need.**

    Like everywhere else in Access, these filters determine what records are copied from the source table. To set a filter condition, just fill in the Criteria box for the appropriate field.

    If you add a filtering field to an append query, but don't want to copy the field's value to the target table, then don't put anything in its Append To box.

    If you add a filtering field to a make-table query, but don't want to copy the field's value to the target table, then turn off that field's Show checkbox.

11. **Right-click the tab title, and then choose Datasheet View to see the rows that your query affects.**

    This step lets you preview the rows you're about to copy.

12. **If you're confident you've got things right, then switch back to Design view, and then choose Query Tools | Design → Results → Run to transfer your records.**

Access warns you about the change it's about to make. Click Yes to copy the records. Access doesn't show you the copies—you need to track those down by browsing the destination table's datasheet.

At this point, you have the same records in two places—the source table and the destination table. You may want to follow up with a delete query to clean out the original versions, as described in the next section.

13. **If you want to save your query, hit Ctrl+S (or close the query tab). You need to supply a name for your query.**

If you don't plan to use your query again, then consider deleting it.

Delete Queries

Delete queries are the simplest—and most dangerous—of the action queries. A delete query works much like a normal select query. You specify a set of filter conditions, and then Access finds the matching records in the table. But the delete query doesn't just display the records—instead, it erases them from the database.

Delete queries are great for clearing out a huge number of records at once after you've finished transferring them to another table. In the append-query example described earlier (page 263), you probably want a way to remove the original records once you've copied them to the new table. A delete query fits the bill perfectly.

To create a delete query, follow these steps:

1. **Create a new query by choosing Create → Other → Query Design.**

2. **Using the Show Table dialog box that appears, add the table that has the records you want to delete. Then click Close to close it.**

3. **Change your query to a delete query by choosing Query Tools | Design → Query Type → Delete.**

The Sort and Show boxes disappear from the column list, and the Delete box appears.

4. **Add the fields you want to use for filtering, and then set your filter conditions.**

   Your filter conditions determine what records are deleted, so make sure you define them carefully. If you don't include any filter conditions—gulp—Access will delete all the records when you run the query.

5. **Add any other fields that you want to inspect to confirm you're getting the correct records in the datasheet preview.**

   It's critical that you verify that you're removing only the records you want to delete. Delete queries have a nifty feature that can help you identify each record before you perform the actual delete operation. To use it, double-click the asterisk (*) in the table field list. The Delete box automatically sets itself to From, which indicates this information isn't being used as part of a filter condition—instead, it's just there to show the list of to-be-deleted records in your previews.

   Figure 7-8 shows a finished delete query.

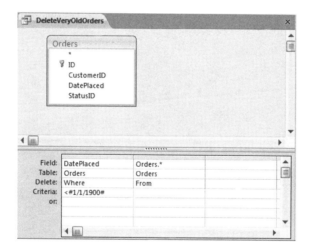

Figure 7-8. This query removes old order records. The first field in the query defines the filter condition (orders with a DatePlaced before 1900). The second field (*) is a shortcut that lets you see all the fields in the preview, so you can carefully review the data you're removing.

6. **Right-click the tab title, and then choose Datasheet View to see the rows that'll be affected by your query.**

   This step lets you preview the rows that you're about to delete. If you used the asterisk (*), you'll see the full information for each record.

7. **If you're confident you've got things right, then switch back to Design view, and then choose Query Tools | Design → Results → Run to remove the records.**

   Access warns you about the change it's about to make. Click Yes to delete the records for good.

8. **If you want to save your query, hit Ctrl+S (or close the query tab). You'll need to supply a name for your query.**

   If you don't plan to use your delete query again, consider not saving it. It's a dangerous tool to have lying around.

PART THREE: PRINTING REPORTS AND USING FORMS

CREATING REPORTS

▶ Report Basics

▶ Printing, Previewing, and Exporting a Report

▶ Formatting a Report

▶ Filtering and Sorting a Report

THERE ARE MANY REASONS TO CREATE A HARD COPY of your lovingly maintained Access data. With a good printout, you can:

▶ **Carry your information without lugging your computer around.** For example, you can take an inventory list while you go shopping.

▶ **Show your information to non-Access users.** For example, you can hand out product catalogs, order forms, and class lists to other people.

▶ **Review details outside the office.** For example, you can search for mistakes while you're on the commuter train home.

▶ **Impress your boss.** After all, it's difficult to argue with 286 pages of raw data.

In Chapter 3 you learned how to print the raw data that's in a table, straight from the datasheet. This technique is handy, but it provides relatively few features. You don't have the flexibility to deal with large blocks of information, you can't fine-tune the formatting of different fields, and you don't have tools like grouping and summarizing that can make the information easier to understand. As you've probably already guessed, Access provides another printing feature that fills in these gaps. It's called *reports*, and it allows you to create a fine-tuned blueprint that tells Access exactly how it should prepare your data for the printer.

Reports are specialized database objects, much like tables and queries. As a result, you can prepare as many reports as you need, and keep them on hand indefinitely. Life isn't as easy if you stick to the datasheet alone. For example, if you're using the bobblehead database, you may want to print a list of bobblehead dolls with the doll's name and manufacturer information for your inventory list, and a separate list with prices for your budgeting process. To switch back and forth between these two types of printouts using the datasheet, you have to manually rearrange and hide columns *every time*. Reports don't suffer from this problem, because each report is saved as a separate database object. So if you want to print your inventory list, you simply run the DollInventory report. If you want the budgeting details, you fire up the Doll-Prices report.

To see one reason why reports are insanely better than ordinary datasheet printouts, compare Figure 8-1 (which shows a datasheet printout) and Figure 8-2 (which puts the same data into a simple report). Notice how the datasheet printout has both wasted space and missing information.

ID	Character	Description	Purcha
1	Homer Simpson	The Simpsons everyman is a classic bobblehead creation, with fine detail.	
2	Edgar Allan Poe	This is one of my least-loved dolls. In fact, I find it disturbing. On several occasions, I've witnessed this doll begin to bob without	
3	Frodo	The quality of this cult bobblehead is lacking. Magiker sinks to a new low of cut-rate production.	
4	James Joyce	This bobblehead adds class to any collection.	
5	Jack Black	The bobbling action of this doll is broken, and the head remains fixed in place.	

Figure 8-1. Ordinary printouts are notoriously bad at dealing with large amounts of data in a single column. Consider the Description field in this Dolls table. Every record has the same-sized box for its description, which fits three short lines. If the information is larger than the available space (as it is for the Edgar Allan Poe doll), it's chopped off at the end. If the information is smaller (as with the James Joyce doll), you have some wasted white space to look at.

Dolls

ID	Character	Description	Pur
1	Homer Simpson	The Simpsons everyman is a classic bobblehead creation, with fine detail.	
2	Edgar Allan Poe	This is one of my least-loved dolls. In fact, I find it disturbing. On several occasions, I've witnessed this doll begin to bob without human intervention.	
3	Frodo	The quality of this cult bobblehead is lacking. Magiker sinks to a new low of cut-rate production.	
4	James Joyce	This bobblehead adds class to any collection.	
5	Jack Black	The bobbling action of this doll is broken, and the head remains fixed in place.	

Figure 8-2. In a typical report, you size the column widths, but the height of each row depends on the amount of information in the record. That means each row is just large enough to show all the text in the Description field. Best of all, you don't need to apply any special settings to get this behavior. Reports do it automatically.

Report Basics

You can take more than one path to create a report. Experienced report writers (like you, once you've finished this chapter) often choose to create a report from scratch. Report newbies (like you, right now) usually generate a quick report with a single click. This section covers the simplest method for generating a report.

Creating a Simple Report

It takes just two steps to create a simple report, and a few more to fine-tune it. If you want to try out this technique for yourself, open the Boutique Fudge database (included with the downloadable content for this chapter, explained on page 19) or a database of your creation, and follow these steps:

1. **In the navigation pane, select the table you want to use for your new report.**

    This example uses the Products table from the Boutique Fudge database. You can also create a report that's based on a query. See the box "Doing the Heavy Lifting with a Query" (page 277) for more about this trick.

2. **Choose Create → Reports → Report.**

    A new tab appears with a simple, automatically generated report. This report arranges information in a table, with each field in the table (or query) occupying a separate column. The Report view looks somewhat like the datasheet, except for the fact that it has nicer formatting and uses space more efficiently, as shown in Figure 8-2.

    When you first create a report, the fields are arranged from left to right in the same order that they live in the table. It doesn't make any difference if you've rearranged the columns in the datasheet. However, any columns you've hidden in the datasheet (page 108) are left out of the report.

    ___ NOTE _____

    You can fine-tune exactly which data appears in your report by removing columns you don't want and adding new columns. Page 279 has more about this trick.

3. Resize the columns smaller or larger until you have the balance you want.

To resize a column, first click the column header to select it. (A dotted line will appear around the column.) Next, move the mouse to the right-side of the column header, so that it changes into the two-way resize pointer. Finally, drag the column border to the left (to make it smaller) or to the right (to make it larger). Figure 8-3 shows this process in action.

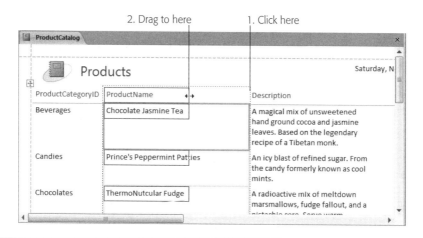

Figure 8-3. *Drag the edge of the column to the desired width. A black box shows you the new width. When you release the mouse button, Access changes the column width and moves all the following columns accordingly. To prevent the last column from leaking off the edge of the page, you may need to shrink some columns after you expand others.*

___ NOTE _____

You'll see a dotted line on the right side of your report that indicates the edge of the page. You can resize a column right off the edge of the page—which may make sense if you have dozens of columns, and the only way you can deal with them is to create a printout that's two pages wide. Generally, though, it's better to make sure all your fields fit the width of the page, and turn the page sideways using landscape orientation (page 125) if you need to accommodate more columns.

4. **Arrange the columns in the order you want by dragging them.**

To move a column, click the column heading, and then drag the column to a new position.

TIP

You can also move columns with the keyboard. Just click to select the right column, and then use the left and right arrow keys to hop from one spot to the next.

---

5. **Optionally, you can tweak the formatting by changing fonts, colors, and borders.**

The quickest way to change the formatting of your report is to select the appropriate part (by clicking), and then use the buttons in the Report Layout Tools | Formatting → Font section of the ribbon. Using this technique, you can change how titles, column headers, and data appear. Page 296 has more on this technique.

6. **Add the finishing touches.**

Now's the time to change the headings, add a logo, and apply page numbers. You'll learn how to fill in these details starting on page 284.

7. **Optionally, choose Office button → Print to print the report now.**

You can also adjust the print settings in Print Preview mode (choose Office button → Print → Print Preview), as described on page 286.

8. **Save your report to use later.**

You can save your report at any time by pressing Ctrl+S. If you close the report tab without saving it, Access prompts you to make the save. Either way, you need to supply a name for your report.

It's possible to create reports that have the same names as tables or other database objects. For example, you could create a Products report that shows information about the Products table. However, in practice it's usually better to pick a more specific report name (like ProductsByCategory, ProductListForDealers, and Top50Products). The report shown in Figure 8-2 and elsewhere in this chapter is named ProductCatalog.

Doing the Heavy Lifting with a Query

The most obvious way to build a report is to base it on an existing table. However, you can also create a report on top of a *query*. This approach lets you use some heavy-duty filtering or sorting on your records before they reach the report. It also makes sense if you want to create a report that uses information from more than one table.

For example, imagine you decide you want to create a product list that includes additional details from another table (like the category description from the ProductCategories table). Although

you can create this report from scratch, it often makes more sense to structure your data with a query first. That way, you can reuse the query for different purposes (like editing), and you can change it any time.

In this example, the first step is to create a query that joins the Categories and Products table (page 229). Then, you save this query, select it in the navigation pane, and choose Create → Reports → Report to create a report that's based on the query. You can then follow the normal steps to perfect your report.

Arranging a Report

You've already learned how you can shuffle columns around in a report. However, that's not all you can move. You can also add space between the rows (see Figure 8-4) and adjust all the following elements:

▸ **The logo** (in the top-left corner). In a new report, the logo looks like a notebook with a circle around it.

▸ **The report title** (right next to the logo). To start out, this is the name of the table or query on which the report is based (like Products).

▸ **The date and time** (which is updated every time you open the report). Initially, this appears in the top-right corner.

▸ **The page number**. This appears at the center-bottom of each page. In Layout view, Access treats the report as though all the data occupies one page, so you need to scroll to the end to find this element.

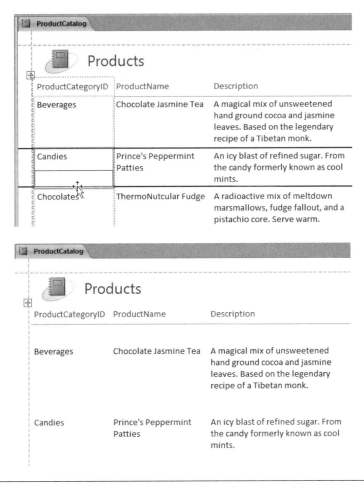

Figure 8-4. Top: To add space between the rows, click a value in one of the rows, and drag it down. Bottom: All the rows are adjusted to have the same spacing.

▶ **The report data** (after the title). To change where the table in the report first appears on the page, click one of the column headers, and then drag it down (to add space between the title and the report data) or up (to remove the space).

▶ **The totals** (at the bottom of some columns). Access automatically adds calculations for numeric fields. For example, when the ProductCatalog report is first created, Access adds a total at the bottom of the Price column that indicates how much it costs to buy one of each product. (This total is of dubious value—to change it, select the column, and then pick another summary option from Report Layout Tools | Formatting → Grouping & Totals → Totals menu.)

Adding and Removing Fields

If you're tired of merely rearranging columns, you may want to try adding ones that aren't already included or removing existing ones that you don't want. Removing a field is easy: just click to select it, and then press Delete. (You can try out this technique with the Discontinued field in the ProductCatalog report.)

When you create a simple report using the quick creation technique described on page 274, you usually end up with all the fields you need. However, there are two reasons why you may need to add an additional field that isn't already in the report:

▶ **You want to add a field that's hidden in the Datasheet view (page 108).** When you create a new report, hidden fields are left out.

▶ **You want to add a field with related information from a linked table.** For example, you could add fields from the ProductCategories table to show information about the category that each product is in.

To add a new field, you need the help of the Field List pane (see Figure 8-5). To show it, choose Report Layout Tools | Formatting → Controls → Add Existing Fields.

When you add a new field, Access uses the field name for the column heading, which isn't always what you want. Maybe you'd prefer *Product Name* (with a space) to *ProductName*. Or maybe you'd like to shorten *ProductCategoryID* to just *Category*. After all, the report shows the name instead of the numeric category ID, because the ProductCategoryID field uses a lookup (page 187). Fortunately, renaming the column headers is easy. Just double-click one to switch it into edit mode. You can then edit the existing text or replace it altogether.

Adding Pictures to Reports

Can I store pictures in a table and show them in a report?

Many tables include embedded pictures using the Attachment data type (page 84). You can use this technique to store employee photos, product pictures, or supplier logos. Depending on the type of picture, you may then want to include them in your printouts.

It is possible to show your pictures in a report (and even print them), provided you meet the following requirements:

* **Your picture is stored in an attachment field.** (See page 84 for more information about the attachment data type.)

* **Your picture is stored in a standard picture format (think .bmp, .jpg, .gif, .tif, .wmf, and so on).** If you have another type of file in an attachment field, you just see the icon of the related application (like Microsoft Word for a .doc file) in your report.

* **Your picture is the first attachment.** If you have more than one attachment, when you select the row in the report, tiny arrow buttons appear above that you can use to move from one attachment to another. But it's way too much work to do this with all your records before you print a report.

The Dolls table in the bobblehead database Products table fits the bill, which lets you create a report like the one shown in Figure 8-6.

Alternatively, you can show the file name or the file type of an attachment in a report. To do this, you need to use the Field List pane (Figure 8-5). For example, if you have an attachment field named Picture, it appears with a plus button next to it in the Field List pane. Click the plus button, and you'll see the three Picture-related details you can display in a report: *Picture.FileData* (the attachment content itself, which is the image), *Picture.FileName* (the name of the file), and *Picture.FileType* (the type of file). If you want to show these details, just drag them onto your report.

The Many Views of a Report

Just like tables and queries, you can use several different views to change a report. When you create a report using the quick creation technique described earlier, you begin in Layout view, which is an ideal starting place for report builders. But

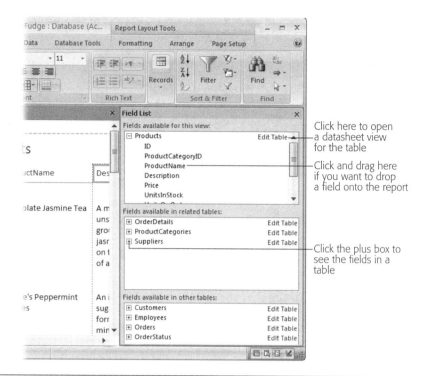

Figure 8-5. The top portion of the Field List window lists the fields from the table (or query) on which the report is based. The middle portion lists the fields in any related tables, and the bottom portion lists unrelated tables (which you probably won't use). To add a field, drag it from the Field List pane and drop it on your report.

depending on the task at hand, you may choose to switch to another view. You have four viewing options:

▶ **Layout View.** Shows what the report will look like when printed, complete with the real data from the underlying table. You can use this view to format and rearrange the basic building blocks of the report.

▶ **Report View.** Looks almost the same as Layout view but doesn't allow you to make changes. If you double-click a report in the navigation pane, Access opens it in Report view so you can see the data it contains without accidentally changing its design. One common reason to use Report view is to copy portions of your

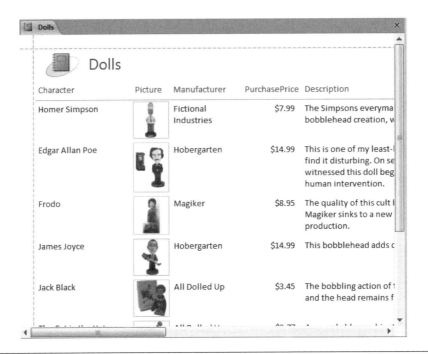

Figure 8-6. You can see this in the sample Bobblehead database examples for this chapter. (They're available on the "Missing CD" page at www.missingmanuals.com.) The report is named DollsWith-Pictures.

report to the clipboard, so you can paste them into other programs (like Microsoft Word). Figure 8-7 shows how that works.

___ **NOTE** _____

If you want to transfer the entire content of a report, you should consider the export features described on page 289.

_____

▸ **Print Preview.** Shows a live preview of your report, just like Layout view and Report view. The difference is that the preview is *paginated* (divided into print pages), so you can figure out how many pages your printout needs and where the page breaks fall. You can also change print settings (like page orientation) and export the complete report, as described on page 289.

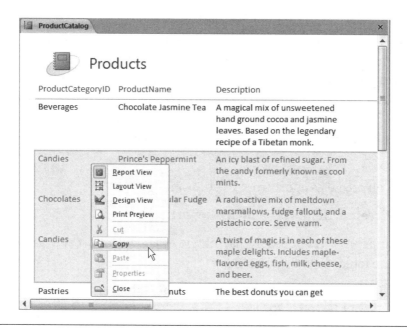

Figure 8-7. To select a bunch of rows, click in the margin on the left next to the first row you want to select, and then drag down to highlight the rows you want. Then, right-click the highlighted portion, and choose Copy to transfer it to the clipboard, so it's ready for pasting into other Windows applications.

▶ **Design View.** Shows a template view where you can define the different sections of your report. It's not nearly as intuitive as Layout view, but it does give you complete, unrestrained flexibility to customize your report. Access experts often begin creating a report in Layout view and then add more exotic effects in Design view. Learn more about Design view in *Access 2007: The Missing Manual*.

You can switch from one view to another by right-clicking the report tab title, and then choosing the appropriate view from the pop-up menu. (Or, you can use the Home → Views → View menu or the view buttons in the bottom-right corner of the Access window. It's just a matter of personal preference.)

After you've closed your report, you can reopen it in the view of your choice. Just right-click the report in the navigation pane, and then choose the appropriate view. Or double-click the report in the navigation pane to open it in Report view.

Creating a Report from Scratch

So far, you've learned how to quickly create a report based on a table or a query. However, you have another choice—you can start with a blank slate and explicitly add each field you want. Both approaches are equally valid. You may prefer to use the quick creation technique when you want to build a report that closely follows the structure of an existing table or query. On the other hand, if you plan to create a report that uses just a few fields from a table, you may find it's easier to start from scratch.

Here's how you create a report from the bottom up:

1. **Choose Create → Reports → Blank Report.**

   A new, empty report appears in Layout view. The Field List appears on the right, with all the tables in your database.

2. **Add the fields you want from the appropriate table, either by dragging them from the Field List onto the report surface or by double-clicking them.**

   You can also use fields from related tables. For example, you can create a report that combines product information and the category details for each product. In this case, the report automatically uses a join query (page 229) to get the results.

3. **Format the columns.**

   When you create a report from scratch, the columns start off with no formatting at all. You'll need the formatting techniques described in the next section to add color and emphasis.

4. **Add any other elements you want, like a logo, a title, page numbers, and the date.**

   When you create a simple report, you get all these ingredients for free. Fortunately, it's just as easy to add them to a report you're building from scratch. Just head to the Report Layout Tools | Formatting → Controls section of the ribbon (see Figure 8-8).

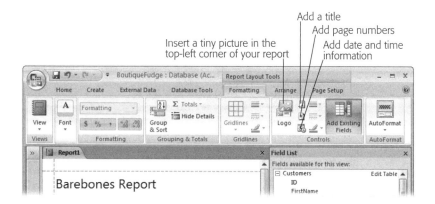

Figure 8-8. The logo and title typically sit at the top of your report. You can use any picture for the logo and any text for the title. Access gives you more options for the date (Figure 8-9) and page number (Figure 8-10).

Figure 8-9. When adding date information, you can choose whether to include the date, the time, or both. You also pick the format. Once you've added the date information, you can change the font, borders, and colors, as with any other report element.

Figure 8-10. With page numbers, you can choose the format, the position, and the alignment. (The position determines whether the page numbers appear above or below the report data. Although you can drag the page numbers around after you add them, Access will shift the report data to make room, based on your choice.)

Printing, Previewing, and Exporting a Report

Once you've created the perfect report, it's time to share it with rest of the world. Most commonly, you'll choose to print it.

Printing a report is easy—simply choose Office button → Print. But before you inadvertently fire off an 87-page customer list in jumbo 24-point font, it's a good idea to preview the end result. Access makes it easy with its integrated Print Preview feature.

> **TIP**
>
> You don't need to open your report to print it. Just select it in the navigation pane, and then choose Print from the Office menu. But beware— when you use this shortcut you don't get the chance to preview the result and make sure it's what you want before it pops out of the printer.

Previewing a Report

To get a preview of what your printed report will look like, right-click the report tab title and then choose Print Preview, or choose Office button → Print → Print Preview. Print Preview mode doesn't let you make any changes or select any part of the report. You're limited to zooming in and out, and moving from page to page (see Figure 8-11). When you're finished looking at your print preview, choose Print Preview → Close Preview → Close Print Preview.

Figure 8-11. In Print Preview mode, to zoom in, click once with the mouse. Click again to zoom back out to the full page view. You can also use the page navigation buttons at the bottom of the window to move from one page to the next, and the zoom slider (not shown) for more precise zooming. But the most useful commands appear in the ribbon, which lets you tweak the print settings and export your report results to another type of file.

In Print Preview mode, the ribbon changes dramatically. The tabs you've grown to know and love disappear, and Access replaces them with a single tab named Print Preview. (This is the same Print Preview tab you saw when you previewed a datasheet printout in Chapter 3.) You can use all the same techniques that you learned on page 125 to move around the preview, see multiple pages at once (which lets you study where page breaks occur), and change the page margins and paper orientation.

For example, the Portrait and Landscape buttons let you quickly switch between the standard portrait orientation (which places the short edge at the top of the page) and landscape (which rotates the page, placing the long edge at the top). Portrait fits more rows, while landscape fits more columns. Generally, portrait is best, provided it can fit all your columns. If portrait mode doesn't fit all your columns, you can try using landscape orientation, a smaller font size (page 296), narrower margins, or a larger type of paper.

> **NOTE**
>
> Reports always use your standard paper size (which is usually 8.5×11 inches, or letter size) when you first create them. However, if you change the size, the new size setting is stored with the report. That means the next time you open your report, it still has the customized paper size. The same applies for the paper orientation setting.

Access has two extra options that aren't provided in a normal datasheet print preview:

▶ **Use the Print Data Only button** to produce a streamlined printout that leaves out details like column headers and titles. This option is rarely useful, because the resulting printout is harder to read.

▶ **Use the Columns button** to fit more report data on a page. This option works only if your report is much narrower than the page width. For example, if your report is less than half the width of the page, you can double-up by using two columns. You'll need half the number of pages.

> **TIP**
>
> You can change a lot of the page layout settings (like margins and paper orientation) without heading to the print preview. You'll find many of the same buttons in the Report Layout Tools | Page Setup tab of the ribbon, which appears whenever you have your ribbon in Layout view.

Exporting a Report

The Print Preview tab is a bit of an oddity, because it includes a few commands that don't have anything to with printing your report. The commands in the Print Preview → Data section let you take a snapshot of the current report data, and then *export* it into some other type of file so you can view it outside of Access or work with it in another program. This technique is a great one to use if you want to share some data with other people (read: impress the boss).

Although Access supports many different formats for exporting a report, you'll use just a few with reports. (The others are more useful when you're exporting pure data from a table or query, as explained in Chapter 10.) The useful formats for exporting reports include:

▶ **Word.** This option transforms your report into a document you can open in Microsoft Word. However, the format Access uses is a bit clumsy. (It separates each column with tabs and each line with a hard return, which makes it difficult to rearrange the data after the fact in Word.) A nicer export feature would put the report data into a Word table, which would make it far easier to work with.

▶ **HTML Document.** This option transforms your report into a rich HTML document, suitable for posting on the Web or just opening straight from your hard drive. The advantage of this format is that all you need to view it is a Web browser (and who doesn't have one of those?). The only drawback is that the formatting, layout, and pagination of your report won't be preserved exactly, which is a disadvantage if someone wants to print the exported report.

▶ **Snapshot Viewer.** This option creates a .snp snapshot file, which anyone can open to view and print the fully formatted report. In order to view the snapshot file, you need Microsoft's free Snapshot Viewer program. (To download it, surf to *http://office.microsoft.com* and search for "Snapshot Viewer.") Although the Snapshot Viewer works perfectly well, most people prefer to use the more standard PDF format (next in the list), which provides the same features. (Truthfully, the Snapshot Viewer is a bit of a holdover from earlier versions of Office.)

▶ **PDF or XPS.** This option lets you preserve your exact report formatting (so your report can be printed), and it lets people who don't have Access (and possibly don't even have Windows) view your report. The only disadvantage is that this feature isn't included in the basic Access package. Instead, you need to install a free add-in to get it (you'll see how on page 292). For more information about the PDF and XPS formats, see the box "Learning to Love PDFs" below.

No matter which format you use, the process is essentially the same:

1. **If you're not already in Print Preview mode, right-click the report tab title, and then choose Print Preview.**

2. **Click one of the buttons in the Print Preview → Data section of the ribbon, depending on the format you want to use for your export.**

   For example, choose Print Preview → Data → Word to copy the results of your report into a Word-compatible document. Some of the options are stored under the Print Preview → Data → More menu, and you won't see a PDF export option until you install the PDF add-in (as described in the next section).

3. Choose a name for the destination file (Figure 8-12).

The destination file is the place where the exported data will be stored.

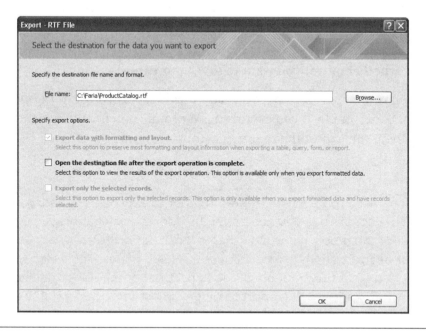

Figure 8-12. Access assumes you want a name that matches your report (for example, ProductCatalog.rtf if the ProductCatalog report is exported to a rich text document that can be opened in Word). However, you can change the file name to whatever you want.

4. If you wish to open your exported file in the related program, check the setting "Open the destination file after the export operation is complete."

Say you're exporting a Word document and you choose this option; Access will export the data, launch Word, and load up the document. This is a good way to make sure your export operation worked as expected. This option works only if you have the program you need on your computer.

5. Click OK to perform the export.

Ignore the other two checkboxes, which are grayed out. They apply only to export operations that work with other database objects.

Remember, exporting a report is like printing a report. Your exported file contains the data that existed at that moment in time. If you decide a week later that you need more recent data, you need to export your report again.

6. **Choose whether or not you want to save your export settings.**

By saving your export settings, you can quickly repeat your export operation later on. For example, if you export to a Word document and save the export settings, you can export the report data tomorrow, next week, or a year in the future.

You don't need to open your report in order to export it. Instead, you can use all the commands you need straight from the navigation pane. Just right-click the report name, and then choose Export to show a menu of all your export options, from PDF files to HTML pages. You'll also see a few options that don't appear in the Export tab of the ribbon, including options for exporting the report to older, almost forgotten database and spreadsheet products like dBase, Paradox, and Lotus 1-2-3.

Getting the "Save As PDF" Add-in

To export a report as a PDF file, you need the "Save As PDF or XPS" add-in. To get it, surf to *www.microsoft.com/downloads*, and search for "PDF". The links will lead you to a page where you can download the add-in and install it with just a couple clicks.

Once you install the add-in, all your Office applications will have the ability to export their documents in PDF format. In an Access report, you work this magic by choosing Print Preview → Data → PDF or XPS while you've got a report in Print Preview mode. Or, you can right-click your report in the navigation pane, and then choose Export → PDF or XPS.

When you export a PDF file, you get a few extra options in the "Publish as PDF or XPS" dialog box (Figure 8-13). PDF files can be exported with different resolution and quality settings (which mostly affect reports that have pictures). Normally, you use higher-quality settings if you're planning to print your PDF file because printers use higher resolutions than computer monitors.

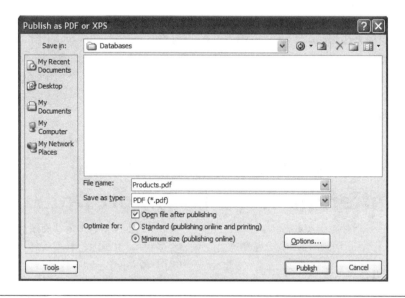

Figure 8-13. The "Publish as PDF or XPS" dialog box looks a lot like the Export As dialog box, except it has a Publish button instead of an Export button. You can turn on the "Open file after publishing" checkbox to tell Access to open the PDF file in Adobe Reader (assuming you have it installed) after the publishing process is complete, so you can check the result.

The "Publish as PDF or XPS" dialog box gives you some control over the quality settings with the "Optimize for" options. If you're just exporting a PDF copy so other people can *view* the information in your report, choose "Minimum size (publishing online)" to save some space. On the other hand, if there's a possibility that the people reading your PDF may want to print it out, choose "Standard (publishing online and printing)" instead. You'll export a slightly larger PDF file that will make for a better printout.

Finally, if you want to publish only a portion of your report as a PDF file, click the Options button to open a dialog box with yet a few more settings. You can choose to publish just a fixed number of pages rather than the full report.

TIP

Getting the "Save As PDF or XPS" add-in is a bit of a hassle, but it's well worth the effort. In previous versions of Access, people who wanted to create PDF files had to get another add-in or buy the expensive full version of the Adobe Acrobat software. The "Save As PDF or XPS" feature was originally slated for inclusion in Office (with no add-in required), but antitrust concerns caused an ultra-cautious Microsoft to keep it out. Best of all, the add-in gives you PDF-saving abilities in other Office applications, like Word, Excel, and PowerPoint.

FREQUENTLY ASKED QUESTION

Different Ways to Export Data

Is it better to export the results of a report, or the entire contents of a table?

There are several ways to transport data out of Access. You can take data directly from a table, or you can export the results of a query or a report. So which approach is best?

Generally, the easiest option is to get data straight from the appropriate table (as described in Chapter 10). However, in a few cases it makes more sense to use a report:

* You want to use the unique arrangement of columns that you've defined in a report. (For example, you may not want the full Products table—instead, the ProductCatalog report lays out exactly what you need.)

* You want to use the filtering, sorting, or grouping settings that you've applied to a report. These advanced options are discussed in depth in *Access 2007: The Missing Manual.*

* You want to take advantage of the formatting you've applied to a report. Depending on what exporting option you use, you may be able to keep formatting details like fonts. If you export to a PDF file, HTML document, or snapshot, all the formatting remains in place. If you export to an Office application like Word or Excel, only some of the formatting is retained. But if you export a table or a query, you get the data only, and it's up to you to make it look nice all over again.

In Chapter 10, you'll take a closer look at how to export tables and queries.

Formatting a Report

So far, you've learned to create simple reports that show all the information you want in a compact table. The only problem with these reports is that they all look the same. If you're working in a cubicle farm for a multinational insurance company, this drab sameness is probably a good thing. But those who still have a pulse may want to jazz up their reports with borders, exotic fonts, and a dash of color.

The quickest way to apply formatting is to use one of the prebuilt AutoFormats (shown in Figure 8-14) from the Report Layout Tools | Formatting → AutoFormat → AutoFormat list. Each AutoFormat applies a combination of fonts, colors, and border settings. AutoFormats let you transform the entire look of your report in one step, but they don't give you the fine-grained control to apply exactly the details you want.

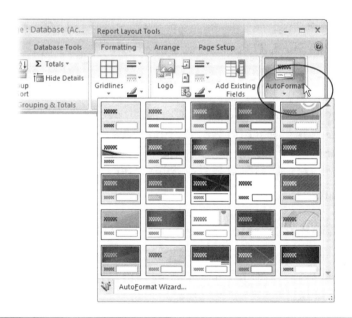

Figure 8-14. Click the drop-down arrow (circled) to see all the available AutoFormats. (Or, if you have a really large monitor, the AutoFormat previews appear right in the ribbon.) Each thumbnail preview shows the colors and a bit of the background that the format uses, but you need to apply it before you can really see what it looks like.

Remember, in order to format a report, it needs to be in Layout view. If you double-click a report in the navigation pane, it opens in Report view. Right-click the tab title, and then choose Layout View to switch over.

You can do a couple other things with AutoFormat:

▶ To apply just *part* of an AutoFormat, choose Report Layout Tools | Formatting → AutoFormat → AutoFormat → AutoFormat Wizard. In the AutoFormat dialog box, choose the AutoFormat you want. Then, click Options to show three check-boxes at the bottom of the dialog box: Font, Color, and Border. Turn off the check-mark next to the types of formatting you *don't* want to apply, and then click OK.

▶ To revert to a plain report with no formatting, choose Report Layout Tools | Formatting → AutoFormat → AutoFormat → AutoFormat Wizard to show the AutoFormat dialog box. Then, choose None in the list of AutoFormats, and click OK.

▶ If you've applied some fancy formatting to your report, and you want to save it as your own custom AutoFormat, choose Report Layout Tools | Formatting → AutoFormat → AutoFormat → AutoFormat Wizard to show the AutoFormat dialog box. Then, click Customize, choose "Create a new AutoFormat," enter a name for your AutoFormat, and click OK. You'll see your AutoFormat appear in the AutoFormats list.

Formatting Columns and Column Headers

AutoFormats are a great way to get a bunch of formatting done in a hurry. However, sometimes you want to use more of a personal touch and format the different parts of your report by hand.

To apply more targeted formatting, you need to follow a two-step approach. First, select the portion of the report you want to format. Second, click a command in the Report Layout Tools | Formatting → Font section of the ribbon (Figure 8-15).

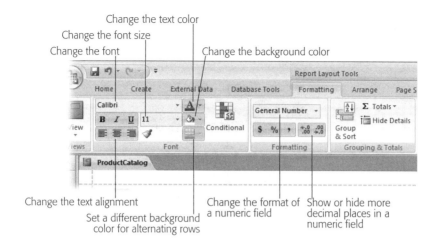

Change the text color
Change the font size
Change the font
Change the background color
Change the text alignment
Set a different background color for alternating rows
Change the format of a numeric field
Show or hide more decimal places in a numeric field

Figure 8-15. The Report Layout Tools | Formatting → Font section is packed with basic formatting tools.

The Layout Tools | Formatting → Font section lets you adjust all the following details:

▶ The font and font size (11-point Calibri is the easy-on-the-eyes standard)

▶ The text alignment (left, right, or center)

▶ The text color and background color

Although you can format the title, date, or page number sections of the report, you'll spend most of your time formatting the column headers and the column values. To format a column header, click it. To format the column *values*, click any one of the values in the column. Figure 8-16 shows an example.

You can't format the individual values in a column. That means that you can format the ProductName column to look different from the Price column, but you can't format Chocolate Jasmine Tea differently from Prince's Peppermint Patties. This limitation makes sense—after all, you could have thousands of records, and keeping track of the formatting of each one would be way too much work for Access.

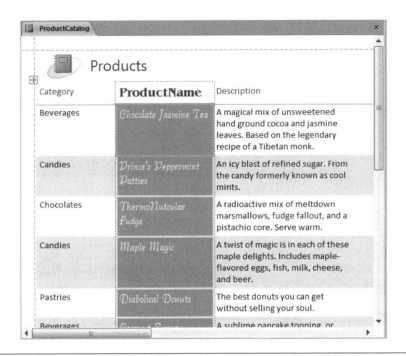

ProductCatalog

Products

Category	**ProductName**	Description
Beverages	*Chocolate Jasmine Tea*	A magical mix of unsweetened hand ground cocoa and jasmine leaves. Based on the legendary recipe of a Tibetan monk.
Candies	*Prince's Peppermint Patties*	An icy blast of refined sugar. From the candy formerly known as cool mints.
Chocolates	*ThermoNutcular Fudge*	A radioactive mix of meltdown marshmallows, fudge fallout, and a pistachio core. Serve warm.
Candies	*Maple Magic*	A twist of magic is in each of these maple delights. Includes maple-flavored eggs, fish, milk, cheese, and beer.
Pastries	*Diabolical Donuts*	The best donuts you can get without selling your soul.
Beverages		A sublime pancake topping, or

Figure 8-16. Here, the ProductName column is singled out for special formatting. Although it looks like only a single value is selected, Access will apply formatting changes to the entire column.

TIP

> One way around this shortcoming: Use conditional formatting to tell Access when it should kick in some extra formatting based on the value in a cell. See *Access 2007: The Missing Manual* for full details on this fancy maneuver.

Formatting numeric fields

You can use the Report Layout Tools | Formatting → Formatting section of the ribbon to adjust numeric fields (like the Price field in the ProductCatalog report). You'll find a drop-down list that lets you pick various options for formatting numbers:

▶ **General Number** gives a basic, no-frills number. Access gives each value the number of decimal digits it needs.

▶ **Currency** makes sure each number has two decimal points and gets the currency symbol that's configured for your computer (based on its geographic locale).

Large numbers get thousands-separator commas to separate the digits, as in $1,111.99.

▶ **Euro** is similar to Currency, except it shows the currency symbol for the euro.

▶ **Fixed** gives each number the same number of decimal places. (Initially it's two, but you can use the Increase Decimals and Decrease Decimals buttons, shown in Figure 8-15, to change this.) Large numbers don't get commas.

▶ **Standard** is the same as fixed, except large numbers do get the thousands separator comma (as in 1,111.99).

▶ **Percent** assumes each number is a fractional value that represents a percentage, where 1.0 is 100 percent. So if you have the number 48, Access changes this to 4800.00 percent. (You can change the number of decimal places with the Increase Decimals and Decrease Decimals buttons.)

▶ **Scientific** displays each number using *scientific notation*, so 48 becomes 4.80E+01 (which is a fancy way of saying 4.8 multiplied by 10^1 gives you the number that's stored in the field). Scientific notation is used to show numbers that have vastly different scales with a similar number of digits. You can change the number of decimal places using the Increase Decimals and Decrease Decimals buttons.

You can also change the number of digits that are displayed to the right of the decimal point by clicking the Increase Decimals and Decrease Decimals buttons in the Report Layout Tools | Formatting → Formatting section of the ribbon.

Alternating row formatting

Here's a simple but powerful formatting trick: Add a shaded background to every second row. Alternating row formatting gives a bit of polish to the plainest report, but it also serves a practical purpose. In dense reports, the shaded bands make it easier for readers to distinguish each row and follow a row from one column to the next.

To apply an alternating row format, you need to click immediately to the left of any row. At that point, the entire row becomes selected, and the Report Layout Tools | Formatting → Font → Alternate Fill button is turned on. (The Alternate Fill button looks like a mini-grid. It appears right under the Fill button.) You can click it, and then choose a color.

If you click one of the values in the row, the Alternate Fill button won't be turned on, and you won't be able to change the alternating fill color.

Gridlines

When you create a new report, your data is arranged in an invisible table. This table doesn't include any gridlines, so your printouts look sleek and lightweight. But if you're a closet gridline lover, you'll be happy to know you can add borders to the report table. It's up to you whether you want to add them everywhere to keep data carefully regimented in separate cells or just use them judiciously to highlight important columns.

> **TIP**
>
> Gridlines are useful with dense reports where the data may otherwise appear to run together into a jumbled mess. Access gurus know that less is more and using just a few gridlines is usually better than adding them between every column and row.

You can apply gridlines in two ways. The simplest and most common option is to apply them to the entire table. To do this, click anywhere inside the table of report data, and then choose one of the gridline options from the Report Layout Tools | Formatting → Gridlines → Gridlines list (Figure 8-17). Next, use the other buttons in the Report Layout Tools | Formatting → Gridlines section to change the thickness, color, and style (dashed, dotted, solid, and so on) of your gridlines.

> **NOTE**
>
> There's one trick to gridlines. You can apply gridlines to the column headings that are different from the ones you use for the rest of the table. To apply gridlines to the column-heading section, just click any column heading, and then choose your gridline options from the ribbon.

Borders

Along with report gridlines, you can also use a similar set of border options. The difference between gridlines and borders is that gridlines apply to the table of report data, while borders can be attached to any ingredient in your report.

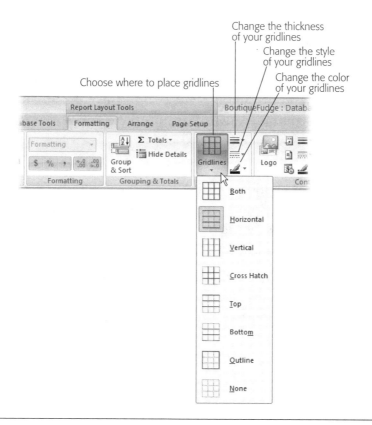

Choose where to place gridlines

Change the thickness
of your gridlines

Change the style
of your gridlines

Change the color
of your gridlines

Figure 8-17. The commands in the Gridlines section of the ribbon let you apply gridlines in the most common patterns: everywhere, between columns only, between rows only, around the outside of your data, and so on. You can also choose a line style (solid, dotted, dashed, and so on), thickness, and color.

You'll find the three border buttons (for choosing border thickness, color, and style) in the Report Layout Tools | Formatting → Controls section of the ribbon. The border options don't make much sense when you use them on column values, because you'll end up with a box around each value. Borders are more useful around other report elements, like the report title.

Filtering and Sorting a Report

Reports offer much the same filtering and sorting features that you learned to use with the datasheet in Chapter 3.

Filtering a Report

The ProductCatalog report presents all the records from the Products table. However, reports often need to filter out just an important subset of information. For example, you may want to analyze the sales of products in a specific category or the orders made by customers in a specific city. In the case of the ProductCatalog, it's logical to leave out discontinued items. After all, there's no reason for Boutique Fudge to advertise items it no longer sells.

You can pare down the results that are included in a report in two ways. You've already learned about one option: creating a query that extracts the results you want, and then using that query to build your report. This option is a good choice if you already have a query that fits the bill or you plan to use this subset of data for several purposes (reports, editing, other queries, and so on).

Another choice is to apply the filtering through report *settings*. The advantage of this technique is that you can change the filter settings quickly and repeatedly. If you plan to use the same report to print several different subsets of data, this approach is best. For example, you could filter out the products in one category, print them, and then adjust the filtering to select products in a different category, which you could also print.

Report filtering works the same way datasheet filtering does (discussed in detail on page 115). You have two options:

▶ If you want to quickly build a filter condition based on an existing value, right-click that value, as shown in Figure 8-18. For example, in the CategoryName field, you can right-click the value "Beverages." The menu that pops up includes several filtering options based on the current value. Depending on the option you choose, you can include records in the Beverages category, records in different categories, records that have a category name that includes Beverages (like "Alcoholic Beverages"), and so on.

▶ If you need more flexibility to create the filter expression you want, right-click any value in a column, and then look for the filtering submenu. The exact name of the menu depends on the data type. For example, if you right-click the CategoryName field, you see a submenu named Text Filters. If you right-click the Price field, you see a submenu named Number Filters. These submenus include a

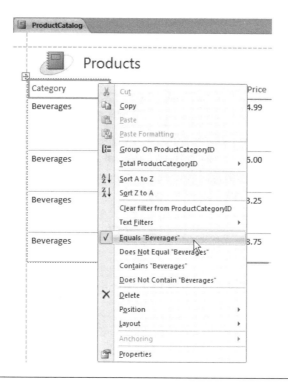

Figure 8-18. The quick filtering options you see vary based on the data type. Here, the filtering options let you set a variety of filters based on the term "Beverage."

range of filtering options that let you set specific ranges. For all the exquisite details and help creating a variety of filter expressions, refer to the instructions on page 115.

You can apply filters to multiple columns at once. To remove a filter, right-click the column, and then choose Clear Filter.

Sorting a Report

Ordinarily, a report has the same order as the underlying data source. If you've built your report on a query, the order is determined by the sort order you used in the query. If you've built your report on a table, the records have no particular order at all, although they'll typically appear in the order you added them.

Either way, you can apply formatting directly in your report, in much the same way that you can with the datasheet (page 112). Simply right-click the appropriate column header, and then look for the sorting options. The sort commands depend on the data type—for example, you can order text fields alphabetically, dates chronologically, and numeric fields in ascending or descending order.

___ NOTE ___

You can sort using only one field at a time. If you want to apply a more complex sort that uses more than one column (for example, a sort that separates products into alphabetical categories and then orders each category by price), you need to build a query for your report.

CREATING SIMPLE FORMS

- ▶ Form Basics
- ▶ Sorting and Filtering in a Form
- ▶ The Form Wizard

SO FAR, YOU'VE LEARNED HOW TO CREATE TABLES that house your data, queries that search it, and reports that prepare it for printing. You've also created action queries that automate big updates. But your actual database users (whether that's you or someone else) will spend most of their time on an entirely different job: daily database upkeep.

Database upkeep includes reviewing, editing, and inserting information. Real databases go through this process continuously. In a typical day, the staff at Cacophoné Studios adds new students, the customer service department at Boutique Fudge places new orders, and the Gothic Wedding planners tweak the seating arrangements. Bobbleheads are bought, addresses are changed, purchases are logged, test scores are recorded, and your data grows and evolves.

You can perform your daily upkeep using the datasheet (Chapter 3), but that isn't the easiest approach. Although the datasheet packs a lot of information into a small space, it's often awkward to use, and it's intimidating to Access newcomers. The solution is *forms*: specialized database objects that make it easier for anyone to review and edit the information in a table.

___ NOTE _____

Remember, if you're using Access in a business environment, different people probably use your database. You may create it, but others need to be able to use it to perform a variety of tasks—usually data entry and searches. These other folks may not be as Access-savvy as you are.

_____

Form Basics

Forms get their name from paper forms that people use to record information when a computer isn't handy. Depending on your situation, you may create an Access form that resembles a paper form that your company or organization uses. If you're working at a bank, you can create an Access form that lays out information in the same basic arrangement as a paper-based customer application form. This arrangement makes it easy to copy information from the paper into your database. However, most of the time the forms you design don't have a real-world equivalent. You'll create them from scratch, and use them to make data entry easier.

To understand why forms are an indispensable part of almost all databases, it helps to first consider the datasheet's shortcomings. Here are some areas where forms beat the datasheet:

▶ **Better arrangements.** In the datasheet, each field occupies a single column. This arrangement works well for tables with few fields, but leads to endless side-to-side scrolling in larger tables. In a form, you can make sure the data you need is always in sight. You can also use color, lines, and pictures to help separate different chunks of content.

▶ **Extra information.** You can pack a form with any text you want, which means you can add clues that help newbies understand the data they need to supply. You can also add calculated details—for example, you can calculate and display the total purchases made by a customer without forcing someone to fire up a separate query.

▶ **Table relationships.** Many tasks involve adding records to more than one related table. If a new customer places an order in the Boutique Fudge database, then you need to create a new record in the Customers and Orders tables, along with one or more records in the OrderDetails table. A form lets you do all this work in one place (rather than forcing you to open two or three datasheets).

▶ **Buttons and other widgets.** Forms support *controls*—buttons, links, lists, and other fancy pieces of user interface matter you can add to your form. The person using your database can then click a button to fire off a related task (like opening another form or printing a report).

Properly designed forms are what the geeks call a database's *front end*. In a database that uses forms, you can edit data, perform searches, and take care all of your day-to-day tasks without ever touching a datasheet.

Creating a Simple Form

As with reports, Access gives you an easy and a more advanced way to construct a form. The easy way creates a ready-made form based on a table or query. Keen eyes will notice that this process unfolds in more or less the same way as when you automatically generate a simple report (page 274).

Here's how it works:

1. **In the navigation pane, select the table or query you want to use to generate the form.**

   Try the Products table from the Boutique Fudge database.

> If you create a form for a parent table that's linked to other tables, then
> you wind up with a slightly different type of form. If you create a form
> for the Categories table (a parent of the Products table), then you end
> up with a two-part form that lets you view and modify the category
> record *and* the linked product records in each category.

2. **Choose Create → Forms → Form.**

A new tab appears, with your form in Layout view. The simple form shows one
record at a time, with each field on a separate line (Figure 9-1). If your table has
lots of fields, then Access creates more than one column (Figure 9-2).

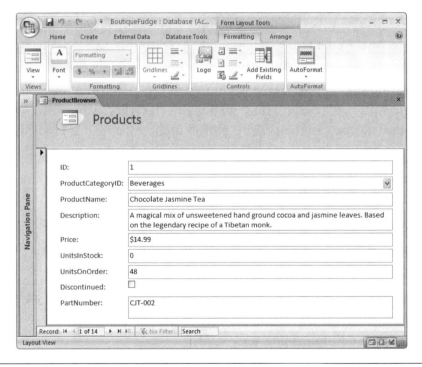

Figure 9-1. This simple form for the Products table already shows a fair bit of intelligence. Access uses
text boxes for all the text fields, a drop-down list box for fields that have a lookup (in this case, Product-
CategoryID), and a checkbox for any Yes/No field (like Discontinued). It also makes some boxes (like
Description) larger than others, because it notices that the underlying field has a larger maximum allow-
able length (page 69).

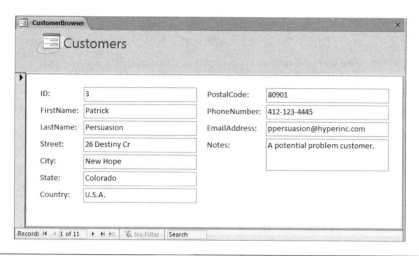

Figure 9-2. In this form for the Customers table, Access can't fit all the fields using the ordinary one-field-per-line arrangement. Instead, it adds a second column.

TIP

Good design practices pay off when you begin building forms. If your text fields store a far greater number of characters than they need (as controlled by the Field Size property described on page 69), then your form winds up with huge text boxes that waste valuable space. You need to resize them by hand.

When you first create a form, Access arranges the fields from top to bottom in the same order in which they're defined in the table. It doesn't make any difference if you've rearranged the columns in the datasheet. However, Access leaves any columns you've hidden in the datasheet (page 108) out of the form.

TIP

You can add or remove fields in a form in the same way you do with a report. If the Field List pane isn't open, then choose Form Layout Tools | Formatting → Controls → Add Existing Fields. Then, drag the field you want from the Field List pane onto the form. To remove a field, click to select it on the form, and then press Delete. However, keep in mind that people often use forms to add records, and if you want to preserve that ability, you need to make sure your form includes all the required fields for the table.

3. **Arrange the fields in the order you want by dragging them around.**

   Although a simple form doesn't look like the simple reports you learned about in Chapter 8, you can actually work with it in much the same way. One of the easiest ways to tailor your form is to drag fields from one place to another (Figure 9-3).

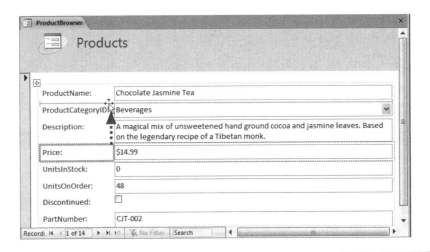

Figure 9-3. To move a field, drag it to a new position. Access reshuffles all the other fields accordingly. In this example, the Price field's being relocated to the top of the form, just under the Product-Name field. Access bumps all the other fields down the page to make room.

4. **Change your columns' widths.**

   When you create a new form in Layout view, Access makes all the fields quite wide. Usually, you'll want to shrink them down to make your form more compact. It's also hard to read long lines of text, so you can show large amounts of information better in a narrower, taller text box.

   To do so, just click to select the appropriate field; a yellow rectangle appears around it. Then, drag one of the edges. Figure 9-4 shows this process in action.

   NOTE

   You may like to make a number of changes that you can't accomplish just by dragging, such as adding a new column or giving each field a different width. To make changes like these, you need to understand layouts, which are covered in *Access 2007: The Missing Manual*.

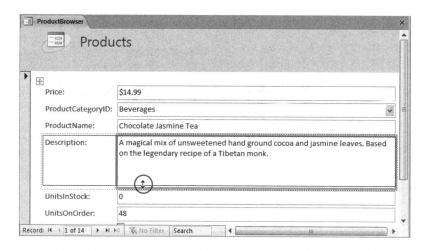

Figure 9-4. Here, the Description field is being heightened to fit more lines of text at a time. You can also make a field wider or narrower, but there's a catch—when you do so, it affects the entire column. In this report for the Products table, every field always has the same width.

5. **Optionally, you can click a field header to edit its text.**

   This option lets you change ProductCategoryID to just Category.

6. **Optionally, you can tweak the formatting to make the form more attractive, by changing fonts and colors.**

   You can most quickly change the formatting of your form by selecting the appropriate part (by clicking), and then using the buttons in the ribbon's Form Layout Tools | Formatting → Font section. You can also use the Form Layout Tools | Formatting → Formatting section to adjust the way Access shows numeric values. You learned about all your formatting options on page 296 when you built basic reports.

   Often, you'll want to format specific fields differently to make important information stand out. You can also format the title, header section, and form background. Figure 9-5 shows an example of judicious field formatting.

TIP

To select more than one part of a form at once, hold down Ctrl while you click. This trick allows you to apply the same formatting to several places at once.

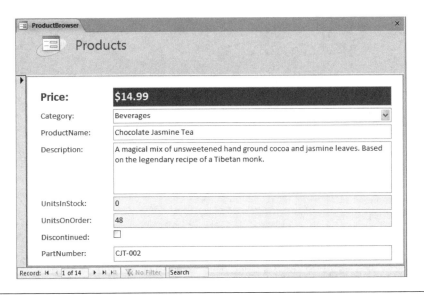

Figure 9-5. You can select the field header (Price, for example) and the box with the field value separately, which means you can give these components different formatting. This form gives a shaded background fill to the Price, UnitsInStock, and UnitsOnOrder fields. It also gives a larger font size to the Price field and Price header, so this information stands out.

If you're in a hurry (or just stylistically challenged), then you can use a nifty Access feature called AutoFormat to apply a whole slew of related formatting changes. Just make a choice from the Form Layout Tools | Formatting → Auto-Format section (which has the same AutoFormat choices you used with reports on page 295).

7. **Save your form.**

You can save your form at any time by choosing Office button → Save. Or, if you close the form without saving it, Access prompts you to save it at that time.

Using a Form

Now that you've created your first form, it's time to take it for a test spin. All forms have three different viewing modes:

AutoNumber Fields in Forms

The best way to uniquely identify each record is with an AutoNumber field (page 87). When you insert a record, Access fills in a value for the AutoNumber field. All the tables you'll see in this book include a field named ID that uses the AutoNumber data type.

Only Access can set an AutoNumber field. For that reason, you may not want to show it in your forms. (If you decide not to show it, just select it in Layout view and then press Delete.) However, there are some reasons that you might actually want to keep the AutoNumber field on display:

✳ **You use the AutoNumber field on some type of paperwork.** Cacophoné Studios puts each student's ID number on their registration papers. When

you need to look up the student record later on, it's easier to use the ID number than search by name.

✳ **You use the AutoNumber field as a tracking value or confirmation number.** After you enter a new order record in the Boutique Fudge database, you can record the order record's ID number. The next time you have a question about the order (has it shipped?), you can use the ID number to look it up.

Depending on how you use the ID number, you may choose to place it at the bottom of the form rather than in its usual position at the top. That approach avoids confusion. (It's less likely that people will try to type in their own ID numbers when they create new records.)

▶ **Layout view.** This is the view you've been using so far. It lets you see what your form looks like (with live data), rearrange fields, and apply formatting.

▶ **Design view.** While Layout view provides the simplest way to refine your form, Design view gives you complete power to fine-tune it. In Design view, you don't see the live data. Instead, you see a blueprint that tells Access how to construct your form.

▶ **Form view.** Both Layout view and Design view are there to help you create and refine your form. But once you've perfected it, it's time to stop designing your form and start *using* it to browse your table, review the information it contains, make changes, and add new records.

___ NOTE ___

> When you open a form by double-clicking it in the navigation pane, it opens in Form view. If you don't want this view, then right-click your form in the navigation pane, and then choose Layout View or Design View to start out in a different view.

To try out the form you created, switch it to Form view if you're not already there. Just right-click the tab title, and choose Form View.

In Form view, you can perform all the same tasks you performed in the datasheet when you worked with a table. With a simple form, the key difference is that you see only one record at a time.

Most people find forms much more intuitive than the datasheet grid. The following sections give a quick overview of how you can use Form view to perform some common tasks.

Finding and editing a record

Rare is the record that never changes. Depending on the type of data you're storing, most of your work in Form view may consist of hunting down a specific record and making modifications. You may need to ratchet up the price of a product, change the address details of an itinerant customer, or reschedule a class.

Before you can make any of these changes, you need to find the right record. In Form view, you have four ways to get to the record you need. The first three of these methods use the navigation controls that appear at the bottom of the form window.

▶ **By navigating.** If your table's relatively small, then the fastest way to get going is to click the arrow buttons to move from one record to the next. Page 111 has a button-by-button breakdown.

▶ **By position.** If you know exactly where your record is, then you can type in the number that represents the position (for example, 100 for the one-hundredth record), and then hit Enter. If you don't get exactly where you want, then you can also use the navigation buttons to move to a nearby record.

▶ **By searching.** The quick search feature finds a record with a specific piece of text (or numeric value) in one of its fields. To use quick search, type the text you want

to find in the search box, as shown in Figure 9-6. If you want a search that exam-
ines a specific field or gives you additional options, then use the Home → Find →
Find command.

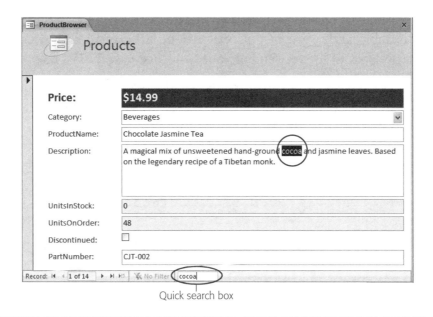

Quick search box

Figure 9-6. When you use the quick search box, you don't need to hit Enter. Access finds the next
match as you type.

▶ **By filtering.** Using filtering, you can narrow down the displayed records to a
small set. Filtering's best-kept secret's that you can use a feature called *filter by
form* to quickly hunt down a single record. You'll see how that works on page 321.

Once you've found the record you want to change, you can edit it in the same way
you would in the datasheet. If you make a change that breaks a rule (like typing the
text "*Exasperated Bananas*" in a date field), then you get the same familiar error
messages.

Access commits any change you make as soon as you move to another record or
field. To back out of a change, hit Esc before you move on. When you do, the original value reappears in the cell, and Access tosses out your changes. And if you do

commit a change by accident, then you can use the Undo button in the Quick Access toolbar (above the ribbon), or hit Ctrl+Z, to reverse it.

Adding a record

As you already know, you add a new record in datasheet view by scrolling to the very bottom of the table, and typing just underneath the last row. In Form view, the concept's similar—scroll to the very end of your table, just past the last record.

You'll know you've reached the magic ready-to-add-a-record spot when all the fields in your form are blank (Figure 9-7). To save yourself the scrolling trip, use the New Record button at the bottom of the form (marked in Figure 9-7).

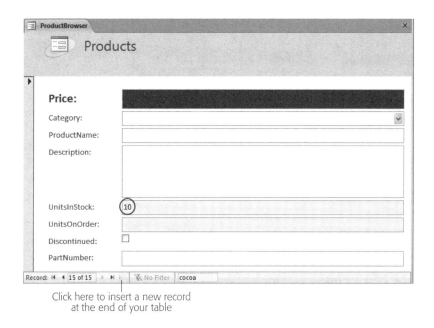

Click here to insert a new record
at the end of your table

Figure 9-7. When you create a new record, you start off with a clean slate that shows your form's formatting but no values. If you've set any default values for the table (page 134), then you see them appear instead of the blank values. In the Products table, the UnitsInStock field has a default value of 10.

If you've decided that you don't want to add a new record after all, then hit Esc twice. The first time you press Esc, Access wipes out the value in the current field. The second time, Access removes all the other values you entered. Now that your form's been restored to its original emptiness, you can safely scroll off to another record.

If you scroll away from your new record while there's still some data left in it, then Access creates the new record and adds it to the table. You can't reverse this action. If you want to get rid of a newly created record, then you need to delete it, as described in the next section.

GEM IN THE ROUGH

Showing Pictures from a Database

As you learned in Chapter 2, you can store a picture file as part of a record using the Attachment data type. Forms handle attachments gracefully using the *Attachment control*. The Attachment control has one truly useful perk—it shows picture content directly on your form.

Here's how it works. If your attachment field stores a picture, then that picture appears in the Attachment control box so you can admire it right on your form. This behavior's a great improvement over the datasheet, which forces you to open the picture file in another program to check it out. Even better, if the attachment field stores more than one picture, then you can use the arrows on the handy pop-up minibar to move from one image to the next, as shown in Figure 9-8.

As you know, attachment fields can store any type of file. If you're *not* storing a picture, then the Attachment control isn't nearly as useful. All you see's an icon for the program that owns that file type. If your attachment field contains a Word document, then you see a Word icon. If it contains a text document, then you see a Notepad icon, and so on. If your attachment fields don't include pictures, you may as well resize the box for the Attachment control so that it's just large enough to display the file type icon. There's no reason to make it any bigger, because the rest of the space will be wasted.

Deleting a record

When you find a record that shouldn't exist, you can wipe it out in seconds. The easiest way to delete the current record is to choose Home → Records → Delete. But you have another option. You can select the whole record by clicking the margin on the form window's left side. Then you can liquidate it by pressing Delete.

Picture:

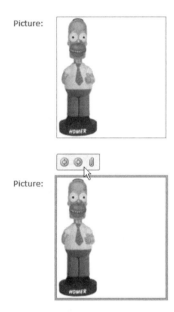

Picture:

Figure 9-8. Top: Here, the Picture field shows a bobblehead doll's picture. Access sizes the picture to fit the Attachment control box (without unnaturally stretching or skewing the picture).

Bottom: When you select the Picture field, you see a minibar with additional options appear right above the image. The arrows let you step through all the attached files for this record. The paper clip icon opens the Attachments window, where you can add or remove attachments, or open them in a different program. (The Attachments window's described on page 86.)

No matter what approach you use, Access asks you for confirmation before it removes a record. You can't recover deleted records, so tread carefully.

Printing records

Here's a little-known secret about forms: You can use them to create a quick print-out. To do so, open your form, and then choose Office button → Print. The familiar Print dialog box appears, where you can choose your printer and the number of copies you want.

When you print a form, Access prints *all* the records, one after the other. If you want to print just the current record, then, in the Print dialog box, choose the Selected Records option before you click OK.

You can also use Office button → Print → Print Preview to check out the result before you send it to the printer (Figure 9-9). Click Print Preview → Close Preview → Close Print Preview to return to your form.

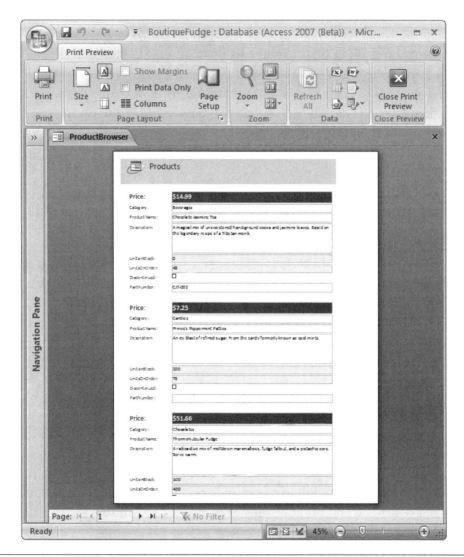

Figure 9-9. This preview shows what you'll get if you print the CustomerList form. The printout closely matches the form, with the same formatting and layout. When Access first creates the form, it gives it the same width as an ordinary sheet of paper. When you print the form, Access crams as many records—three in this case—as it can fit on each page.

Although you might be tempted to use forms as a convenient way to create snazzy printouts, you'll always get more features and better control if you use reports.

Sorting and Filtering in a Form

Sorting and filtering are two indispensable features that Access gives you with Form view. Learning how to use them could hardly be easier—in fact, you already learned everything you need to know when you tackled the datasheet in Chapter 3. The creators of Access took great care to ensure that filtering and sorting work the same in forms as they do in the datasheet. You use the same commands, on the same part of the ribbon, to put them into action.

Sorting a Form

As you've probably realized by now, forms show your data in raw, unsorted order. So records appear in the order you created them. (The only exception is if you create a form that gets its data from a query, and that query uses sorting.)

Fortunately, sorting's easy. In fact, you can sort the records that are shown in a form in exactly the same way you sort records in a datasheet. Choose the field you want to use for sorting, right-click it, and then choose one of the sorting options. In a text-based field, you'll see the sorting choices "Sort A to Z" (for an alphabetical sort) and "Sort Z to A" (for a reverse-alphabetical sort). You can also use the Ascending and Descending buttons on the ribbon's Home → Sort & Filter section.

For more information about your sorting options (including how to sort by multiple fields), see page 112.

Filtering a Form

Filtering's a feature that lets you cut down the total number of records so you see only those that interest you. Filtering can pick out active customers, in-stock products, expensive orders, and other groups of records based on specific criteria.

In a form, you have the following filtering choices:

▶ **Quick filter** shows you a list of all the values for a particular field and lets you choose which ones you want to hide. It's easy to use, but potentially time-consuming. If you want to hide numeric values that fall into a certain range, then you'll get the job done much faster with the "filter by condition" approach (as described later). To show the list of quick filter values, move to the field you want to filter, and then click Home → Sort & Filter → Filter. Page 115 has full details about quick filters.

▶ **Filter by selection** applies a filter based on an existing value. First, find the value in one of the records, right-click it, and then choose a filter option. You can right-click a price value of $25, and then choose "Greater Than or Equal to 25" to hide low-cost items. For more information, see page 117.

▶ **Filter by condition** lets you define the exact criteria you want to use to filter records. You don't need to base it on an existing value. To add this sort of filter, right-click the field and then look for a submenu with filtering options. This menu item's named according to the data, so text fields include a Text Filters option, number fields have a Number Filters option, and so on. You can learn more about this type of filter on page 119.

▶ **Advanced filters** are filters that you design using a window that looks just like the query designer. The advantage of advanced filters is that you can apply filters on more than one field in a single step. To create a set of advanced filters, choose Home → Sort & Filter → Advanced Filter Options → Advanced Filter/Sort.

___ **NOTE** _____

If you insert a new record that doesn't match the currently active filter conditions, your new record disappears from sight as soon as you add it. To get it back, remove the filter settings using the ribbon: Select the Home tab, click the Advanced button in the Sort & Filter chunk, and then choose Clear All Filters. Or, use the Toggle Filter button to temporarily suspend your filter settings (and click Toggle Filter later to get them back).

_____

Using the Filter by Form Feature

One other filtering technique works with forms: *filter by form*. Essentially, "filter by form" transforms your form into a full-fledged search form. Using this search form, you supply one or more criteria. Then you apply the filter to see the matching record (or records).

Although you can use "filter by form" with the datasheet, it really shines with forms. "Filter by forms" is particularly useful for searching out a single hard-to-find record. (If you want to use filtering to pull out a whole group of records, one of the other filtering options is generally easier.)

Here's how to use the "filter by form" feature:

1. **Choose Home → Sort & Filter → Advanced Filter Options → Filter By Form.**

    Access changes your form to search mode. In search mode, your form looks exactly the same, except all the fields are blank.

    If you've already used the "filter by form" feature and you're returning to change the filter settings, then you should start by clearing the previous set of filters. To do so, right-click a blank spot on the form surface, and then choose Clear Grid.

2. **Move to the field you want to use for filtering.**

    A drop-down arrow appears in the field.

3. **Click the drop-down arrow, and then choose the value you want to *include* in your results.**

    The drop-down list shows all the values from the different records in the table (Figure 9-10). When you choose one, it appears in the field box in quotation marks.

4. **If you want to apply a filter to more than one field, then return to step 2.**

    Use multiple filter conditions if a single filter condition may result in more matches than you want. If you don't remember a customer's last name, you could apply a FirstName filter. But if that customer has a common first name, then you may also want to apply a filter on another field, like City.

    If you don't want to use exact matches, then you can write in more complex filters using an expression. Use *<10* to find numeric values under 10, and *Like Jon** to find text values like "Jones," "Jonathon," and "Jonson." This trick's particularly useful with date fields. Page 221 has the full scoop on filtering expressions.

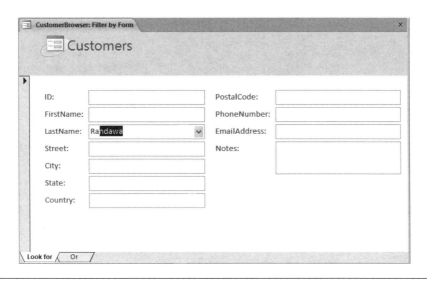

Figure 9-10. Here's the Customers form in "filter-by-form" mode. Using the drop-down list, you can quickly find a customer by last name. Or you can find a name by typing the first few letters rather than scrolling through the list, as shown here. In this example, typing "Ra" brings up the first alphabetical match: the last name Randawa.

5. **If you want to perform more than one filtering operation and *combine* the results, then click the Or tab and fill out more filter settings (Figure 9-11).**

   If you fill out your first search form so that it matches the LastName "Gorfinkel," and the second search form to match the FirstName "Jehosophat," your results will include all the records that have the last name Gorfinkel *and* all those that have the first name Jehosophat. However, if you put both those filter conditions on the same search form, your matches include only people named Jehosophat Gorfinkel.

6. **Right-click a blank spot on the form surface, and then choose Apply Filter/ Sort.**

   Access switches back to your normal form, and then applies the filter settings. At the bottom of the form, between the navigation buttons and the search box, you see the word "Filtered" appear to let you know that you aren't seeing all the records.

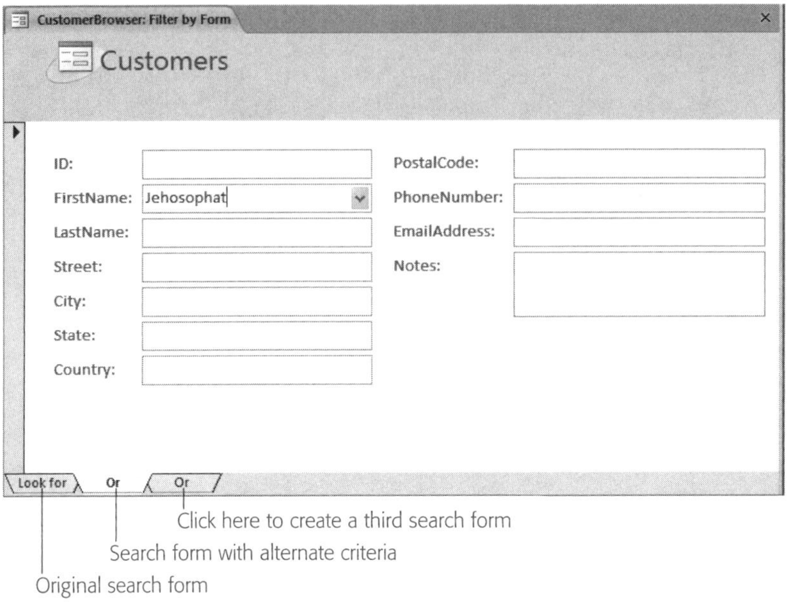

Figure 9-11. The Or tab appears at the bottom of the form. When you click the Or tab, a second copy of your search form appears, where you can fill out additional filter conditions. Each time you click the Or tab, another Or tab appears. You can repeat this process to fill in a dozen search forms at once, but there's rarely any reason to go to such lengths.

If you decide not to apply the filter settings, just close the search form. Access switches back to your normal form but doesn't apply any filtering.

___ TIP ___

To remove your filter settings but keep them handy for later use, choose Home → Sort & Filter → Toggle Filter. To reapply the filter settings later on, click Toggle Filter a second time. Access stores the most recent filter settings with your form, so they're always available.

Saving Filters for the Future

One of form filtering's limitations is that Access remembers only your most recent set of filters. If you've perfected a complex filter expression that you want to reuse later, this quality's a problem. As soon as you apply a different filter, you'll lose all your hard work.

Fortunately, you have several solutions to this dilemma. One option's to create a whole new query that performs the filtering, and use that query in a whole new form. This choice is a good one if you want to use your filter criteria to perform a specific task, and you also want to customize the way the form works or the way it displays its data.

On the other hand, if you don't plan to use your filtering settings very often, but you just want to have them on hand for the next time you need them (or if you need to store dozens of different filter settings, and you don't want to be stuck with dozens of nearly identical forms), there's a better option. You can save your filter settings as a query in your database. Then, when you want them back, you can load them up and apply them to your form.

Here's how to pull this trick off:

1. **Apply your filters.**

   Use any of the techniques described on page 320.

2. **Choose Home → Sort & Filter → Advanced → Advanced Filter/Sort.**

   This action opens a query window. This query uses the same data source (table or query) as your form, and it applies your filtering using the Criteria box under the appropriate field (page 217). You don't need to make any changes in the query window because Access automatically fills in the Criteria box (or boxes) based on the current filter settings.

3. **Choose Home → Sort & Filter → Advanced → Save as Query. Supply a name for this query, and then click OK.**

   Although you can use this query like a normal query, you probably won't. So to prevent confusion, use a different type of name, like CustomerBrowser_Filter, that clearly indicates this query's designed for form filtering.

The next time you want to retrieve your filter settings and reapply them, open your form and follow these steps:

1. **Choose Home → Sort & Filter → Advanced → Advanced Filter/Sort.**

   This action shows the query window.

2. **Choose Home → Sort & Filter → Advanced → Load From Query.**

   Access shows all the queries that use the same table and don't involve joins (page 229).

3. **Pick the filter query you created earlier, and then click OK.**

   The filter settings for that query appear in the query window.

4. **Right-click anywhere on the blank space in the query window, and then choose Apply Filter/Sort to put your filter settings into effect.**

   TIP

   You can use this trick to apply the same filter expression to *different* forms, as long as these forms include the fields you want to filter. (You can use the filter settings that you created for the CustomerBrowser form to filter another form that shows a list of customers, but not a form that shows products.)

The Form Wizard

By now, you've learned how to create a number of common forms. Access gives you one other way to build a form: using the *Form wizard*. The Form wizard has an uncanny similarity to the report wizard you used in Chapter 8. It asks you a series of questions and then builds a form to match. However, the questions are fairly rudimentary, and the form it builds is little more than a good starting point for further customization.

Here's how to put the Form wizard through its paces:

1. **Choose Create → Forms → More Forms → Form Wizard.**

   The first step of the Form wizard appears.

2. **From the drop-down list, choose the table you want to use.**

   In the Available Fields list, the wizard shows all the fields that are in your table.

The Access Form Family

Access forms manage to please just about everyone. If you're in a hurry, then you can create a ready-made form with a basic layout and a dash of formatting. Or, if you're feeling creative, you can pull your fields out of the standard layouts and place them absolutely anywhere. In other words, forms are flexible—time-pressed types get the convenience they need, while serious artistes get the creative control they demand.

Here's a roundup of some of your form choices:

✽ **A simple form** shows one record at a time in a basic stacked layout. To create a simple form, choose Create → Forms → Form.

✽ **A layout-less form** lets you place controls anywhere you want on a form. It's up to you whether you want to show a single record at once, or several records at a time. When creating a layout-less form, you need to do all the work. You can get started by choosing Create → Forms → Form Design (to start in Design view) or Create → Forms → Blank Form (which starts you in Layout view).

✽ **A tabular form** shows records in a tabular layout. Usually, tabular forms show several records at once (which gives the appearance of a table). To quickly create one of these babies, choose Create → Forms → Multiple Items.

✽ **A datasheet form** looks exactly like the Datasheet view you get with a table. This form's not as powerful as other form types, but it's still useful if you want a customized datasheet-like view of your data. You can create a datasheet form that shows fewer columns, uses filtering to hide certain records, prevents record insertions, uses different formatting, and so on. To create a datasheet form, choose Create → Forms → More Forms → Datasheet.

✽ **A split form** combines two types of form in one window. One portion of the window shows the current record in a simple form. The other portion of the window shows a datasheet with several records. To create a split form, choose Create → Forms → Split Form.

The advanced form types, pivot table and modal dialog, are covered in depth in *Access 2007: The Missing Manual*.

3. **Add the fields you want to include, as shown in Figure 9-12. When you're finished, click Next.**

You can choose fields from more than one table, provided these tables are related.

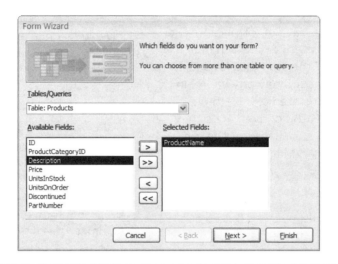

Figure 9-12. To add a field, select it, and then click the > button to move it from the Available Fields list to the Selected Fields list. To add all the fields, click >>.

4. **Choose a layout option for your form.**

Your layout options include:

▶ **Columnar** creates a form with a stacked layout. It's similar to clicking Create → Forms → Form in the ribbon.

▶ **Tabular** creates a form with a tabular layout. It's similar to clicking Create → Forms → Multiple Items in the ribbon.

▶ **Datasheet** creates a datasheet form. It's similar to selecting Create → Forms → More Forms → Datasheet in the ribbon.

▶ **Justified** creates a form that doesn't use any set layout. Instead, it packs controls closely together, combining several fields on a single line if they're small enough to fit. A justified form's the only kind of form you can't create directly from the ribbon using another command.

Justified forms are difficult to modify later on. For example, if you need to add a field into the middle of a layout form, you're stuck with the painstaking task of moving many more fields out of the way to new positions. Often it's easier to recreate the form from scratch using the wizard.

5. **Choose one of the preset styles, and then click Next.**

   The styles determine the formatting that Access applies to your form. Unfortunately, it's difficult to get a feeling for what the final result will look like unless you actually try each option.

6. **Enter a name for your form.**

   When the Form wizard finishes, it immediately saves your form using this name.

7. **Choose "Open the form to view or edit information" if you want to start using your form to work with data, or "Modify the form's design" if you want to adjust it in Design view first. Then, click Finish.**

   Access saves your form and opens it in Form view or Design view, depending on your choice.

PART FOUR: SHARING ACCESS WITH THE REST OF THE WORLD

Chapter 10   Importing and Exporting Data

IMPORTING AND EXPORTING DATA

10

▶ Case for Importing and Exporting

▶ Using the Clipboard

▶ Import and Export Operations

AN ACCESS DATABASE IS LIKE A CAREFULLY BUILT FORT. It takes strictly organized and error-tested information, and locks it up tight. Very few programs guard their data as protectively as database software does. Word processors and spreadsheet programs accept just about any content and let you build your document structure on the fly. Databases aren't nearly as freewheeling.

Most of the time, databases live in an independent world. But every once in a while, you need to bridge the gap in one of two ways:

▶ You want to take the information from another program and *import* it—basically, stuff it into your database.

▶ You want to take some of the information in an Access database and *export* it, so you can work with it in another program.

Access has several different options for transferring information. You can use the lowly clipboard, or sophisticated import and export features. In this chapter, you'll learn about all your options.

___ NOTE _____

The ever-popular XML standard is yet another option for importing and exporting, which is great for Access power users. You can learn more about Access and XML in *Access 2007: The Missing Manual*.

_____

Case for Importing and Exporting

If you haven't thought much about importing and exporting, it's probably because you don't need to use these features—yet. Many databases are completely happy living a quiet, solitary life. However, importing and exporting might come in handy for a few reasons. Sooner or later, one of these reasons will apply to you.

Understanding Exports

Exporting is the easier part of the equation. Exporting's simpler than importing, because it involves moving information from a stricter storage location (the database) to one with fewer rules (another type of document).

Here are some of the most common reasons people decide to export information:

▶ **You want to email some information to a friend.** You don't want to send the Access database because your friend doesn't have a copy Access, or you want him to see only some—not all—of the data.

▶ **You're creating a presentation in PowerPoint.** The easiest way to dazzle and convince your peers is to show them some impressive information from your database.

▶ **You want to analyze the information in Excel.** Access is great for storing and managing your data, but it doesn't give you the tools to help you figure out what it all means. If you want to crunch the numbers with heavy duty formulas and slick charting features, it makes sense to move it to Excel.

Some programs are intelligent enough to pull the information out of an Access database all on their own. One example's Word, which provides a *mail merge* feature that lets you take a list of names and addresses from a database, and then use them to create mailing labels, personalized forms, or any other sort of batch paperwork. When using this feature, you don't need to perform any exporting—instead, you can just point Word to your Access database file. (For more information about Word's mail merge feature, see *Word 2007: The Missing Manual*.)

Understanding Imports

You need importing whenever there's information outside your database that belongs inside it. Suppose you create a state-of-the-art e-commerce database for your buffalo farm. However, some of your sales associates still fill out forms using an old Excel spreadsheet. Now, you need a way to get the information out of the Excel spreadsheet and into your database.

___ TIP ___

Your sales staff has let you down. They really shouldn't enter data into a document for another program. Instead, they should use a form that's designed for logging sales, as described in Chapter 9.

Import operations have two key challenges. The first is making sure the data fits the database's strict requirements. As you learned in Chapter 1, databases are rule-crazy, and they rudely toss out any information that doesn't fit (for example, text in a date field). The second challenge is dealing with information that doesn't quite line up—in other words, its representation in the database doesn't match its representation in the external document. This headache's more common that you may think.

In your database, you might use status codes (like 4302), while the spreadsheet you want to import uses status *names* (like High Priority). Or, you may need to break the information you're importing into more than one linked table, even though it's stored together in a single document. The customer order spreadsheet for your buffalo farm could include customer information (which corresponds to the Customers table) and order information (for the Orders table). Sadly, you don't have any easy way to solve these problems. If the external data doesn't match the representation in the database *exactly*, you'll need to change it by hand before or after the import operation.

Using the Clipboard

Anyone who's spent much time using a Windows computer is familiar with the clipboard—a behind-the-scenes container that temporarily stores information so you can transfer it from one program to another. Using the clipboard, you can copy a snippet of text in a Word document, and then paste it into a field in an Access table, or vice versa. That much is easy. But you probably don't realize that you can copy an entire *table* of information.

___ TIP ___

Almost all Windows programs respect the same shortcut keys for the clipboard. Use Ctrl+C to copy information, Ctrl+X to cut it (copy and delete it), and Ctrl+V to paste it.

Before you try this trick out, you need to understand two key facts about the clipboard:

▶ **The clipboard can store many different types of information.** Most of the time, you're using it to copy plain text. However, depending on the program you're using, you could also copy shapes, pictures, tables, and more.

▶ **Some types of information can convert themselves to other types.** If you copy a selection of cells in Excel, then you can paste it as a formatted table in a word processing program like Word or WordPerfect. Of, if you copy a diagram in Visio, then you can paste it as a picture in Paint. In both examples, you copy a specialized type of object (Excel cells or a Visio diagram) to the Windows clipboard. However, this object can *downgrade* itself when it needs to. You can paste a full-fledged copy of the object in the original program without losing anything, or you can paste and convert it to something simpler in a less powerful program.

This flexibility is the secret to transferring data to and from Access. The following sections explain how it works.

— **NOTE** _____

The clipboard approach is simpler than the import and export features in Access. As a result, it's a faster choice (with fewer steps). Of course, it also gives you fewer choices and doesn't work with all programs.

_____

Copying a Table from Access to Somewhere Else

Access lets you copy a selection of rows or an entire table to another program, without going through the hassle of the Export wizard. Access copies these rows to the clipboard as an intelligent object that can convert itself into a variety of software-friendly formats. You can paste them as Excel cells, HTML text (the formatting language of the Web), or RichText (a formatting standard created by Microsoft and supported by all major Word processors). Since HTML and RichText are so widely supported, you'll almost never have a problem copying your rows into another program when you use this technique.

Here's how to try it out:

1. **If you want to copy an entire table, then, in the navigation pane, select the table. If you want to copy only a few rows, then select them in the Datasheet view, as shown in Figure 10-1.**

   You're not limited to copying tables. You can also copy a query's results. Just select the query in the navigation pane. You can't copy reports or forms, however.

   When you copy rows or an entire table, Access takes your column hiding settings (page 108) into account. If you've hidden a column so it doesn't appear in the datasheet (by selecting it, and then choosing Home → Records → More → Hide Columns), Access doesn't copy it to the clipboard. This technique helps you leave out information you don't want to copy.

	Products				
	ProductCategoryID	ProductName	Price		
	Beverages	Chocolate Jasmine Tea	$14.99	A magical mix
	Candies	Prince's Peppermint Patties	$7.25	An icy blast o
Click here →	Chocolates	ThermoNutcular Fudge	$51.66	A radioactive
	Candies	Maple Magic	$52.75	A twist of ma
	Pastries	Diabolical Donuts	$6.99	The best don
	Beverages	Coconut Syrup	$36.00	A sublime pa
	Beverages	Vanilla Bean Dream	$13.25	Do you drean
Drag to here →	Fruit and Vegetables	Chocolate Carrots	$6.99	The surprise
	Fruit and Vegetables	Fudge Spice Bananas	$14.99	Ripe bananas
	Chocolates	Mini Chocolate Smurfs	$1,112.00	Hand-carved
	Candies	Gummi Bear Sandwich	$108.99	Two lightly tc
	Beverages	Salt Crusted Coffee Beans	$8.75	Weird but no

Record: ◄ ◄ 3 of 15 ► ►I ►☆ No Filter Search

Figure 10-1. When selecting rows in the datasheet, click the gray margin just to the left of the first row you want to select. Then, drag down to select as many rows as you want. If you don't want to take your hand off the mouse, then you can copy these rows by holding down the Ctrl key, and right-clicking one of them. Then, from the pop-up menu, choose Copy.

NOTE

You can copy only a contiguous selection of rows, which is a fancy way of saying you can copy only rows that are right next to each other. If you have 10 rows in a table, then you can copy rows three to six, but you can't copy just the first and last rows. (Of course, you can use several smaller copy operations to get the stragglers.)

---

2. **Hit Ctrl+C to copy your selection.**

This action places the records on the Windows clipboard. You can now paste it inside Access or in another program.

3. **Switch to the program where you want to paste your information.**

If you're just trying this feature out for the first time, then take a whirl with Excel or Word (shown in Figure 10-2).

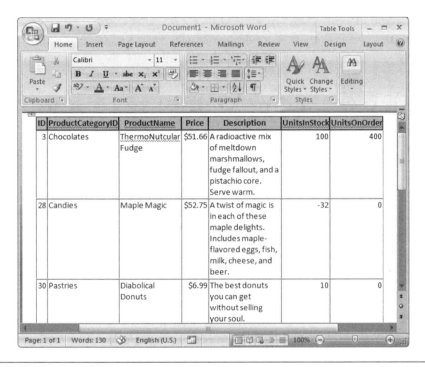

Figure 10-2. Using cut and paste, you can transform a database table into a table in a Word document (shown here). Once you've pasted the content, you may need to fiddle with column widths to make sure it all looks right.

4. **Hit Ctrl+V to paste your selection (see Figure 10-2).**

Access pastes the rows from your selection, complete with column headers. If you've applied formatting to the datasheet (page 103), then most of that formatting comes along.

Depending on the program where you paste your records, you might see a smart tag icon appear at your newly pasted content's righthand corner. In Office applications, you can use this smart tag to change options about how the data's pasted (for example, with or without formatting).

___ NOTE _____

Copying text, numbers, and dates is easy. However, some data types don't make the transition as well. If you copy an attachment field, then the pasted content shows the number of attachment fields, but the files themselves are left out.

_____

TIMESAVING TIP

Copying from One Database to Another

You can also use the copying trick described on page 337 to copy data from one Access database to another Access database that's open in a separate window. However, it works only if you're copying a complete table (or other object), not a selection of rows.

To try it out, right-click the object you want in the navigation pane, and then choose Copy. Then, switch to the second Access database, right-click in the empty space in the navigation pane, and then choose Paste. Access asks you what you want to name the pasted table, and gives you three pasting options:

* **Structure** creates the table structure, but leaves it empty.

* **Structure and Data** creates an exact duplicate of the table, with all the data.

* **Append Data to Existing Table** doesn't create a new table—instead, it adds the data to the table that you specify. For this to work, the table must have the same structure as the one you've copied.

This trick also lets you create a duplicate copy of a table (or other object) in the *same* database.

Copying Cells from Excel into Access

You can copy information from Access into another program easily enough, but you probably don't expect to be able to do the reverse. After all, a database is a strict, rigorously structured collection of information. If you try to copy a table from a

Word processing program, then you'll lack vital information, like the data types of each column. For that reason, Access doesn't allow it.

However, Access makes a special exception for everyone's favorite spreadsheet program, Excel. You can copy a selection of cells in Excel, and then paste them into Access to create a new table. This procedure works because Excel *does* distinguish between different types of data (although it isn't nearly as picky as Access). For example, Excel treats numbers, dates, text, and TRUE/FALSE values differently.

Here's how to use this feature:

1. **In Excel, select the cells you want to copy.**

   If your spreadsheet includes column titles, then include those headers in the selection. Access can use the titles as field names.

   ___ NOTE _____

   It doesn't matter what version of Excel you have—this trick works with them all.

   _____

2. **Hit Ctrl+C to copy your selection.**

3. **Switch to Access.**

4. **Click anywhere in the navigation pane, and then press Ctrl+V.**

   Access notices that you're trying to paste a group of Excel cells, and it tries to transform them into a table. First, it asks if the first row in your selection includes column titles.

5. **If you selected the column titles in step 1, then choose Yes. Otherwise, choose No.**

   If you choose Yes, then Access doesn't need to create random field names—instead, it can use your headers.

   Access creates a new table to deal with the new data. This table's named after the Excel sheet. If your sheet's named Sheet1 (as so many are in Excel), you now have a Sheet1 table.

Once Access finishes the paste, it shows a confirmation message to let you know everything's finished successfully.

6. **Click OK.**

Now you can refine your table to make sure the data types and field names are exactly what you want.

Import and Export Operations

Although the clipboard cut-and-paste approach is neat, it doesn't always work out. If you need to export data to a file and you don't have the corresponding program installed on your computer (or you just don't want to bother running it), then you need a different way to transfer your information. Similarly, if you're downloading data from the Web or fetching information from a program that doesn't support Windows cut-and-paste, you need the full-fledged Access import feature.

When Microsoft designed Access 2007, they spent a fair bit of time making the import and export features clearer and more straightforward. Nowadays, you can do all the importing and exporting you want from a single ribbon tab, which is named External Data (Figure 10-3).

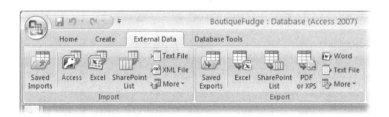

Figure 10-3. The External Data tab's Import section lets you pipe data into Access using a variety of formats. The Export section does the reverse—it takes your table, and exports it in a bunch of different flavors.

___

NOTE
___

The Import and Export sections have easy-to-access buttons for the most popular file formats. If you don't see what you want, then click the More button to see an expanded list of choices.

___

Whether you're importing or exporting data, the process is essentially the same. You answer a few questions about what file you want to use and how you want to make the conversion, and then Access does your bidding.

Once you finish performing an import or export operation, Access gives you the option of saving all your steps. If you do, you can reuse them later on. This method's a great way to save time if you need to perform the same export or import process again (like if you need to import some data every day, or export a summary at the end of every month).

Importable File Types

Most of the time, you'll import data that's in one of these five common formats:

▶ **Access.** When you use this option, you aren't performing a conversion. Instead, you're taking a database object from another Access database file, and copying it into the current database.

▶ **Excel.** Pulls the data from an Excel spreadsheet.

▶ **SharePoint List.** Pulls the data from a list that's hosted on a SharePoint server (which big companies use to help workers collaborate). You don't need to import SharePoint information in order to work with it. You can also edit SharePoint lists directly in Access. *Access 2007: The Missing Manual* has much more about getting Access and SharePoint to work together.

▶ **Text File.** Pulls the data out of a plain text file. Typically, plain text files use some sort of character (like a comma) to separate field values. This universally understood format's supported by many programs, including just about every piece of spreadsheet software ever written. When using this option, Access takes a look at the text file as it tries to figure out how it's organized. However, you get the chance to confirm or correct the hunch before you import any data, as described on page 349.

▶ **XML File.** Pulls the data out of a structured XML file. XML is a cross-platform format used to represent any type of information.

Using the More button, you'll find several other, more exotic import choices:

▶ **ODBC Database.** Grabs information from just about any database product, provided it has an ODBC driver. This option works particularly well if you need to get data out of a high-end server-side database like Oracle, SQL Server, or MySQL.

▶ **HTML Document.** Extracts information from a list or a table in an HTML Web page. Since HTML's a standard that's notoriously loose (and at times downright sloppy), you should try to avoid this option. You're likely to have importing problems.

▶ **Outlook Folder.** Pulls information out of a folder in Outlook or Outlook Express.

▶ **dBase File, Paradox File, and Lotus 1-2-3 File.** Pulls information out of a file created with one of these Paleolithic programs.

Importing Data

No matter what type of data you want to import, you'll go through the same basic steps. Here's an overview:

1. **In the ribbon's External Data → Import section, click the button that corresponds to the type of file you want to import.**

   When you choose a format, Access launches the Import wizard (Figure 10-4).

2. **Enter the name of the file you want to import.**

   If you don't remember the file path (or you just don't want to type it in by hand), then click Browse, and then navigate to the right place in the File Open window. Once you find the file, double-click it.

3. **Choose where to place the imported content in your database.**

   You have three possible choices for placing your data. Depending on the file format you're using, all these may not be available.

   ▶ **Create a new table.** This option creates a fresh new table for the data you're importing, which saves you the headache of worrying about conflicting records. However, if a table of the same name already exists in the Access database, then this option wipes it out.

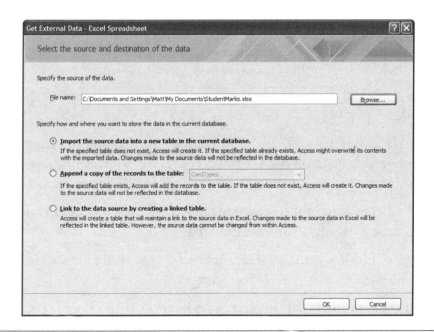

Figure 10-4. No matter what format you choose, the Import wizard's more or less the same, although certain options may be restricted. In this first step, you choose the source file name, and the way Access inserts the information into your database.

▶ **Append to an existing table.** This option takes the rows you're importing and adds them to an existing table. In order for this option to work, the structure of the data you're importing must match the structure of the table you're using. For example, the field names much match exactly. However, the data you're importing can leave out fields that aren't required (page 131) or have default values (page 134).

▶ **Create a linked table.** If you use this approach, then Access doesn't actually transfer the information into your database. Instead, every time you view the linked table, Access checks the original file to get the most recent information. The neat thing here's that your linked table always shows the most recent information. With any other option, the imported table's left untouched if you change the original file. However, linked tables are also risky, because you don't have any guarantee that the file won't travel to another location on your hard drive (where Access can't find it).

— NOTE —

Linked tables are a good way to bridge the gap between different
Access databases or other databases (like SQL Server). However, they
don't work well with other more limited formats, like text files.

4. **Click OK.**

   A wizard launches that collects the remaining information that Access needs. If
   you're importing an Excel file, then Access asks you which worksheet to use. If
   you're importing a text file, then Access asks you how the fields are separated.

5. **Answer all questions in the wizard to tell Access what it needs to know about
   the structure of the data you're importing.**

   Once you're finished with this stage, Access asks you its final question—whether
   or not you want to save your import steps.

6. **If you want to perform this import again later on, then select "Save import
   steps". Then, click Close.**

— NOTE —

If Access finds any errors while importing your data, then it creates
another table with the same name as the table you're importing to, with
ImportErrors tacked on the end. Access adds one record to that table
for each problem. If you try to import a bunch of information into a
table named SalesData, and Access can't convert the values to the data
type you want (for example, there's text in a column that should only
hold numbers), you get a table named SalesData_ImportErrors.

The following sections walk you through the specifics for two common data formats
that need a few extra steps: Excel workbooks and text files.

Importing from an Excel File

In order to import from an Excel file, your data should be organized in a basic table.
Ideally, you have column headings that match the fields in your database. You
should trim out any data that you don't want to import (like other cells under the

table that aren't a part of the table). You should also remove values calculated using Excel formulas. (As you learned on page 98, you shouldn't store calculated values in a table, because they introduce the risk of inconsistent data.)

NOTE
Earlier in this chapter, you learned how to take Excel data, and cut and paste your way to an Access table. However, when you perform a full-fledged import, you get the opportunity to change field names, fine-tune data types, and use indexing.

Once you have a cleaned-up table of data in an Excel file, you're ready to start the import process:

1. **Choose External Data → Import → Excel, choose your Excel file, and then specify how you want to add the imported information to your database. Then, click OK.**

    You learned how to make these decisions in steps 1 to 3 on page 344.

2. **Choose the worksheet that houses your data (Figure 10-5).**

    Excel files, or *workbooks*, begin with three worksheets. Most people plop their data on the first one, which is initially named Sheet1. If you're an Excel expert, then you might have designated a section of a more complex worksheet as a *named range*. If so, you can pick that named range from the list.

3. **Click Next.**

4. **If your Excel data has a row with column headings, then choose First Row Contains Column Headings.**

    These headings become the starting point for your field names. If you don't choose First Row Contains Column Headings, then Excel treats the first row as an ordinary record.

5. **Click Next.**

    If you're creating a new table for your imported records, then Access asks you to configure the fields you're creating. If you're appending the records to an existing table, then skip ahead to step 7.

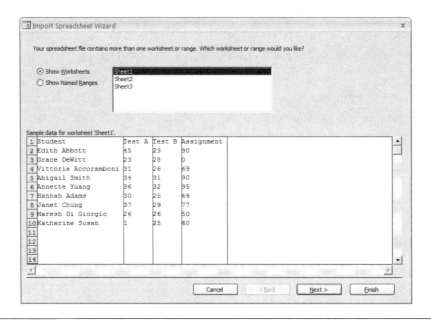

Figure 10-5. This Excel workbook file has the standard three worksheets: Sheet1, Sheet2, and Sheet3. When you make a selection, you see a preview of the data.

6. **For each field, you can choose a field name, the data type, and whether or not the field should be indexed (page 135). Then, click Next.**

   Access makes some intelligent guesses based on the data that's there, but it's up to you to fine-tune the details. For example, if you have a column with whole numbers, you may want to change the data type from Double (which supports fractional numbers) to Integer, as shown in Figure 10-6.

7. **Choose whether you want Access to create the primary key.**

   Choose "Let Access add primary key" if you'd like Access to create an autonumbered ID field (which is generally a good idea). If the data you're importing already includes a field you want to use as a key, then select "Choose my own primary key", and then pick the right field.

8. **In the Import to Table text box, type the name of the table you want to create or add your records to.**

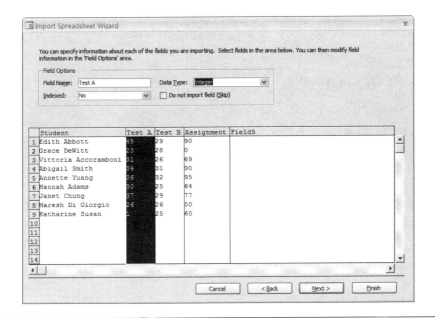

Figure 10-6. To configure a field, select it in the preview, and then adjust the settings. If you decide you don't want to import a field at all, then you can choose "Do not import field" to ignore it altogether.

9. **Click Finish to finalize your choices.**

Once the import's complete, you can choose whether or not to save your import steps for reuse.

You'll find some potential stumbling blocks when importing data from Excel. Blank values and fields, the commonest problems, occur when the Import wizard assumes there's data in a part of your worksheet that doesn't contain any information. (This could happen if there's a cell with just a space somewhere on your worksheet, or even if you have a cell that used to contain data but has since been deleted.) After you perform your import, you may need to clean up your table to fix problems like these by deleting empty fields and records.

Importing from a Text File

Text files are the lowest common denominator for data exchange. If you're using a program that creates files Access can't import, then plain text may be your only avenue.

Once again, you start by choosing your file, and then choosing how you want to add the information to your database. Then, the Import wizard takes you through a few more steps:

1. **Specify the type of text file.**

   Access can import from two types of text files:

   ▶ **Delimited text files** use some sort of separator to indicate where each field ends. For example, *Joe,Piscapone,43* is a line of text you may find in a delimited text file—it's three field values separated by commas.

   ▶ **Fixed-width text files** separates a record into separate fields by position. Each field has a certain number of characters allocated to it, and if you don't use them all up, then Access fills the remaining space (up until the next field) with space characters.

   > **NOTE**
   >
   > Delimited text files are more common and more flexible than fixed-width text files (because they can accommodate data values of vastly different lengths).

2. **Click Next.**

   If you're importing delimited text, Access asks you what character's the *delimiter*—in other words, what character separates the fields (Figure 10-7). Commas and tabs are common delimiters.

   If you're importing fixed-width text, Access lets you set the field boundaries by dragging column lines to the right position in the preview window.

3. **Complete the wizard.**

   The rest of the wizard unfolds in exactly the same way as it does for Excel data.

   If you're creating a new table to hold your imported data, then the next step asks you to configure the fields you want to create by setting their names, data types, and indexing options (Figure 10-6). Once you've finished this part, you can choose whether or not you want Access to create an autonumbered ID field, and then use it as the primary key.

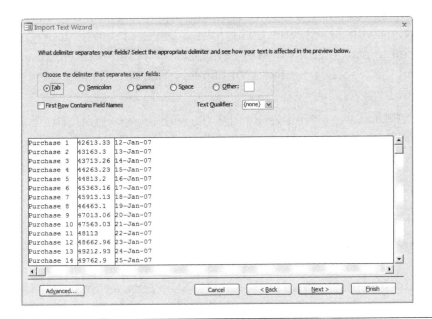

Figure 10-7. In this example, fields are separated using tabs.

Finally, in the last step, you need to enter the name of the table you want to create or add to. You can then click Finish (and, optionally, choose to save your import steps for later reuse).

Exportable File Types

Just as you can import information from other files and pop it in your database, you can also take the existing information and ship it out to another format. You'll most often undertake this step to let some other person or program get their hands on your information without needing to go through Access.

When exporting your data, you can use all the same formats that you can use in an import operation, plus a few more. Here's a rundown of the most popular choices:

▶ **Access.** Transfers the Access table (or a different type of object) to another Access database file. This feature isn't as powerful as importing Access objects, because you're limited to one object at a time. For that reason, people don't use it as often.

▶ **Excel.** Puts the data into the cells of an Excel worksheet. Perfect if you want to use Excel's tools to analyze a sales trend or plot a profit chart.

- **Word.** Puts the data into a Word document, separating each column with tabs and each line with a hard return. This format leaves a lot to be desired, because it's difficult to rearrange the data after the fact in Word. (A nicer export feature would put the report data into a Word table, which would make it far easier to work with.)

- **PDF or XPS.** Creates a print-ready PDF file with the exact formatting and layout you'd see if you sent the table to your printer. Unlike Excel or Word documents, you can't edit a PDF file—you're limited to reviewing the report and printing it out.

> **NOTE**
>
> The PDF or XPS option appears only if you've installed a free add-in for Office. Page 292 describes how to get it.

- **HTML Document.** Creates a web-ready HTML Web page that you can post to a Web site or a company intranet. The HTML format that Access generates looks remarkably like your real, printed report.

- **Text File.** Dumps the data into a plain text file, with tabs and spaces used to arrange the data. You lose colors, fonts, borders, and other formatting details. This format isn't very useful—think of it as a last resort to transfer data to another program if none of the other export options work.

- **XML File.** Saves the data in a text .xml file, without any formatting. This option makes sense if you're using some sort of automated program that can read the exported XML file and process the data.

Exporting Data

To perform an export operation, follow these steps:

1. **In the navigation pane, select the table you want to export.**

   Unfortunately, you can't export more than one table at once. However, you can export just a *portion* of a table. One way to do this partial export is to open the table, and then select the rows you want to export. (Once you start the export process, you see an option that lets you export just the selected rows.) You can also create a query that gets just the rows you want. You can export the query results by selecting the query in the navigation pane instead of the underlying table.

2. **Click the button that corresponds to the type of file you want to export.**

When you choose a format, Access launches the Export wizard (Figure 10-8).

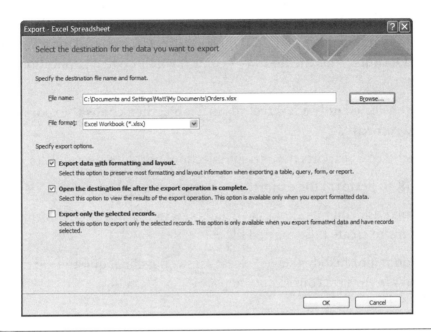

Figure 10-8. The Export wizard varies depending on the export format you're using. But the first step's always to pick your file, and then set the export options shown here.

3. **Enter the name of the file you want to create.**

Access creates this file during the export operation. In some cases, you may have a choice of file format. For example, if you're exporting to Excel you can use the newer XML-based spreadsheet format (the .xlsx standard), or the older .xls standard that supports older versions, like Excel 97.

4. **If you want to keep the formatting that's in your database, then choose "Export data with formatting and layout".**

If you've tailored the datasheet with fancy fonts and colors (as described on page 103), Access preserves these details in the exported file. Obviously, this option doesn't work for all formats. For example, simple text files can't handle any formatting.

5. **If you want to double-check your exported document, then choose "Open the destination file after the export operation is complete".**

   It's always a good idea to make sure you got the data and the formatting you expect. If you use this option, then Access launches the exported file, opening it in the program that owns it (Excel for spreadsheets, Notepad for text files, and so on). Of course, this method works only if you have that application on your computer.

6. **If you've selected only a few records in a table, then choose "Export only the selected records".**

   This way, Access exports the current selection, not the entire table or query.

7. **Click OK to perform the export.**

   Access may ask you for additional details, if it needs any more information about how to create the exported file.

   Once you're finished this stage, Access asks you its final question—whether or not you want to save your export steps.

INDEX

Symbols

A

Quick Access toolbar
  depicted, 10
  overview, 13
  Save button, 64
  Undo command, 45
quick search feature, 119
quotation marks ("), 222

R

**Random option (New Values field
    property)**, 88
**RDBMS (relational database
    management system)**, 173
**Recent Document list (Office
    menu)**, 47
records
  action queries and, 252
  adding to forms, 316
  appending, 261–266
  AutoNumber data type in, 88
  blank values for unlinked, 181
  copying in one step, 43
  defined, 31
  deleting, 39, 266–268
  deleting from forms, 317–318
  editing, 38, 42
  exporting selected, 354
  expressions and, 243
  filtering in tables, 115–119
  finding unmatched, 237
  finding/editing in forms, 314–316
  identifying before deleting, 267

  inserting, 39
  linked, 185
  many-to-many relationships, 196
  one-to-one relationships, 193
  printing from forms, 318, 320
  searching, 119–122
  setting default values, 134
  sorting in queries, 216
  sorting in tables, 112–115
  transferring, 263
  updating, 254–261
  viewing top, 223–224
Redo command, 14
redundant data, 98, 167–169
references, circular, 244
**referential integrity, relationships
    and**, 178, 180–185, 192
**Regional and Language Options dialog
    box**, 81
related data, redundant data vs., 167–169
**relational database management
    system (RDBMS)**, 173
relationship diagram, 179, 180
Relationship window, 180
relationships
  Chocolate Store practice, 204–208
  defining, 173–179
  defining between tables, 231
  deleting, 188
  editing, 180
  error handling and, 173
  explicit, 173

U

Undo command
  automatic save feature and, 44
  cascading deletes and, 182
  form changes and, 316
  Quick Access toolbar, 14
unfreezing columns, 110
Unhide Columns dialog box, 108
unhiding columns, 108
universal dates, 152
Up Arrow key, 41
update queries, 254–261
updates
  cascading, 184
  Design view and, 62
  modifying records, 254–261

V

Validation Rule property, 148, 149
validation rules
  date expressions, 151, 153
  expressions for numbers, 151
  field, 148–155
  filters and, 223
  overview, 147
  table, 155–157
  for text, 153–155
Validation Text property, 149

views
  for forms, 312, 314
  queries as, 221
  reports and, 280–283
  switching, 18

W

width, column, 107
Windows environment, regional settings, 81
Windows Task Scheduler, 45
Windows Vista, XPS format, 290
Word (Microsoft)
  Attachment data type support, 84
  exportable file type support, 352
  exporting reports to, 289, 290, 291, 295
  mail merge feature, 335
workbooks, 347
worksheets (Excel), 347

X

XML (extensible markup language)
  exporting to, 352
  importing from, 343
XPS format
  exportable file type support, 352
  exporting reports as, 289
  overview, 290

Y

Z

COLOPHON

Sanders Kleinfeld was the production editor for *Access 2007 for Starters: The Missing Manual*. Philip Dangler and Colleen Gorman provided quality control. Lucie Haskins wrote the index.

The cover of this book is based on a series design originally created by David Freedman and modified by Mike Kohnke, Karen Montgomery, and Fitch (*www.fitch.com*). Back cover design, dog illustration, and color selection by Fitch.

Tom Ingalls designed the interior layout, which was modified by Ron Bilodeau. Abby Fox converted the text and prepared it for layout. Robert Romano and Jessamyn Read produced the illustrations.

Related Titles from O'Reilly

Missing Manuals

Access 2003 for Starters: The Missing Manual

Access 2007: The Missing Manual

AppleScript: The Missing Manual

AppleWorks 6: The Missing Manual

CSS: The Missing Manual

Creating Web Sites: The Missing Manual

Digital Photography: The Missing Manual

Dreamweaver 8: The Missing Manual

eBay: The Missing Manual

Excel 2003 for Starters: The Missing Manual

Excel 2003: The Missing Manual

Excel 2007 for Starters: The Missing Manual

Excel 2007: The Missing Manual

FileMaker Pro 8: The Missing Manual

Flash 8: The Missing Manual

FrontPage 2003: The Missing Manual

GarageBand 2: The Missing Manual

Google: The Missing Manual, 2nd Edition

Home Networking: The Missing Manual

iMovie HD 6: The Missing Manual

iPhoto 6: The Missing Manual

iPod: The Missing Manual, 5th Edition

Mac OS X: The Missing Manual, Tiger Edition

Office 2004 for Macintosh: The Missing Manual

PCs: The Missing Manual

Photoshop Elements 5: The Missing Manual

PowerPoint 2007 for Starters: The Missing Manual

PowerPoint 2007: The Missing Manual

QuickBooks 2006: The Missing Manual

Quicken 2006 for Starters: The Missing Manual

Switching to the Mac: The Missing Manual, Tiger Edition

The Internet: The Missing Manual

Windows 2000 Pro: The Missing Manual

Windows XP for Starters: The Missing Manual

Windows XP Home Edition: The Missing Manual, 2nd Edition

Windows XP Pro: The Missing Manual, 2nd Edition

Windows Vista: The Missing Manual

Windows Vista for Starters: The Missing Manual

Word 2007 for Starters: The Missing Manual

Word 2007: The Missing Manual

Other O'Reilly Titles

Excel 2007 Pocket Reference

Writing Excel Macros with VBA, 2nd edition

Excel Hacks

Analyzing Business Data with Excel

Excel Scientific and Engineering Cookbook

Better than e-books

Buy *Access 2007 for Starters: The Missing Manual* and access the digital edition FREE on Safari for 45 days.

Go to www.oreilly.com/go/safarienabled
and type in coupon code SDWPCFH

Search
thousands of
top tech books

Download
whole chapters

Cut and Paste
code examples

Find
answers fast

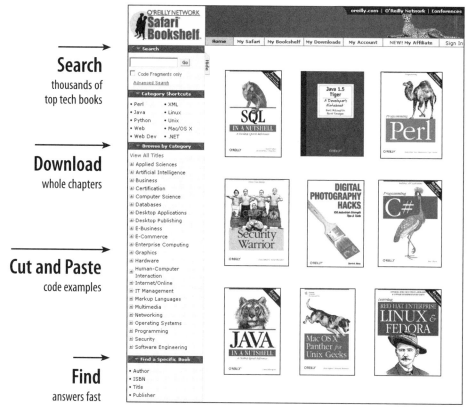

Search Safari! The premier electronic reference
library for programmers and IT professionals.